TATSIMOU, HOLD ON

Find your truth!

Andrea E. Claudis

Also by Andrea Cladis:

Forgotten Coffee

A Collection of Poems (Adelaide Books, 2018)

Finding the Finish Line:

Navigating the Race of Life through Faith and Fitness

(CrossLink, 2017)

Tatsimou, Hold On!

A Memoir By

ANDREA CLADIS

BOOKS

Adelaide Books
New York / Lisbon
2018

TATSIMOU, HOLD ON!
a memoir
by Andrea Cladis

Published by Adelaide Books, New York / Lisbon
adelaidebooks.org

Editor-in-Chief
Stevan V. Nikolic

For any information, please address Adelaide Books
at info@adelaidebooks.org
or write to:
Adelaide Books
244 Fifth Ave. Suite D27
New York, NY, 10001

ISBN13: 978-1-949180-07-7
ISBN10: 1-949180-07-7

Printed in the United States of America

To my parents, Peter and Jane, for creating "tatsimou" moments in my life, wanting the best for me, choosing to be present at all times for our family, and fighting without end to rescue me from the most devastating personal pain.

To my sister, Stacey, for always seeing me as a whole person, loving me through the lens of an angel, and walking with me in the way of Christ.

To my husband, Matthew, for continually pursuing me through unconditional love and affirmation. Thank you for reminding me every day of my worth. Thank you for being my lighthouse.

And to my Lord and Savior, Jesus Christ, the forever heart of my tatsimou and my eternal purpose, I praise you without end for the gift of grace and redemption in this life.

Contents

"For where you have envy and selfish ambition, there you will find disorder and every evil practice"
(James 3:16)

Prologue

Elegant and glamorous, the delicate white lace sheath dress hugged every curve of my womanly silhouette. With a swooping, revealing back showing off a somewhat unflattering swim suit tan line from the outdoor aquatic fitness classes I taught all summer, I watched over my spirited family crowd the dance floor in preparation to commence a traditional Greek circle dance to accompany the song, "Orea Pou Ine Nifi Mas," an iconic Greek wedding song which translates to, "How Beautiful our Bride is." It had not really sunken in yet, but for that night of my life, I was the beautiful bride of the song. My calves still burned from the triathlon I had gotten third place in, and the heels I was wearing were causing blisters on my feet. But even with tan lines, blisters, and amplified emotions of a wedding – my wedding, I would be dancing, and I would be drinking, and I would be celebrating for the new life I was about to begin.

My new husband, Matthew, a strappingly suave 30-year-old man with a brunette undercut and handsomely masculine jawline picked up my left hand to adjust the now completed diamond ring on my fourth finger. The ring was slightly loose as nerves caused weight loss in the months before our wedding, but Matthew wanted to ensure that the diamond was visible for others to see and to admire. A man from a working-class family who had sweat long and hard for every penny he paid for that large round, dazzling, exquisitely cut center stone had not vanity, but pride for the gift he had carefully procured for me, his new wife.

After making sure the diamond was set just in place atop the center of my fourth finger on my left hand, Matthew led me towards the far end of the oversized white marble dance floor in the center of the dimly lit room that smelled of Grecian lamb, old women's floral perfumes and Roditis wine, where our tiered wedding cake waited for us to ceremonially cut it and thus, officially set off the boisterous partying that would last well into the evening.

Soon, my entire Greek family – the entourage of cousins, parents, uncles, aunts, nieces, nephews, people I never met, but were somehow related to because all Greeks claim blood allegiance were encircling us on that stunning, polished marble dance floor that was the reason I had chosen that venue, just north of Chicago, for our wedding reception in the first place. They were all anticipating eating indulgent desserts and participating in long episodes of raucous dancing. Ouzo-drinking, spanakopita-loving, baklava-eating, passionate people. The nexus of my family swelled my already swooning heart.

The vanilla frosting on our cake was smooth in texture and sweetly satisfying and the endless layers of chocolate cake beneath the thick covering of frosting were most and rich. Matthew and I laughed and smiled for photos and I eagerly smeared cake all over his nose and mouth, making sure I did not dirty his bowtie, which he was splendidly particular about. I allowed my left hand to remain frosting-free as to best show off the brilliance of that diamond for Matthew.

As the DJ began to coalesce the troops to commence some Greek dancing, Matthew helped clean the sugary frosting from my face and kissed my long, Greek nose. There was no mistaking me for being a Greek. Yes, I was one of them. Straightening Matthew's ivory bowtie and smoothing out the lines of his tuxedo jacket, I leaned in towards him, gliding onto my tip toes to reach his left ear and whispered, "Tatsimou." A few of the Greeks whistled and cheered assuming I said something sultry or provocative to turn on my man, but that was far from the case. "I found it here. Tatsimou," I said again over the crescendo of "Zorba the Greek."

Matthew winked and gave a head nod and chin lift to the whistling Greeks but furrowed his brow in my direction not knowing what I meant by the word, but too distracted in the moment of our wedding day to really care. He kissed my forehead in the way he always did. It was a placating kiss of affirmation in his love and his way to convey that everything was okay, I was fine, and he was there for me. Matthew had no idea that that obnoxiously loud Greek family he married into had once been encircling me, this woman he promised to love and cherish, not in celebration, but in languished, tormenting grief as I slowly, compulsively withered away into suicidal starvation.

I tugged on his hand gently, not wanting to move or get swept into the dance, but to forever hold onto the moment. He squeezed back, looking at me with brightened, lightly intoxicated eyes, and suddenly shouted, "Honey! They're wanting us to dance! Let's go! Opa!" He clapped his hands and soon lost his grasp on mine as he was enveloped by my family, unified in ritualistic dance. I watched his fumbling dance steps, amused, as he was finally being officially welcomed into the Greek family circle.

"Tatsimou, hold on." I mumbled as one of my crazy, forceful uncles placed another shot of the anise-tasting Greek liquor in my hand, reeling me into the dance. "You're a wife now! Let's go! Dance for Yia-Yia! She would want this! Ella! Ella!"

And so, I took that shot of Ouzo, let it ride over the frosting dissolving into my throat, held up the long train of my lace dress with my diamond studded hand, linked arms with some proud, sweaty groomsmen, and I danced. *How beautiful our Bride is*, I sang aloud to the reveling music. It was in that moment wherein I experienced love of the highest caliber. Love I had not felt in such degree for many years. It was the bountiful love of family. Of joy. Of warmth and of beauty. It was love that supported the pinnacle of meaning in life – the very zenith of my tatsimou.

PART I

Self-Inflicted Atrophy:
Resist. Control. Maintain.

1
The Mocking Mirror

Bubblegum pink and navy blue flannel bed sheets rested atop my body as a palate of unforgiving ice against my thirsty, pallid skin. Immobilized by a weighted comforter restricting my efforts at movement, my eyes refused to open to the chilled air that pooled on the nape of my neck, delicately covered by a smooth layering of lanugo hair. An angry alarm clock blared its final warning as the numbness of my frozen, bony feet pulsed from my heels to my calves and up through the silhouette of my skeletal frame. Nine golden bells clamored in chorus from the top panel of my bedroom door frame as Dad barged into my room with a bright spirit, eager for the day. Those bells had been attached to my door one year as a Christmas decoration designed by my older brother, yet I no longer understood why they remained. On most mornings, they only served as piercing indications that another painful day was to begin.

"It's twenty after five, time to get up, kid!" Dad called. I grumbled as I felt my left hip sink deeper into my permanently dented mattress. As usual, Dad offered several wake-up call attempts to each of his three children and wife, always to the disruptive detriment of his own sleeping patterns each morning, so I expected his offer to come again before I would have to respond. "When do you want me to come back, sweetheart?"

"Five minutes, Dad. Just give me five more minutes," I said turning my head to drown my breath in my pillow that still smelled from the wetness of my thin hair and the floral scent of this strange brand of Silken Hair shampoo I had been using to try to re-grow my hair. I did not want five minutes. I did not want ten minutes. I wanted eternity to lie there until sleep took me to a place of warmth and freedom from pain.

I heard the bells jangle softly as Dad exited my room and retreated to his own to set the snooze on his alarm clock for me. I heard three short clicks and a beep; I squirmed as best as I could. I began fervently rubbing my feet in between the comforter and the bottom flannel sheet to create friction enough to generate some heat. It was a hapless effort as it was when I tucked my knees into my body, cradling them for warmth. I still could not open my eyes, but the light and cold wanted to come in. I burrowed further under the comforter maintaining my tucked position, my icy toes coiled snugly beneath me, and my bruised left hip pressing deeper into the mattress.

I wanted everything to be warm—even for just a moment—to experience the relief of being warm. I had craved that for several months and was yet to feel it. I heard a far off alarm clock tick, beep, and pulse in crescendo followed almost immediately by Dad's steady footsteps nearing my door. The bells jangled a bit more aggressively this time, but did not distemper my ears quite as raucously as they did on the first wake up.

Though my eyes were closed, I could picture Dad standing in my doorway wearing a white V-neck night shirt, Calvin Klein briefs, those skinny legs of his hanging out - having the hair worn off from mid-calf down from the dress socks he wore every day - and the upright posture of his strong shoulders, chest, and lean body.

"Honey, you there?" he said. I moaned in response.

"Time to wake up! Is your bag packed? We are leaving in fifteen minutes! Get up, sleepy head!" The gusto and enthusiasm in his voice alone made me tired. I did not hear the bells ring as he left my room and I hated when he would leave my door open on the final wake-up call letting more cold air from the hallway enter, exposing me like my raspberry colored beta fish when I removed the security of the large bamboo leaf from his containment. Unable to hide from the world outside my room I felt like anyone could see me. Only fifteen minutes, I thought. I can't F-ing move. My thoughts scrambled and I thrashed under the weight of my covers still unable to open my eyes. My head was throbbing. Today was supposed to be the day. The crowning moment of my swimming career loomed in fifty meters of chlorinated competition in an event that was going to begin in less than five hours' time.

It was 2005 and for the first time in my high school's history, our swimming team, and specifically, the four person women's relay team I was on had qualified for state, was favored to win, and proceed to Nationals. And if successful there, possibly even a time trial at the Junior Olympics. It was an honor and accomplishment; my teammates and I were all very proud. I certainly was not the fastest leg on our relay team, but I had done my part all season and I never wanted to disappoint. Unfortunately, we did not have any back-up swimmers or second-tier swimmers to take the place of someone if they missed a meet. So if I could not get to that meet, my absence would mean automatic forfeit for my entire relay team as well as the burden of letting down my coaches, my family, and the pride of an entire school.

I mustered all the strength I could cajole from my feeble body to shove aside the heavy covers. Shivering, I crawled out of my bed and onto the floor towards my bathroom where my swimsuits and swimming bags were packed and ready to go. My blue-tinted goggles in the clear compartment on the side of my bag mocked me as the straps frowned in my direction. I turned on my small space heater to diminish the cold air from aggravating my body any more. Still failing to keep my eyes open, I hovered over the heater. The darkness outside was less than encouraging to me and the January hoarfrost on my windows reminded me of the icy, painful entry into a competition swimming pool. 77 degree competition pool water would have felt like a frigid lake to me – an icy layering entombing my feeble body. Leftover snow draped the edges of the skylight in my bathroom, and as I looked up at it I could see the sparkles of feather dust snow absorbing the reflection of the dissolving moonlight. Crawling even closer to the heater, I fidgeted just enough to begin undressing.

"Five minutes!" My Dad called up to me.

"Okay, doc," I murmured inaudibly as I heard him sorting through newspaper pages to find the sports section as he awaited the days until the despised football season would end and spring training for baseball would begin. He was also busy taking calls from the hospital as I gathered that he was on call the entire night prior, and still had some unfinished business to attend to. I smelled coffee brewing and the scent of cinnamon raisin toast; the man was so goddamn efficient, it was impossible to keep up. He lived ten lives in the same space of time that his family slept or coddled space heaters in efforts for warmth or any source of energy. I felt nauseated at the thought of an entire piece of bread. I heard the crunch of the raisin toast between his teeth, the wrestling of newspapers… "Yes, this is Dr. Cladis speaking, what is her current status? Yes, give her the insulin shots and keep her on bedrest until I get there. Yes. Okay. Thank you. No, Ramone is out today, I'll be on call again tonight." Call after call after call – the man never took a break from work. Diagnosing and prescribing and problem solving and visiting and performing surgeries and delivering babies and…it exhausted me. I remembered that as a little kid whenever Dad left in the middle of the night to go deliver a baby I thought he would come home and I would have another sibling. Of course that was never the case, but my dad sure did have a lot of babies and now those babies were having babies and the cycle of life perplexed me and…

"Andrea! It's time to go. Come on!" He yelled up to me and I felt the urgency in his voice as the phone rang again. "Yes this he. Admit one, yes. She's a DNR. No, keep him on watch until the blood tests come through. Call me with the results. Hah. Of course, it's a busy time post holidays. I understand."

Hah? I wondered. Sometimes when he joked with the receptionists and nurses I wondered what in the world these people could possibly be laughing at. Their business was sick people. Sure their business was in supporting new life too, but also in seeing people through the end of life. Only cynics could laugh at that or maybe they had to keep a sense of humor or they'd all end up like me, just hating themselves because of the cruel, bitter reality of the world. DNR. There were always a lot of those phone calls right after the holidays.

As though crippled, I dismantled my four layers of long underwear beneath my white cotton pajamas and slid into my faded black and green TYR racing suit. As I slipped the arm holes over my shoulders, the suit did not grip my body, but merely hung over me like I was a mere hanger for its display.

Maybe the latex got stretched out…

Maybe the suit is too old…

Maybe I need another suit over it…

Maybe when Mom washed it last week and the elastic got ruined…

Maybe, maybe, maybe.

Hugging my heater for warmth close enough to burn my bare skin, I felt wetness whelm my eyes as I watched single strands and then larger clumps of my long, dark, brunette hair fall to the ground covering new spots on my light blue, shag carpeting. I removed the sagging suit from my body, grabbed my knees into my chest and sat naked on the floor, shaking, but unable to cry. I went through the slow, painful process of trying on another smaller suit, but it hung on me in a more mocking fashion than the last.

I caught a glimpse of my protruding ribs in the closet mirror and quickly grabbed a towel from my swim bag to conceal the harrowing self-image. Wearing the sleek, black racing suit as nothing more than an oversized diaper just around my bottom half, I cowered underneath the towel, eyes still closed, and inched my way back towards my bed. The height of my two and a half foot tall twin bed was a daunting climb. I'd lost track of time and space and the reason for scattered suits and goggles and my hair on the carpet and burnt cinnamon toast and coffee and it's only 50 meters...it's only 50 meters. Meters to where? Meters for whom? Whom was Dad talking to?

Aware of the cold, but not the nudity of my physical state, I pulled the red beach towel further over my body and sunk into the pile of bedside pillows on the floor at the foot of my bed. They relieved me from the bruising ground. My eyes squeezed shut to keep cold air from blistering my naked eyeballs, blurred images danced in front of me, thoughts spiraled to buttered toast and the calories in a single tablespoon of butter was 50 and it contained 11 grams of fat and the saturated fat would make me gain weight and the sodium would cause bloat and an entire piece of bread crunching between teeth...and parchment paper on my lips and cold, cold, icy, freezing, unrelenting cold only a few feet from my heater.

Bells jangled aggressively above my door and I thought Santa was real for a moment and I felt my body try to stand, but only realized it was sinking down through my shoulders and sunken chest. The physical dissolution of my body contaminated my mental will to fight for another day.

"Honey," I thought I heard Dad. "Get up, get up. We are late. Would you get up and eat something? Please!" He cringed in impatience standing in my doorway upon seeing my face buried in pillows and towels. "Aren't you going to the meet? We have to leave. Andrea! We are going to be late. Get up." His voice trailed off and I was thinking about how 60 calories were in an apple and that 50 meters of competitive swimming would surely burn 60 calories and what about the carbs and 72 jumping jacks and 100 sit-ups and...

"Andrea! Andrea! Andrea!?" I heard an elevated voice of concern, but I didn't know where it was coming from. Soon I felt long arms around me pressing into my sides and moving my body. Dad lifted me up as though I was an empty chair and placed me back into my bed, pulling the covers up over me.

2
Is there a Doctor on call?

Dad found me lifeless and naked in a mangled heap of pillows and ill-fitting swim suits on my bedroom floor. As he retreated into the hallway, I felt a heavy tinge of both disappointment and welling anger on his behalf. And in that anger I know my dad finally confronted what Mom had been telling him for months, which until now he had willed himself to ignore. Momentarily adjusting and silencing the pager on his right hip, the strong Greek man sighed deeply and walked back into my room careful not to disturb those dangling bells he wanted taken down several Christmases ago.

Kneeling at my bedside, Dad, the doctor who was always on call for the Family Medical practice he owned was only on call for me. He checked my vitals and felt my cold, dry skin. I was breathing, but slowly, and my weakened body needed rest and nourishment. Knowing I needed to change which side I was lying on as to avoid further bedsores, Dad effortlessly moved my body and tucked me in applying an ample covering of blankets on top of my comforter and turned on the space heater. With his large, calloused, working hands, he caressed the soft hair covering the skin on my arms and picked up the fallen clumps of hair from my head that were resting on the floor next to the bed.

"Honey? Sweetheart?" he cooed. "Andrea?" Purring gently in response to his touch, I recoiled upon feeling the forehead kiss that he gave as the wetness of his lips added to the heightened state of cold I felt. His face held dismay, fear, concern, and dejection. He knelt at my bed, as he did every morning at the end of his own bed to pray. Before he began to pray, I thought of him closing his eyes and envisioning me as a bouncing, happy, young girl wearing just a slip and tights after we got home from Greek church services together on Sunday mornings when I would run around chanting, "Ooo la lah! Ooh la lazzie, do I look sexy!" And he would heartily laugh at me and I would prance and dance and sing until he knelt down by his bed to pray and the curious girl I was wearing my favorite pink heart-embroidered tights and silky slip would come near him and stand behind him, now that he was at her height when in a kneeling position, and I would rest my chin on his right shoulder and lean into his body to listen to his prayer. And if he forgot anything important to pray for I would nudge him at the end and say, "Daddy, what about the doggy?! Daddy, daddy what about mommy?! Daddy, you forgot to pray for yourself again. You know God loves you, too!" And he would finish his prayer and we would say, "Amen" in communion and I would prance off again to find my mother with hopes that Sunday morning pancakes were cooking and I could go sneak chocolate chips in the batter when Mom wasn't watching.

One tablespoon of chocolate chips has 55 calories and 10 grams of fat and 15 grams of carbs and 7 grams of sugars. If you count eight, that's a tablespoon, so if you eat them never eat more than four.

A tear fell from his right eye as he looked at me — his once ebullient, dancing daughter—now lost beneath blankets for warmth. He squeezed his eyes shut, kneeled closer to my bed, resting his elbows next to the small bump in the blankets that was my body, bowed his head, and prayed:

"God, please protect this girl. Please guide her, love her, cherish her, hold her, remind her that she is yours. Give her the comfort and gift of your embrace. Show her the love that you have shown me. Dear Lord, please help her to be strong and courageous and to fight another day. This is my little girl – the sweetest gift I know - and I feel helpless to make things right again. I want her to feel wholesome, worthy, and important. Allow me to be a better father to her. Allow me to love her dearly and hold her closely each moment that I get. Let me be the one to shower her with your love. I want her to keep fighting and hanging on to life. She is worth it. You are worth it. I love her with a heart that only grows with compassion and knows love without condition. Dear Lord, give me strength to understand and wisdom to follow your plan for her life. I need courage, too. She is mine and we are yours. God bless this girl. Let her see you. Amen."

Finishing his prayer by making the sign of the cross, he stood up. Re-arranging my pillows and picking up the abandoned swim suits and placing them atop my swim bag so Mom would not come in asking too many questions, he turned his pager on again and left my room to go wake his wife, willing, but I am more than certain, not wanting to confront her with news of the situation.

3

50 Yards too far

Dizzy, but regaining a state of consciousness, I overheard Dad in the hallway outside my room speaking with my swim coach about my condition.

"She's not going to be able to make it today. I'm so sorry and I know she doesn't want to let the team down," he said. There was a long pause until I heard him insert words into the dialogue such as, "sick," "tired," "weak...body needs to rest," "virus," and he trailed off, but I knew even though he was trying to medically persuade of something other than the truth of what was going on with me, that in his forthright manner it was evident why I would not be at the meet. Everyone but me saw what was going on, but didn't seem to have the heart to mention that some girl who was once an accomplished swimmer was too weak to make it 50 yards at the most important meet of the year and probably her entire swimming career.

"I will keep in touch," he said. "Thank you for understanding and good luck at the meet today." I think coach said something about how the other swimmers would miss him cheering them on because he ended the conversation with a slight chuckle and indication that he wished he was going to be there. I heard his beeper's vibration interrupt my headspace as I became aware of the noise, too of Mom's waking. I felt like I needed to throw up or have an accident in my bed as my stomach churned, but all I could do was shiver in place as tears trickled down my face pooling into the well of my left ear. I was upset with myself, disappointed I had let my teammates down, and I felt even weaker in spirit upon hearing my father's conversation. After all, this was my father saying these things. My father! The man who had been there for everything in my life. From school events to family functions to tee ball games to softball and baseball games and to more baseball games! But mostly to all things involving sports. We shared a special bond over sports as he was the one who taught my siblings and I to play – baseball, softball, basketball, soccer, anything! He coached many of our teams growing up and he willingly paid for countless private lessons for tennis and softball for me. He showed up. And that was probably what mattered the most. He showed up. He was there for us. Always and without question. In his work clothes, his scrubs from the hospital sometimes, in between seeing patients, after long days without eating standing in hunger or thirst, it did not matter to him. What mattered was that he was there to motivate, to encourage, to tell us not to ever again take a call-third strike even though we crushed his heart in many circumstances when we still did. But he'd be there nevertheless telling us to hustle, hustle, hustle! Because if not, we were going to be benched, riding the pine next game. When he coached us, he never favored us as his kids over the other players and we never got special treatment just because we were related to the coach.

one of the greatest lessons he ever taught me. From my father I learned that hard work and merit trump all else. Sometimes I learned the hard way through the many deflated tears after games when I felt I didn't perform up to my potential for him. But even so, I was still thankful I did not win a trophy for not accomplishing anything of merit and I was glad I did not develop an inflated ego when I wasn't deserving.

Tears came flooding back uncontrollably as I recounted every long afternoon tennis session baking in the sun with Dad there picking up balls for me. Every soft toss hitting practice in the batting cage he rigged up in our garage, so we could practice through the winter. Every time we spent hours practicing in our backyard sandlot and I threw pitch after pitch in the dirt, but he somehow still scooped up to catch and laugh at me while saying, "Hit the glove next time, kid. You're killing me, smalls!" Every early morning wake-up for a swim meet or double-header with a drive over two hours away and every time he would wrap a towel around me to keep my muscles warm between events at long meets or when he'd turn the ball cap on my head into a rally cap when I'd come in off the mound from a bad inning of pitching and he'd playfully tap my backside and say, "You'll get 'em next time! C'mon now, chin up! Let's get those bats moving!" And every time he held his clipboard into his chest and furrowed his brow looking dejected when I struck out and every time he beamed and jumped with joy and slammed that clipboard in the dirt and beat the air with his fists and shouted, "You can put it on the board, Yes!!!!" Every time I scored a run or slide into base.

And each time I scored or did not score or I struck out or I got last place in my heat in a meet or I missed an easy break-away lay-up or I won my tennis match or lost in a grueling tie-breaker by making "stupid" errors as he would say, he was always there to pick me up and to cheer me on, and to tell me sarcastically that the players on the other team were big enough to eat me for lunch or that I was an "idiot" or even better, "a stupid idiot" for not keeping my eye on the ball.

From the time he first coached an all-girls park district basketball team for me and learned that you can't pat girls on the butt like you can with the boys teams he coached for my brother, to the time he was selfishly proud of me for fouling out in a late winter basketball game because I charged the lane and body-slammed the biggest bully in the league who was physically five times my size and pushed her off the court ramming her into the wall. To this day that is still one of the greatest highlights of my short-lived basketball career. It was the pride that overwhelmed his face in moments like that one that made me the absolute happiest girl alive. I needed nothing but my daddy and I knew everything would be okay. I was always more of a dancer than an athlete, but my father's endless investment in me and my siblings in the arena of sports made me want to learn, want to grow, want to play, and want to be the best.

I snuck a glance towards my door which had been slightly cracked open because I heard those pestering bells jingle again. My eyes opened and I tried to lift my head, but my abdominal muscles were too weak to support the action. I was still able to turn my head enough to allow the salty water from my tears to fall from my ear into the pillow and enough to see my Dad's face looking in at me. It was that same disconsolate coach's face that I got to know so well during my 8th grade year as a pitcher. It was normally one of disappointment, sadness for me and my team, angst on account of my rocky performance, and impatience to some degree. But this time his face read pain more than anything else. He mouthed inaudibly, "I love you," and closed the door. Those everlasting bells were an ongoing nuisance as they jangled and jingled louder and louder. Now, lying on my back, both of my ears pooled with the lost calories of my tears.

All too soon the morning erupted with its usual cacophony of sound with dogs barking, my Mom making demands of my Dad, my brother's alarm clock blaring this obnoxious drumbeat band cycle, my sister asking for someone to make her breakfast and help load her car, Dad washing dishes and cleaning the kitchen, making another fresh pot of coffee in preparation for the day.

"Why haven't you left yet?" I heard my Mom questioning Dad about why he was not on his way to the swim meet. "Did you get her up? It's getting late, Peter. You normally take care of this."

"Honey, hon----", he was abruptly interrupted.

"Is she going to eat anything today? Peter, you have to take her something, anything. Maybe some hot tea, crackers, toast, fruit or some peanut butter. Where is she? Did you drop her off for the bus? You knew she wanted to ride with you, correct?"

In what felt like 100 questions later, Dad re-surfaced in the conversation finally able to get a word in to slow Mom's speech.

"Janey, honey. She is not going today. She's still in bed. Andrea is far too sick. You were right. You were right." It was an empowering thing for her to hear she was right but in this context she wished that she wasn't. The questions ramped up from Mom again followed by a litany of impatient demands.

"What in the world are you going to do? You've ignored this thing for months." Exasperated, she continued. "Get her help! That's our daughter. Peter! Peter! Peter, please!"

She cried, she screamed, she wailed in both palpable anger and agony. The dogs broke into the chorus and amidst the pained intersection of sounds my father tried to reason and calm Mom.

"Sweetheart, it's going to be okay. She is going to be okay and so are we as a family." The calm logic in his reasoning failed to suture his wife's irrational flame of emotions.

"Peter! I have not seen her eat for weeks and you think this is all okay. This is all your fault. You kept saying she's fine, she's okay, leave her alone, and she would get better. Where is she right now? Did she sneak out to the gym again?"

Biting his upper lip to refrain from launching into a tirade at his now hysterically venting wife and sparing details about their daughter's state of prior unconsciousness that morning, Dad continued to calm the situation.

"Janey, we are going to take care of things and get on top of this. Please believe me," he said.

Failing to express any form of a rational thought, she rambled on. "I think she needs to be hospitalized. We are dragging her to therapy, don't tell me 'no.' I will do it myself if I have to!" The bickering and heightened emotions rang on, but doors closed and I could no longer hear the sounds. I think at some point that morning between my states of waking and sleeping my mom came into my room and cried by my bedside and kissed me and had our two black and white Tibetan Terriers stay with me while she went to shower after my dad left to visit patients and complete rounds in the hospital because his daughter's swim meet no longer had precedence on his time.

Mom had a right to be fearful for me, my health, and my life. She grew up with a father hell bent on perfectionism and making sure his children did everything to the best of their abilities. I only remembered my grandfather, Mom's dad, when I was a very young child because he died in his early sixties from colon cancer, which now would have been easily treated or prevented. My mother wore the loss of her father heavily and in ways I think she adopted many of the traits he was so well remembered for after his death. She instilled those upon her children with pride. I don't think it was out of any kind of malicious intent to control us even though that is what I liked to believe. Mom's sister and brother told me that they never felt good enough for their father and never felt able to live up to his standards. I could echo that sentiment with my own mother so well. Mom mirrored her father's attitude in her methods of parenting. She loved her father and maybe acting like him was, by her standard, doing the right thing for her own children. It was what she knew. And she knew her father loved her. So she loved us the same.

Mom also had high anxiety about my situation because of the struggles her older sister went through. Often when she and Dad would argue about me she would mention how her sister had an eating disorder and because of living through that experience she worried and easily diagnosed that I did, too. And that Aunt of mine still very evidently lives with the struggle because proper help because treatment for that disease was not available to her at the time and in her adult life she never received any professional help. I was not able to see it at the time, but Mom's fear of my illness was obviously much greater because she witnessed her sister go through the same thing and not receive help.

Perhaps, in a slightly different context, though, as her sister's anorexia was fueled by feminism and cultural narratives of the 60s era and the pressure Mom's dad put on her older sister to be perfect and to conform. He was the force against my aunt's youth rebellion and her control of her physical form was her counter to his desire for control of her life and choices. She too, wanted to be an artist as did I. But art was not acceptable as a venture for her father whose parents lived through the Great Depression and who saw creative endeavors as folly. Mom never chastised my art, but she certainly did not see it as a viable avenue for making a career. In that sense, though, Dad was the one who would be there for anything sports related, but when it came to my interests in dance, writing, or theatre he would play the part of an engaged father but he did not support those things as a way to make a career or make a living. Then again, he grew up with immigrant parents from Greece who owned a restaurant, a grocery store, and worked tireless hours to make their way in the America and raise a family. It was not easy for him to place merit in dollar signs and success on those artsy whims of mine. And so he pressed those values onto me in the same way my mother instilled her own father's pressure to be the absolute best. Excellence was the only option. It was no wonder I felt like a failure most of the time for both of my parents. I was not a great athlete, to the disappointment of my father, and I wanted to be an artist. In the shadow of Mom's expectations, I felt I would never be good enough at either.

Looking back, Mom must have felt utterly helpless with me. And I was cruel to her in response to her ever mounting pressure to fix the situation of my dwindling health. At the time I was defending myself against her because I wanted to prove I could overcome her desires for my perfection, but now I know I was only further hurting myself. Mom was a good woman who had lived through cyclical traumas with the people she loved and she certainly did not deserve it. Her life's passion was caring for the ones she loved. She gave up a successful career in finance so Dad could pursue his own dreams and ambitions and she could raise a family. She sacrificed herself for her children and we were her entire world. It is no wonder she had so much energy to pour into us. She stopped pouring it all into herself. She used to tell me, "Andrea, when you hurt, I hurt. And then I hurt some more." I did not give her much credit. She cared so much that my pains were her pains and she felt them even deeper. I never really thought about what it would be like for Mom to watch both her older sister and her daughter fight the same demon. Perhaps the worst kind of deja-vu. I know now what it is to watch another person suffer through physical and mental illness, and it only generates pain and the human desire to love and to serve. My family has a history of depression. Mom battled breast cancer, and I have seen mental illness take the lives of friends. I do not have a daughter, but if I ever do, I know I will come to sympathize with Mom in knowing the cavernous depths of pain I caused her. She became overweight during the time of my illness, she developed depression, and her anxiety was so great she had to start taking multiple medications. All because of me and my selfish desire for control against the burden of perfection I felt from her. She was not out to "get me" as I thought she was, but during those bitterly cold years of my sunken life, my heart felt about as much care and remorse for her as the pissed off faces my swimming teammates would hold for me when I returned to school.

Later that day, in the early afternoon, I woke up and regained a more lucid state of consciousness. I found myself in the family room wrapped beneath a wool blanket. That iconic family blanket. That supposedly ferociously warm blanket. Heavy, dry-clean only, carefully knit and emitting the scent of a chilled, gravel-filled attic crawl space. Throughout my childhood that beloved blanket we kept from my grandmother's house after she passed away was a hoarder of tears, a mask for uncertain fears, an escape and a destiny, a friend and a far-too-distant memory. It was known for causing episodes of profuse sweating if used for too long. A soft, cream color accented its dark green and navy geometric pattern and its fringed yarn-like edges, many of which had been braided over the years, never left the confines of our family room. Every night it was carefully draped over the end of the couch to mimic the way it rested at my grandma's house. Always perfectly laid to rest by my mother's tired, working hands, that blanket was the perpetual guardian of our family and all I could feel being under it was itchy skin and biting cold.

The side table next to the recliner I was resting on held saltine crackers and several glasses of yellow Gatorade and Dad was there instructing me to drink that sticky yellow substance that coated the lining of my throat liked overstretched saran wrap. It was unbearably disgusting, but I did obey his order. Later, after my family finished dinner, I tried to gum down the abandoned crusts of leftover pizza, but I started regurgitating them just as soon as they reached my stomach. I could not eat anything and with all that Gatorade coming back up my throat, I felt full and nauseous. As the evening wore on I heard light conversations in the kitchen as my family talked about me briefly, but mostly about their plans for the rest of the weekend and if I was going to be returning to school on Monday. I sipped on Gatorade the best I could through the evening and had burning urine two times from the hyper burn metabolic state my body was in. My vision kept getting blurrier as I tried to focus on the sitcom, "Everybody Loves Raymond" that had been playing on a Saturday afternoon marathon repeat all day. However, with each passing minute, the sounds from my family and the television became louder and more overwhelming and the prospect of forever sleep sounded all the more enticing.

4
God goes Silent, Bullies vie for Vengeance

I did not go to church that Sunday, nor did I go to school the following Monday. I rarely missed going to church, but there was nothing there for me from a God who had been silent for so long. And the straight-A, perfect attendance, book nerd officially missed her first day of school since second grade. Guilt ridden, I took to resting, crying, and attending to Mom's belligerence towards Dad and her fear for my life as it elevated to unmanageable levels. She kept mentioning how I was like her sister and saying I was going to wither away and perish. I thought if I did, I would be relieve of my pain. But, of course, I reminded myself I was okay and I was not really sick. The taste of Gatorade was getting far more bearable. Dad brought some Purple Frost flavored Gatorade home on Monday night and that kind was not as bad as the yellow lemon-lime one and I discovered that if you mixed the Blue Thunder flavor with the Purple Frost, it muted the flavor and made a grayish color that for some reason I liked sipping on and looking at.

After a full week of unwarranted wool blanket time, twelve bottles of mixed, gray Gatorade, a half-gallon of apple juice, forced oatmeal that was unintentionally thrown up, and fitful sleep accompanied by conversations about

about arrangements for potential interviews with counselors, and the looming prospect that I needed to be placed in an in -patient treatment facility, Mom agreed to let me return to school the following Monday. Though I did not have any sincere desire to go back to school for fear of the looks people would give me and the knowledge I held of disappointing my swimming teammates, the other option of staying home, being interrogated by my mother, and being constantly told to eat seemed a far worse alternative.

When I entered the balking brick high school building at 7:00 AM that Monday morning at the end of January, a time far too early for any teenager to be awake and functional, the petite woman with the curly, brown hair and fake rubber snake on her desk in the front office feigned a smile at me as she saw me walk into the building. I could tell it was a look of minor horror. Dad was her doctor, so somehow maybe she cared for me to some degree, or secretly, she was probably thinking, what kind of doctor lets their daughter starve?

"Good morning, sweetie. Good to see you back!" she said. I waved as the weight of the books in my backpack pulled my shoulders down into a slouched position. I tried to smile, but the dry, taught skin on my face made it difficult. As I proceeded to my locker on the second floor, I was shoved by the men's basketball team gloating through the hallways as well as the marching band playing nonsensically behind them. I had forgotten how noisy a high school hallway was and it had only been a week. The good thing about crowds, however, is that it is easy to feel invisible or at least to think that somehow you are. No one really talked to me as I made my way to my locker. Wearing three scarves around my neck and two pairs of spandex under my jeans that were being held up by two separate belts and a layering of under armor and a fleece vest on the top half of my body, I felt that no one could see me.

Then again, maybe they could, like the one punk freshman I knew as a neighbor growing up who sneered as I made my trek through the hallways, "Yo, ready for the arctic or what, Cladis?" I laughed at his joke to play along, but I was still feeling cold, despite the layers hiding my skeletal frame. As I approached my locker, I noticed a hoard of neon yellow-t-shirt-wearing swim team members waiting for me. My head drooped lower and I wanted to turn around. Crowding my locker, the swim team Captain, Jeannie, saw me first and her overly defined shoulder muscles seemed to threaten as she looked at me and said, "What it the f-ing hell, Cladis?! You screwed all of us. I could have gotten a scholarship."

"This is bullshit," Katy, the brunette anchor of our relay team pealed in. "You really let us down."

"I'm sorry, I'm sorry," I forced a response. My feet were numb in the ends of my shoes and my back was breaking and I couldn't even remember my locker combination so I could shed those gosh darn books from my cumbersome bag.

"What the heck happened?" Jeannie chided.

"I've been really sick with the stomach flu and I am beyond sorry I let you all down. I feel awful," I clarified.

"Well you should. It was a selfish move on your part," Katy added.

"I, I wasn't trying to be..." I tried to justify the situation or to explain my perspective and apologize but it was to no avail.

"Try eating something next time," Captain J retorted. "Our squad can't be made up of sissies like you."

I shrugged off my backpack and faced my locker not knowing how to feel or what to do as the first hour bell rang. Katy threw one of the neon shirts from the meet in my face as they walked away and gossiped together. I left it at the foot of my locker as I made my way to French class with Madame "I think I know it all" Francine. What a wench. Was there a French word for that? *Je suis désolé,* I thought to myself. *Désolé, désolé* I repeated.

That afternoon I took the shirt my teammates threw at me and left it outside Coach Jim's office with a note saying I was sorry about what happened in regard to the meet and that I was quitting the team. They didn't need me anymore and I certainly did not need them. I did still crave the water of a swimming pool though for I wanted to experience it as it would envelop my body and make me feel weightless. I wanted the smooth, chilled water to numb my pain and surround me in gentle waves of chlorinated submersion, removing self from the world. What I hated most about being an athlete was not winning. I was not a consummate champion in any regard and looking back I wanted that above all else. I was good enough to get second and third place, but I was rarely good enough to get first place. This aggravated me because Mom always told me I needed to win and to be the best! Quitting swimming was probably symbolic for me in that I was no longer going to be first, second, or third. Giving in meant I was going to be last. What I did was forfeit and because of that swimming forfeit, I was not going to allow myself to give up or forfeit my personal quest for bodily perfection and control. I know now that as my eating disorder magnified in its scope and intensity, it was not only me wanting control of my life, it was me wanting to be first. And first in anorexia can also mean first to the grave. In swimming if you beat your time, it is referenced as hitting a "Personal Best' or in running, a "Personal Record." In my enduring mission, I wanted to shatter both.

The following day when I walked into school, I avoided any form of eye contact with the front office staff entirely. I went straight for my locker and attempted to ignore the weird looks all the misfit malaperts gave me or the fact that no one was even talking to me. I saw my former best friends, Jenna, Hannah, and Samantha chatting in the hall about ten feet from my locker holding their fancy Starbucks drinks and pointing over at me with fake waves of pretention. I didn't even bother trying to say hello. All I could think about was the ringlets of my tightly coiled hair lining the inside hood of my jacket because that stupid shampoo was not keeping it from falling out. And also pride that I knew the entire Starbucks menu by heart. Those snitty girls were probably having caramel lattes with extra syrup and whipped cream. Before 8:00 AM they were ingesting around 450 calories, 28 grams of fat, nearly 50 carbs and 65 grams of sugar. All for nothing. I felt sorry for them as they sipped and sneered. I was winning. They just didn't know it yet.

During lunch, I avoided sitting in the cafeteria as was custom for me and to no surprise, heard people whispering facetiously outside my bathroom stall. "How long has she been in there? What shoes is she wearing? Is that the same girl from a few weeks ago? Does she have a hall pass?"

Seated on the hard, black plastic toilet seat surrounded by the rusty water smell in chorus with nose-swelling girly perfumes and fruity Teen Spirit deodorant, I squeezed my knees into my chest carefully to sit sideways on the toilet or else I would fall in. I did not want the hall monitors to see my feet or again identify me by the shoes that I was wearing. They were red Converse sneakers with double-tied shoelaces; and were loose on my shrinking feet. They were still trendy cool though and that made me feel a dwindling trace of athleticism and strength. I shivered and closed my eyes for escape. I didn't dare go out into that lunchroom chaos of food and fries and high calorie cookies and the cheerleaders who would call me fat just by looking at me. They were all so thin and I secretly hated them for that.

I quietly removed my brown paper lunch bag to find a sandwich neatly wrapped in a double layering of saran wrap. It was made exactly how I had instructed Dad to prepare it. The crusts were removed. I told him a thin layer of tomato basil hummus instead of mayo, to only use the 35-calorie sliced wheat bread, and to only place one thin piece of turkey on it. And also to cut it into four cubes for me, that way it was easier to eat. Dad followed my strict orders and I felt honored by that, but also somewhat like a total jerk inside. Packing his kids' lunches was one of those sources of pride for him throughout our childhood and even though I was in high school, he still wanted to do it. I'm not sure what he got out of it other than the act of provision and he also made healthy choices for us. He normally cut up a pepper, gave us a small piece of fruit, and we had a sandwich of some variety, but rarely, very rarely was it a peanut butter and jelly one. On special occasions we would get maybe half a brownie or a cookie, but that was it. I never minded the anal "three-item-limit" that he held for brown bag days, but I do remember how uncool it was in elementary school to pull out a bag of peppers to the dismay of classmates who said how horrible they smelled and for some reason never wanted to exchange their bag of Oreos for red and yellow pepper slices.

It was during second grade when Dad was so busy growing his medical practice that my Mom had to take over making our lunches and suddenly, they were beyond filling and delicious. We normally got six items, some kind of yummy dessert, a note, and her signature cream cheese and strawberry or grape jelly sandwiches on white bread. Those sandwiches were so good. The smeared whipped cream cheese and succulent, fruity jelly oozing out the edges of those sandwiches was heavenly. I ate every last bite and even licked the inside of the bag she packed them in. The leftover jelly at the bottom was sweetly satisfying to me. Maybe that was the year I became a "fat" kid, but I can't recall when all the teasing began. It was chalked up to baby fat by my piano teacher and I was told I would grow out of it and it was said some kids are just bigger boned and chunkier than others and it's okay if you're always fat because the world loves its fat people.

Staring at the three item limit lunch bag in front of me, with the slim sandwich, peppers, and small bag of precisely 22 grapes, I felt tears welling in my eyes and I felt sick to my stomach. I couldn't remember the last time I felt hungry. Even the year before when I was at school, I would take my lunch in the bathroom, but for a while I actually sat in the stall and ate it. I normally physically used bathroom once a week at school. If I had a bowel movement it was a something to be celebrated because somewhere in those twisted, malnourished intestines of mine constipation created a sensation of fullness and thus acted as a barrier preventing me from experiencing the natural feelings of hunger.

I would enjoy the half hour break between classes sitting in the bathroom stall where I would eat alone, and write Mom or Dad a note. I wrote to them every single day as sometimes they felt like my only friends. Those notes were more of a diary-style journal than anything else, but I think I wanted to write those diaries out as colorful notes for sharing, using highlighters and stickers and colored papers and sometimes even including poems because I could give the diary away in a beautiful way and would never have to read it again. I liked sharing the good parts of my life, but I did not have any desire to re-live it. I think my mom enjoyed receiving them. She kept every single one and usually followed the origami-like folding patterns I used to fold them back up for safe-keeping. Dad, too. Usually Mondays through Thursdays from middle school through my junior year in high school I would write a note at lunch time to my mother, and on Fridays, I wrote to my father. Dad was off on Friday afternoons and so he frequently picked me up from school if I had not driven to school that day. I knew I had a good chance on seeing him on those days so I made sure I always had an uplifting note for him in hand. When writing to Dad I could write a lot about my faith and the way I witnessed God working in my life. Sometimes I believed what I wrote about God's hand in my life and other times I wrote those things because I knew Dad was steadfast in his belief and God's provision. I loved Mom and Dad a lot and knew I was lucky to have them. Whether they simply appeased me in reading those notes or if they actually genuinely enjoyed them, I may never know, but either way, prior to my fall into illness, I did not care at all what sort of attention they gave to those letters torn from my the back of my red spiral notebook for math. I rarely took worthwhile notes in math class, anyway. No use in writing down what I already did not understand.

During September of my senior year was when I started writing longer notes to my parents and on the way into school each morning I picked up the habit of throwing away my lunch so I wouldn't be tempted to eat it. It was a control thing at that time with Mom. I had been intentionally losing weight and I wanted her to think I was eating at school so I told my dad I would pack my lunch for a while and I packed these overstuffed bags of treats and candies and thickly layered peanut butter sandwiches and sometimes fruit snacks and cookies because I knew my mom would look in the fridge to see what I put in my specially labeled brown lunch bag with an obnoxious 'A' in permanent marker on the front. Mom probably knew I was not eating it, but I had to pretend, nonetheless. Then, I'd proceed to walk into school each day and chuck the whole bag in the garbage can when my sister wasn't looking. It was so empowering and so freeing to do that. What a great lunch I enjoyed every day during the fall of my senior year. Control of my life through my weight was a valued aim of mine, but at that junction in time at least I still felt I was human.

Back in that stall going into the second semester of my senior year, I no longer even had the energy to pack a lunch and throw it away. I could merely command my ignorant father of my lunch demands and still avoid ingesting anything he carefully packed for me. The tears didn't want to come out of my eyes anymore and I crumpled my paper lunch bag into the small stall trash can, perhaps a bit too vociferously.

"Excuse me? Excuse me?" I heard one of the whispers say. A knock came at my stall.

I was well-accustomed to this hide and seek game. "Yes, I'm fine. I'll be out soon. Just have a bad stomach-ache today, nothing to worry about," I said.

"Do you need to visit the nurse?" the more cunning woman of the two probed at me while her bleach blonde, fuchsia and lime green clothed sidekick sneaked in a chuckle.

What the heck, I thought. *Laughing at someone in the bathroom? That's beyond any decorum of normality.* But these were high school hall monitors who got paid $50,000 a year to walk around a high school, laugh, and give students a hard time. What a deal!

"No, no. I'll be okay," I meekly assured. "I'll be out soon." I peeled back the layering of dual sweatshirts in concert with Under Armour and long-sleeve shirts from my left arm and I glanced down at my watch. I still had five minutes to kill before the bell would ring and I would see my sister walking towards the lunchroom and I would latch onto her as a buffer so I would not have to walk alone to my sixth hour class.

In my backpack, which was nestled behind the toilet so those pesky hall monitors would not see it or see me when my feet were off the floor, I kept a special pocket-sized steno notepad engraved with the first letter of my name on it. It had been one of those silly, twelve-year-old personalized birthday presents that rested in my bedside drawer for several years until only a twisted teenager would seek to repurpose it for such vile note-taking tasks. I heard the hall monitors scurry out of the bathroom gossiping like overgrown children as they left. I was amused when I pictured them walking out and slipping on an abandoned ketchup packet or having some fat kid throw mayonnaise covered pickles at them or…I sighed. Relieving the pressure from my tailbone I finally placed my feet back on the ground using my lap to write on. With a pencil and my steno pad in hand, I reviewed the previous weekend pages and started filling in my Tuesday notations. Each day I had a template as follows:

TUESDAY: Current Weight – 92 lbs.

Morning: Juice box (50 calories), Oatmeal (threw away, 0 calories)

Lunch: Orbit Bubblemint Gum (2 pieces, 10 calories)

Dinner Strategy: Extra napkins, dog near feet for scraps, tell them you had some food with friends after school, not that hungry

Calories Consumed: _____

Exercise Completed:_____

Pounds to lose this week:__4.5_____

Self-Statement: You are strong, stay the course, be in control of your life. You are winning!

> **Daily intake log:**
> **400 Max Cal**
>   50
>   10
>   _____
>   340 remaining for dinner

The bell rang as I completed my daily log update. It made me feel secure and in control to write everything down. I slid my second piece of Orbit Bubblemint gum into my mouth and slowly let it soften before I chewed. My jaw would hurt if it was too hard to clench down on immediately. I bypassed the mirror on my way out and waited in the hallway for my sister. At the time, she was a freshman and I, a senior. She was strong, sporty, and really smart. I envied her in many ways then as I still do now, as I was no longer the social, confident, competent student and athlete that she was. A few people said hello to me as the mass of high school humor, flirtation, and hidden angst marched by. Other students stared at me with chapfallen faces or turned their noses up. I smiled either way, but my cheeks always hurt when I did. Leaning against the scratchy brick wall, now only four minutes left in the passing period, I was getting anxious and chewing on my gum harder. The gums in my mouth started to bleed and the nauseating taste of iron was seeping into my mouth again. Bubblemint and blood – it is a menacing flavor I will never outlive.

Swallowing forcefully, I heard the sweet, melodious voice of my sister gently chime out at me, "Hey, Andrea! How was lunch?!" Finding a smile for her knowing she somewhat knew my struggle and worried for me, but always maintained an angelic, happy, accepting presence for me, I lied and said, "Good. It was good. I am glad to be back at school this week and see people again!" I didn't want her to know that I was suffering and had spent my entire lunch period in the bathroom because I knew it would hurt her too much. I always told her I was fine and I lied and I lied and lied some more. I was cold and I was miserable and I wanted everything in my life to fade away and to end. I wanted to disappear forever. The wad of gum in my mouth had been overwhelmed by blood and had lost its flavor.

Stacey's other friends walked ahead of us as we walked together and I listened to her share out about her participation in Scholastic Bowl and softball tryouts and adjusting to high school, now in her second semester. My chest felt heavy as I listened.

"I'm so proud of you," I encouraged.

"Thanks!" She said. "Oh and I have a joke for you!"

"Go on, girlie," I said.

Walking together towards my next class, she laughed as she said, "How do bees get to school?"

"Ummm…they fly to the Honeycomb!"

"No, silly! They take the school buzz!" She laughed and laughed. She was always tickled and amused by the simplest humor, while I usually only laughed not because a joke was particularly funny to me, but because her laughter was so contagious and often a hilarious sound of joy. I loved her for it.

"School buzz…" I quietly mumbled and giggled to myself. "Thanks, Stace."

We made it to my next class and I watched her tall, statuesque frame walk away from me until she turned abruptly to look back at me and shouted out, "See you after school, sis! We can play 'Locate the Civ!' Love you!"

"Love you, too," I said back to her as I felt tears coming into my eyes as loneliness sunk in and I was again aware of the bloody Bubblemint taste in my mouth. I thought about our little game, 'Locate the Civ!' I drove a 2004 Gray Honda Civic to school and at the end of the day we played a challenge game to try to find my car in the massive parking lot a few blocks from school littered with hundreds of high school student's vehicles. Even though we carpooled, we rarely remembered where I parked. She usually won the location contest, but 'Locate the Civ!' was one of my favorite distractions of the school day. Stacey and I connected, we laughed, and it was the brief moment of freedom between school and facing home and cold and Mom and Dad staring at me while I re-organized food on my plate at dinner. Mom kept the heat on low and it was always so cold in our house, I didn't like thinking about it and how many layers of clothing I would need to wear. Nor did I like thinking about dinner. It made me feel anxious and stressed and my steno notepad had no control over how many calories I would be forced to consume.

5
Death be Thy Birthday

By February my levels of fatigue worsened, my loss of hair was more noticeable and my steno pad daily weigh in was hovering around 83 pounds. Five feet, five inches, 83 pounds. I doggedly believed that once I got into the 70s range I would really be happy. I would be so proud if I could achieve that.

I continued to make up lies around the dinner hour - things about going out to eat with friends – the ones I did not actually have, or needing to be at the library to do school work or my overused argument that cherry-flavored, sugar-free Jell-O would be ideal for dinner because it felt so good on my throat and eased swallowing since my throat was dry and irritated much of the time. As my parents battled each other over therapy options for me, whether to do in-patient or whatever form of treatment I would actually agree to, I continued to scoff at the notion that I needed help. Somehow with each dip on the scale I felt stronger and more secure in myself and the ultimate aim of control.

Back at school, I was pulled from gym class with a doctor's note about my physical condition and had to sit in study hall each day during that class period and write reflection papers about various health topics. I got an A on each paper and I grew to prefer doing that activity much more than running around in over-sized, skin-chaffing gym uniforms. For some reason I got stuck on researching the topics of addiction and alcoholism for those papers. I avoided the realization that I related to those topics at a personal level, but I still think I could host an AA class if I ever needed to.

In health class we talked about "Simon the Sperm" and "Ava the Ovum" and the reproductive immaturity of high school nonsense quickly got out of hand. A few weeks into the unit, we got paired with a sex partner to learn about spreading STDs. Some fortified asshole named Brian Hinkler was my "sex" buddy and said I was starting to look hot and thin last year, but wasn't really hot anymore and then had the gall to ask me if anorexic girls can get pregnant because he heard they didn't have periods (he was right on that part) so he figured… "Well I could get a good fuck out of you, no consequences, right? What do you say?" I wanted to slap him or do something, but I smiled innocently because sex sounded horribly painful and just thinking about being naked or being touched in any way mortified me. I had bruises that hadn't healed for over two months from an overbearing hug my older brother had given me so sex would be utter abuse to my feeble body. And if I did by chance get pregnant, that would have been worse. Having a baby meant getting fat. I couldn't even let my mind wander there. It was also the first time I was specifically called anorexic by another student. I think I knew people thought I had a problem, but I never saw myself as anorexic and never labeled myself in that way. In my mind, I wasn't anorexic. I wasn't even trying to be thin anymore; I merely was not hungry. Apparently anorexic – in the denotative sense, literally means, 'lack of appetite.' I did not know that at the time, but I did know first-hand that the connotative meaning of anorexic was widely damaging. I did not have an appetite for food, nor did I have an appetite for life. No one seemed to understand that.

My birthday came in the middle of the month and Mom made me my favorite birthday dessert, which was a white, Pillsbury Funfetti Cake. I watched her make it and I noticed she lacked joy in doing so as I stood in the corner of the kitchen studying the calories on the boxed mix and frosting container.

"Use eggs whites," I instructed her. "I think it will taste better."

"You don't need it made with egg whites," she quipped. She knew my game and as a dieter herself, likely knew every calorie cutting trick in the book. In a snarky fashion I thanked her for making me a cake and I grabbed the wool blanket from the end of our couch to go sleep somewhere until someone woke me and flung candles in my face and gifts and the promise of wishes in flames on a cake of sugared calories I wanted to torch.

Later that same evening my family got news that my grandfather had passed away. He had been fighting lung cancer for nearly two years, so in some ways his death was expected. But it is never something you can ever truly be ready for and somehow God thought it would be great to take him on my birthday. As though my family needed more stress to consume them? Despite that news, my family still sang, "Happy Birthday" to me and I had a few bites of cake with them. It tasted so sweet to me I wanted to throw up, but I was still stronger than what I perceived to be the cop-out desire to purge.

"Happy Birthday, honey," Dad said with welling tears in his eyes before he was going to drive an hour and half towards the city to see his mother and relatives at the hospital where his father had passed away. He kissed me on the cheek and in his ever-strong, fatherly fashion, cupped his hands around my tiny, bony shoulders and said, "I love you."

"I'm sorry, Dad. I'm so, so sorry about Papou. We all loved him dearly." I did not know what else to say. He lost his father and was at risk of losing me, too. Dad nodded in affirmation of my condolence and opened the garage door to get into his car. I do not know where his strength came from or how he ever held it together for our family in the rockiest of times. He had just lost his father. And I witnessed his tears. I had never seen him cry before in my life. It takes a lot to break a Greek man, but the loss of a father might be one of them.

"We love you," Mom and Stacey added, both shattered with emotional trauma and heartbreak.

"Where's the ice cream?" My hunger prone brother, Dennis, asked in attempt to lighten the mood and the reality of what had just so heavily impacted our entire family. We all felt helpless.

I thought Mom was going to fall apart at that table. There were still pink glitter sprinkles on her shirt and dried, crusty frosting on her fingertips. Her eyes were red and bloodshot as she looked across at me.

"I made it with egg whites for you. I hope it tasted okay," she said. She so desperately wanted me happy and to willingly eat something, anything. Even if it was only a bite of a lower calorie birthday cake. There was white and purple frosting on my cake and she had decorated it beautifully for me with the love only a miraculously gracious mother who is under siege of fear, stress, and unbridled emotion, but still loves without condition, can do.

I was 17 years-old and 76 pounds. I had just learned Dad's father died. I could not decide if there was a God anymore. I felt sad, but I was unable to cry. I had not been able to cry for months. I lost that ability after the last time I ate a small bite of barbequed pork at 115 calories and 560 milligrams of sodium, chewed, and spit it out in my napkin for one of my dogs to eat. When I offered my dog, Chip, the pre-chewed piece of meat, he nudged my knee refusing to eat it and then only wagged his tail when I brought that napkin full of meat closer to my mouth pretending like I was going to eat it. Even our dogs had begun to feel sorry for me.

After everyone in my family went to bed that night I shamefully licked all of the pink-sprinkled, white vanilla and dye-your-tongue-purple frosting off the remainder of the cake like a sugar crack addict, reprimanded myself for doing so, did 100 jumping jacks and 17 kick squats (I didn't make it to 20) until I fell to the tile floor and finally garnered energy enough to get up. I threw away the rest of my unfrosted, leftover birthday cake, shoving it aggressively down the sink disposal as to hide the evidence.

We held my grandfather's funeral four days later. That pain is worse than hunger.

6
Winning Control

I can't recall the day when I began resenting my parents. But there's a good chance it was when they forced me to go to therapy sessions for what they called a "depressive, psychosocial eating disorder."

As a child I always remembered looking up to them for everything and also needing their constant assurance to temper my highly emotional personality. And for now, I find my perspective is still much the same. I always knew that they would be there for me and that I was not alone. I deeply feared leaving them and I was unable to sleep anywhere besides home for an overnight period of time. They sheltered me from that cavern of fear because I thought if I fell asleep somewhere else and died or something that I would leave them here alone on earth without me. Mom was always organizing the events and things in our family's life. For this she was indeed the servant-leader of our family. Mom was the hum and the churn. Dad was traditionally the breadwinner. He was a successful man making money to support his family and lead us in a spiritual way. Together they made a balanced team and all my needs were met. I never questioned food, wealth, riches, or activities, because I had it all, but I didn't know what it took to provide and give that opportunity and privilege to another until I worried I would be unable to do that if I ever had a family of my own. They were good people with sacrificial hearts. Yet when they inserted themselves into my personal aims, I wanted nothing to do with them.

For now, those teary-eyed, arguing parents of mine were the enemies of my progress, of my winning, of my, of my, everything. I didn't know what that "everything" was, but I knew I did not need therapy and I did not have a problem. My grandpa who had moved in with us the previous year because he was dying of Lung Cancer, he had a problem! He was sick and he needed treatment. I remember vividly the stress that placed on Mom and our family. She had her over-bearing Greek in-laws move in with her and her husband wanted her to hospitably dote on them. Meanwhile, the rest of the family got front row seats to the slow dissolution of their grandfather's life. It was during that time I started becoming obsessed with controlling what I ate and how much I exercised and how I looked and how sensitive I became to the way I felt when I ate food. Eating became a trigger for empty sadness and the unshakable feelings of being hollow. Eating amplified the loss my family was experiencing, and it made the void of pain far greater. That is precisely why I stopped eating normally in the first place. It made me feel better; or rather, not eating did not make me feel any pain at all.

Tension was high. The tension was always high in my family. From the time when Dennis went on a worrying school trip to study in Guatemala during college to my mother's arduous battle with breast cancer, to the loss of her mother and father, to the death of family pets, and apparently now, I was the new fulcrum of the long pattern of family stress and upheaval. Consequently, they were somehow going to "fix" me. "Fix, fix, fix!" They would say that word like I was a mistake and needed repair. The way they talked about me, even right in front of me or to my face, I no longer felt like I was human. I no longer felt like having anything to do with them. They could not make me go to therapy. I could not allow that to happen. I had to remain in control.

On a late Thursday evening after I had lied to my parents about going to the library to work on a project for history class, but in reality had spent three hours driving East towards the city and back again in avoidance of having to eat dinner with the family, I pulled into the driveway around 9:30 pm.

Dad waited in the doorway looking both worried, angry, and more tired that I had ever seen him. His face was worn and I knew Mom had laid into him about something. He was strong, but she was persistent in her demands on him and her obsession with perfection. Dad messed things up for her all the time, but willingly tried to make things right or uphold her impossible standards. He rolled his eyes from time to time or sighed heavily, but he always complied with her wishes. He was a good husband. I never questioned that. Pulling into the garage he watched me get out of my car and squeeze past him into the house without saying a word as he closed the door behind me. I retched my far-too-loose pants up my body as I walked towards the spiral staircase to go hide out in my room. I heard Mom sobbing in the kitchen. My sister was playing the piano in the living room and I think tears were coming out of her fingers disguised in mourning, playing solemn notes in a minor tone. I hated being there.

"Get over here, Missy," Dad quipped.

"I just want to go to bed. Leave me alone, Dad. Please." Mom was now wailing. I wanted to curse at her if only for that, but I can still hear that wailing now when I go back to that moment. It was a shrieking cry of unconditional love facing a most vicious, agonizing rejection.

"Peter! Peter!" She cried. "Don't let her leave again. Don't let her leave. Is she okay? Where was she tonight?" she questioned between her sobs and heavy breaths. The woman and her everlasting questions never ended. They never ceased even in the throes of physically emotive conflict, they remained.

"Andrea, we need to talk. Put your stuff down and come into the kitchen. NOW," he continued.

I became belligerent and was in a state of nausea, cold, and anger. Lacking any form of the ability to think straight, I walked towards to the front door and fidgeted with the lock so I could leave and walk away to anywhere, somewhere, and never return. I felt my father behind me and with one hand on the door, I looked back at him through my piercing eyes being pulled taught by the tight, translucent skin of my face and said, "We don't need to talk. I'm fine. I'm fine. I'm fine."

"Then come tell your mother that, Andrea. Convince her and then you can leave. You can go wherever the hell you please," he said with retaliation rising in his voice.

Looking up into Dad's dark eyes, observing his ever-tanned Mediterranean skin, I noticed wrinkles for the first time and an abundance of freckles on his face that didn't used to be there. He looked old to me in that moment and I wanted my eyes to tell me they were playing tricks on me. I could tell he was in pain. He was significantly thinner, too. I should have cared, but I only wondered what kind of diet he was on to lose weight. Maybe it was the same one as me. Later I learned that his "diet" is the stress of adulthood – the hardship of getting through life working, living, and raising a family. If that was all to come, perhaps I had forced a spiteful diet upon myself all too soon.

Knowing there was not going to be an escape for me, I skulked into the kitchen where my mother sat next to our black, granite countertop that contained expensive bronze fleck accents that blinded my eyes. They were all uneven and it had bugged me since we moved into that home they designed and built. Near the sink I noticed a plate of food covered in foil with an "A" written in permanent marker on the top. It was my cold, untouched dinner. My mom sure wasted a lot of foil saving plates of food for me.

"Sit down," Dad instructed.

"I don't need to sit," I snapped back. "What do you want?"

"We want you to start taking care of yourself, Andrea. And stop lying to me. I know every single one you tell," Mom pressed her lips together. She looked angry, but I didn't feel any morsel of remorse for her wet eyes, the labor of love evident in the dinner she prepared for me, or for her mounting distress for my life.

"Mom, I'm fine," I said. "I will be fine."

"No, Andrea. No you are not fine and you won't be." Her voice started getting louder and I knew she was about to unload on me. I would have to sit there and listen and take it and nod and smile but it would end as always. It would have to end. I knew it would end. I grew up with her and knew she had to have angry fits and once I learned that you could not win the battle against her and that she always had to have the last word, she would get pissed off more easily if you didn't fight back, but it would end sooner. She did not jump at me as I expected, so I waited.

"You are going to be starting therapy tomorrow afternoon at 3:30 pm. Your mother will take you directly from school," Dad calmly informed.

I did not say a word but callously stared at my mother, pressing my eyebrows together in a growing rage of betrayal and disgust. My anger fueled a surge of heat that undulated from my chest to my ankles.

"You're forcing this, aren't you, Mom," I said. "I know you are! You never believe me. You never trust me! You just think something is wrong with me. I'll never be perfect for you. Never!" I yelled holding my stare, fixing my eyes into hers, but she wasn't going to back down.

"You've lied to me for months now, Andrea. You're not eating. You look terrible and you need to get healthy again. I want to help you. I'm your mother. Stop acting like you know best," she jumped back. Dad sat down on the other side of the counter as I paced near the fridge. I wanted something like sugar-free Jell-O and fat free cool whip to put in my mouth so the taste of the blood seeping from my gums would not be so pronounced. But I knew if I opened that refrigerator door Mom would gain a slight victory and there was no way that I was about to allow that to happen.

"Andrea!" She picked up momentum. "I care about you and I love you and this is what's best for you," she barked at me, securing her victory.

"You don't know what's best for me, Mom. I'll never be good enough for you. I'll never be enough for you. I'll always be a disappointment," I forced a response, more blood spilling down my throat. The surge of angry heat swarmed my toes and flushed out of my body. I was quivering with cold.

"Take this blanket," Dad said as he wrapped me in that itchy wool blanket from our couch.

"What, are you going to force me to drink some Gatorade, too?" I quipped back at him snagging the blanket from his grip.

The fluorescent lights of our kitchen felt blinding and the randomized bronze specs flashed incongruently into my eyes. Mom pulled out a navy blue three-ring binder full of notes and folders and phone numbers and resources. The name of a local hospital was written in bold print on the front.

"What is all that?" I questioned. She never liked when she was the one being interrogated.

Not wanting her to spin off on me again, Dad responded, "This is all for you, Andrea. We have scheduled several appointments for you over the next few weeks until we find someone suitable for you to work with."

"Mom? Mom? What in the heck is going on?" I wanted a response and I wanted one quickly.

"You need help and we are tired of playing these games," she said.

"What help? Are you kidding me? This is completely unfair. If you guys loved me then you would just leave me alone. I am fine. What don't you understand? You can't force me to do this. You can't make me!" The bones of my feet were sinking deeper into my Red Converse shoes and the blanket was itchy and the lights were too bright and Dad was standing beside my mother and it was two on one and I wanted Jell-O and the blood in my mouth had calories of its own and the whites of my eyes felt like ice as I tried to keep them open. I tried to scream, but no sound would come out. I tried to cry, but my eyes were dry. I sunk into the floor, taking the blanket with me.

"Andrea, this is what is best and you're going. No more of this playing around with us." Dad was firm in his recourse and now I knew he was fully on team 'Mom.' There was no winning this one.

"There's several different options for treatment," Mom started up again. I tried to block out the sounds that her lips made. Wrapped snuggly in the wool blanket on the floor looking over at her rustling through papers on the counter with Dad, I felt disgust deep in my heart and anger in my soul. She looked like she was on this perch of pretention with all those papers and these doctors and all these people she had called and my Dad now in her grasp and no longer on the defense for me. Her perfectly coiffed short brown hair and manicured nails that said wealthy housewife and this incessant need to tell me what to do and to control my life. I thought her only goal in life was to control mine and make it what she wanted it to be. Now, I was weakened on the floor and she was there calling the shots again.

"Tomorrow we will meet with Elizabeth Parker. She's a therapist out of St. Vincent's. We will meet a few others on both Saturday and Sunday and see who is best for you," Mom said coming down from her offending throne as though I suddenly was agreeing and had given up all will to fight. "I'll go with you."

"We'll see," I said. "We'll see."

"Andrea, there's no 'we'll see,'" Dad said. I watched Mom punch numbers into a calculator and pull out some checks from her nearby checkbook. "You're going and that's that. If not, we'll admit you to in-patient treatment. We are doing what is best for you."

I recoiled even further into the floor as I shot daggers from my eyes at my mother and her check-writing abilities and her 'do this and do that' and all those 'have to be in control of me' traits she had.

The lights were bothering me. The bloody cotton taste in my mouth was becoming unbearable. I began crawling towards the staircase as my parents planned my life for me once again. "What good are you doing for me? You can't make me do this," I said. "What good at all if I even live anymore? You won't miss me anyway." I felt my parents look at me and I don't recall what the message of the next tirade of my mother's remarks was until my father interrupted her and the storm passed, at least for the moment. I crawled away with the blanket like a dog under a towel. I made it to the second step on our spiral staircase, collapsed, and fell asleep.

7

My Daughter Doesn't Need Therapy

The office of the first counselor we met with was on the top floor of a refurbished, brick apartment building. It was only a few blocks from my high school and was now being utilized as a business center with private offices for different sorts of products and services. The place had creeped me out as an apartment where old people lived when I was a kid and now it appeared even more cumbersome and underwhelming as an independent business facility.

Begrudgingly, I went to the appointment after school that day with Mom; Dad took off work to be there, too. I think Mom was worried she would not be able to get me there alone, so he accompanied her. The united front of my parents. I hated that.

When we entered the building, I immediately noticed at first how very cold it was and that it smelled musty with a hint of mint, almost like a dentist's office. It had an aged, sterile feel. It was a most repulsive place to be.

Dad walked over to the receptionist and found out what floor we needed to go to for the appointment. 5th floor, office 252. There were 252 calories in the Oatmeal Raisin Clif Power Bars I used to eat for breakfast my freshman year. I didn't even know why I knew that, but I refused to touch them anymore.

Dressed in a suit and tie, ever the utmost professional, Dad confabulated with the receptionist as it just so happened, as it often did, that she knew him and he used to be her doctor and he saved her son's life and…I was accustomed to these stories. Everyone loved Dad and his successful medical practice was well-known in every surrounding community. I stood up and walked over to the front desk. The woman he was chatting with looked at me and said, "You look just like your father! He's such a handsome man, isn't he?" She chuckled. I felt Mom's eyes roll behind me. She had heard these things her entire life and I, for the sake of being a mirror image of my father, heard them as well. "Oh, you must be a Cladis!" People would say. "Are you Dr. Cladis' daughter? I have to tell you a story…" And so it went my lack of identity as nothing but the good doctor's daughter. I used to resent it, at least that I was never addressed by a first name and random strangers befriended me on account of him, but in time I knew it was a blessing. If people hated my father and I walked around looking like him, that would have been a different story. It felt like I had secondary celebrity status and I became okay with that over time. He was a good man and I was proud and thankful to claim him as mine. I still rolled my eyes about it all with Mom. She needed that validation from me.

"Great to see you, Sandy!" Dad said as he left the counter. We made our way to the elevator to meet with this "Parker" counselor lady.

"She is supposed to be really good with eating disorder awareness and healing," Mom said to me on the elevator.

"So now I have an eating disorder? Whatever," I said. Dad was still smiling from his conversation in the lobby and was unfazed by the discourse between my Mom and I. He was so good at compartmentalizing life and enjoying small moments that it was beyond me. I think that's why he never cried, sans those brief moments after his father's death, and always kept his head on straight and…I looked at him as I normally did – amazed, bemused, and in wonderment of what it must be like to be powerful, humble, loved, and successful. My mother gripped her binder in anticipated excitement as the elevator opened.

We walked down the long, narrow hallway together searching for the caloric Clif Bar numbered office. The door was open and I peered around the corner to see two large plants near the window that faced the street and the wooden desk behind which Mrs. Parker appeared. The walls were white and there were four upholstered tan and cranberry colored tall-back chairs facing her desk. It looked like we were going to be interviewed.

"Come in, come in," Mrs. Parker said. Her voice was raspy like a smoker and her shoulder-length, curly red hair gave her the appearance of a mad woman concocting evil plans in a secret lair. She wore slacks that accentuated her thick legs and frumpy frame. The vomit yellow and green argyle sweater vest she wore was surely an icon of the 60s. Maybe my parents appreciated that sort of thing. She looked to be in her early forties, maybe younger, but I wasn't about to be generous with her.

She grabbed her clipboard and settled it in her left arm so she could extend her right arm out to me to shake my hand. "You must be Andrea," she said. "I am so happy to meet you." Her voice gave me uncertain chills and I had no intention of responding.

I barely extended my right arm to shake her hand, but I touched her extended hand anyway. It was one of those smooth, cool hands that felt like it didn't have any noticeable texture. I wondered if certain people like the ones who sat with curly red hair in high offices of overgrown plants and hidden ash trays didn't have fingerprints. They were the people that could escape the law. She was a fugitive; I was sure of it.

"Dr. and Mrs. Cladis," she greeted my parents. "It is nice to meet you as well," she said.

"Do you want us to be a part of the meeting?" Dad asked.

"Yes, I think for this first meeting we can all meet together," Parker responded. "Please have a seat."

We filled the empty chairs near her desk and I could see Mom's eyes light up. It was like all her twisted toiling to get me help was sinking in and she sighed heavily. I sympathized with her for a few seconds and then fixed my trance on the red-headed con-artist sitting across the table. Not surprisingly Dad opened the conversation using medical terms to explain my situation and why we were there. "Andrea has lost a significant amount of weight and we believe she has an eating disorder of some degree. Her BMI has rapidly plummeted in the past three months. My wife thinks this would be beneficial to her and we will support her in any way we can," he said. At that last comment, Mom dug the heel of her shoe into his ankle. He threw her under the bus like that relatively often, and even though I was mad at her, she didn't deserve it.

"Well I will begin with how therapy usually works so you understand the process for depressive eating disorder patients and then we will go from there. I can set up a schedule with Andrea after our meeting today for her to have appointments twice a week. Patients usually need constant, attentive therapy to see progress," she explained as her crusty voice seemed to compliment that nasty sweater of hers even more. *What were we paying for this?*

I played with the drawstrings of my aqua blue hoodie, layered as usual over several undergarments. It was a lot of work to stay warm.

"Typically it takes four or five sessions to get to the root of a patient's eating disorder," she said. *Oh, look.* I thought. *Now I was a 'patient' and I for sure had a 'disorder.'*

"What is the goal of treatment?" Mom asked.

"I just do the therapy side. You know, we talk, we learn, we discuss and I will get to know how Andrea is feeling about things in her life," Parker said.

Dad seemed impatient with her explanation. "Therapy side?"

"Yes, with this sort of thing there's the psychological therapy as well as the nutritional therapy once a patient gets to that point. It's both a medical and physical disease," she said. I think Dad was frustrated by her seeming lack of knowledge of what she was even talking about, so he questioned her further.

"What are you going to be doing with my daughter to improve her health? That is the question," he affirmed. Mom took notes as I sat quietly and studied the plants and wondered how their leaves grew so big. They were fat plants and therefore, I didn't like them. She was a chunky woman, and therefore, I did not respect her lack of self-control.

"I will need to analyze your daughter's mental state and I will learn about what got her to this point," Parker said.

"We need progress, not analysis," Dad added.

"This is not about progress, this is about the whole person. This is a holistic process and it can take several months," she said.

Dad knew that medically, in my state, I didn't have several months and I didn't need some red-headed shrink to tell me that my emotions were whacked and that I wasn't healthy. He needed progress and he needed it fast. It was always awkward having two medical professionals in the same room. Dad outsmarted them all and any sort of "holistic" medicine with no tangible proof of results was not going to cut it for him. He needed to feel confident about the process and the result.

The conversation turned to me as Parker asked, "Andrea, how are you feeling today?"

"Fine," I mumbled. I watched as she sipped some coffee and snuck a bite of a stale sugar cookie. It disgusted me. I hated watching people eat and hearing the sound of food mashing in their mouths. It made me physically ill.

"Excuse me as I munch here, I missed lunch today," she said. Yes and I skip lunch every day, you don't see me interrupting with coffee and cookies, do you? "Are you happy to be here today and ready to tell me about what's going on?" she said. Even I could tell that was an elementary question in the realm of therapy, but I think she wanted me to open up to feel comfortable talking to her.

"I like your sweater," I returned in a snarky fashion, aptly avoiding her stupid question about my apparent excitement to be there. Mom glared at me. She knew my sarcasm all too well.

"Thank you," she said and actually seemed authentically flattered. Probably because no one had ever bothered to compliment her on that horrendous article of clothing before.

She began talking about where she got it and as she trailed off, Dad interrupted, "Excuse me. We are here for Andrea. What is this process you are speaking of?"

"It is a combination of psychotherapy and then nutritional support," she explained again. Dad was not buying in and to this day I am not entirely sure why. I could talk around her and he saw that, but I think his defiance to her diagnosis and recommendation of treatment went much further. He didn't want to accept that his daughter had severe anorexia nervosa. He diagnosed and labeled patients every single day, but he refused to do so with his own daughter. She was Daddy's little girl and he was a prideful physician. His kids didn't get self-inflicted illnesses. She did not have the disease that stole lives, atrophied bodies, and caused heart attacks from potassium imbalances. Not his baby girl. Not. His. Baby. Girl.

The sun was starting to set as we parted ways with Parker and Dad said a friendly goodbye to Sandy down in the lobby. Mom was unusually quiet the entire time. I think the weight of the situation had hit her, too. There was a public humiliation certain wealthy families desperately fought to avoid and I was getting in the way of that.

We never returned to that counselor.

8
*Echocardiogram: BPM < 35**

As Dad began to slowly accept the disappointment that was me and he relinquished his reticence to my treatment, he worked with Mom to set up more counseling appointments and doctor visits. If only to make themselves feel better, the fourth counselor they sent me to, which happened to be the one I stayed with, was a Christian counselor. She focused on utilizing the guidance of God and growing through faith in healing. I think above all else, the imagery of it all looked good. Cladis' daughter needed therapy, but what good parents they were to have the rationale and will to send her to a Christian counselor. Maybe I was too hard on them. And in all likeliness they wanted to do right by me. After all, she wasn't that bad. Her name was Sarah and the hair she had that went down to her waist had a slight red hue, but it was not curly like the strange Parker lady we met. Sarah was tall and thin herself, which made it sometimes difficult for me to be told I needed to gain weight by a thin person, but aside from that she did not wear ugly argyle sweaters, a quality which I learned to greatly appreciate about her.

*An Echocardiogram is a test of the action of the heart using ultrasound waves to produce a visual display, used for the diagnosis or monitoring of heart disease.

Sarah was gentle and easy to approach, but perhaps not quite savvy enough to outsmart me. I ended up sort of liking her, so in that sense, I'm not entirely sure.

Sarah's office did not have plants, but it did have a comfortable couch and a heater that kept me warm. There were lots of Bibles and Christian books and an abundance of soft pillows. It was a cozy place and eventually she became a friend that I did not mind going to visit. I did not always tell her the truth, but at least I was not afraid of her.

Our schedule included meetings on Monday and Wednesday afternoons and occasionally some Friday evenings. After my third appointment with Sarah, she commented on the medical notes she had been given and ordered me to get an echocardiogram. She wanted to determine if I needed in-patient treatment or not in my current state. Everyone seemed to be pushing that, but my parents, who knew I could not even sleep overnight at the neighbor's house, also knew that would be a very taxing form of treatment for me. To have to move out of my home and stay away somewhere for several months would have killed me. And to their credit, to this day, I thank them for fighting for me in that regard. I had concocted detailed plans to kill myself before I would allow that to happen and I cannot say with confidence that I would not have followed through with them. Rather, I know that I would have.

Dad said I did not need a separate appointment at the hospital to have the echocardiogram and that he would complete it in his office some evening that same week. I did not look forward to having it done because I knew it was a test that I could not mask or alter the results from. I also desperately did not want Dad to know my weight and medical history that the other doctors had collected through the whole treatment period thus far. He might have already known it, anyway, but I liked to tell myself he didn't.

On Thursday evening that week, Dennis, Stacey, Dad, and I went to his office to perform the test. Dad prepared the machine and the table that I was going to rest on while he did it. I was shivering head to toe as usual and when he asked me to take my clothes off, I was horrified.

"Dennis and Stacey, can you please place these tabs on Andrea's chest in the following locations?" Dad said as he presented them with a diagram to follow. I was embarrassed to be naked and their appalled faces when they saw me without clothing said more than I could bear to take.

"Don't move, Andrea," Dennis instructed as he participated in placing the suction cups on my body. "We have to get this right," he said. It was strange that my brother was so serious in that moment. Up until then he didn't seem consumed by the focus on me at home, nor did he appear to care what was going on. "This is important," he continued. "Stop fidgeting." Dad turned on the monitoring machine and hooked up all of the cords to perform the test. The suction cups and tape buzzed and tickled as Stacey covered me with a blanket the best she could while preparations were being made.

The first run of the test showed that I did not have a notable heartbeat. In other words, the machine was not picking up any heart rate at all. I was still breathing, and now shaking on the table from being exposed to the irritating air.

"We are going to have to use the smaller suctions. We need to use the electrodes and tabs from the children's set," Dad said. My brother peeled off the set he had carefully placed on my chest, shoulders, and right hip and looked at the diagram for the children's set.

"Can we go home yet? I'm cold," I pleaded. "I don't want to be here anymore," I said.

"Andrea, someone else can do this and you certainly would not like that," Dad said. Stacey joined forces with my brother to re-attach the monitoring system and place the delicate suction cups for kids age 3-6 in an "M" pattern on my sunken torso. It hurt when they pushed the tabs into my ribs and my skin was so sensitive that when they placed the tape over them to adhere the mini-suctions cups to my body, it felt like a match being lit up on my skin.

"All right, I think we are good to go. Let's try this again," Dad said. I opened my eyes and stared at the paint cracks in the ceiling above my head in the dimly lit exam room. I heard the machine buzz and click like a fax machine and my father repeated the test several times to find a signal. Even with the smaller cups and tabs on my chest it still was not recognizing a heartbeat. Dad was becoming impatient and fussed with the machine and connecting cable cords. Finally, on the fifth try, it registered my heartbeat and the test could be completed. The printout showed that my heartbeat ranged between 25 and 30 beats per minute. An average resting heart rate is 60 BPM. A well-trained athlete around 40 BPM. A person on their deathbed? 30 BPM. Dad was alarmed and repeated the test several times, but still got the same result. The echocardiogram said my heart was failing. He panicked briefly as he tried to explain to us what the numbers meant.

The last thing I remember hearing in that room before I fell asleep on the table was Stacey nervously asking, "Is she going to be okay, Daddy? Is she going to be okay?"

His medical mind whelmed his role as father and rather than fear for me as my mother had, he wanted to act quickly to heal and to correct, and more importantly to save his daughter's life. He knew how strong I was and he knew I could fight on would fight on. But if he hospitalized me, it would be all but over. I would end the fight right there. He also knew, though, that if he returned those results to the counselors and therapists whom they had been working with, that he'd have to argue against all principled evidence to bypass the recommended, or at this point, possibly even forced in-patient therapy. He was never a man to lie, especially not about anything in relation to ethics in medicine, but sometimes I still wonder if he fabricated the results of that test when he met with Sarah later that week. I hardly had a pulse. There was a lot on the line.

9

I'll pass on the Nurse

Despite bi-weekly counseling sessions and my distressingly low heart rate, I kept up my old habits at school. From lunchroom avoidance to wearing fleece-lined gloves, a full winter jacket, and a stocking hat to each class because the air conditioning was too aggressive for me to endure, to specialized weight and calorie notation at lunch followed by slowly chewing on two pieces of Orbit gum at exactly 12:10 and 12:15 pm, my mental and physical instability worsened.

In late March, on the Friday before spring break, those same annoying hall monitors were back, this time in a different bathroom where I was hiding away before school was to start. They thought I was in there throwing up, as was their conditioned premonition, but I never made myself vomit. I was not bulimic like people claimed I was and that greatly aggravated me. However now in looking back I can understand why they made that assumption. I was skeletal skinny and was often spending abnormal amounts of time in the bathroom. Yet never once did I participate in the activity of regurgitating food. After all, that would have been too easy. Not eating and having the will to abstain from food was far more of a challenge than the cyclical esophagus tearing binge and purge. I thought people who did give into that means of controlling weight were weak and I was not a weak person. Not once, not ever. There were times after I ate wherein I thought about throwing up if I felt overly full or was worried that I ate too much and those calories were morphing into fat molecules swimming beneath my skin, but instead of purging, I would go exercise for two or three hours or until I could not handle the forced exertion anymore.

"Excuse me?" The hall monitor called into the echoing chamber of the oily, silver-stalled bathroom. I was tucked away in the large, handicapped stall at the end of the long corral of toilets and sinks.

"You can't be in here before school," she said. "You need to get out of here and go wait in the library for the first bell."

What kind of garbage was that? Students can't use the bathroom before school? That was a lie and I knew it. I did not want to be manipulated by the hall monitor who wanted to scold me and send me to the nurse. Pretending I did not hear her, I did not respond, so she came and knocked loudly on my stall door.

"Hello? Hello?" Her voice vibrated in her questioning.

"I'll be out in a moment. I'm sorry. Please give me a moment," I pleaded.

"I'll wait right here. You have three minutes," she forcibly replied.

Frustrated, I gathered my things, powered through the stall door past her, and defiantly walked out of the bathroom with my backpack and brown bag lunch that I had not yet gotten a chance to throw away. As I exited the bathroom she followed me and her flighty, moronic side-kick appeared in her ever-sparkly fuchsia and green vest paired with boots and skinny jeans that she was too fat to wear.

"Here's a pass to the nurse. I hope you feel better," the blonde nuisance mocked me. I knew she did not care if I was actually sick or how I felt; she just wanted to assert herself as being superior to me. At least I could fit into skinny jeans, size XXXS. I figured she only secretly wanted that. Poor thing.

I took the pass that smelled of her floral tulip perfume and smiled faintly as my heart started beating faster in my chest and I felt a light tickle of warmth as fear whelmed my body. As snarky as I might have been on the surface, I hated being corrected or reprimanded or being told what to do. And I especially hated when women who thought they were smarter than me, but were nothing more than flighty, judgmental bimbos, tried to control me. God, forgive me for my critical ways, I prayed.

The bathroom I had been hiding in was near my locker so I told the women I wanted to stop at my locker and then would proceed to the nurse before school started. They nodded and marched away in unison towards the stairs and main commons where I hoped they were going to pick on some other unassuming student hanging out in a bathroom getting high, smoking weed, or sneaking vodka into their expensive designer water bottles. Those students were the ones who deserved to be suspended, but rarely were caught, while I, just sitting in a stall to mask my social anxiety from peers wandering halls before school, felt like I was hunted down every day, laughed at, and told to go to the nurse or sometimes to see the principal. What a joke. What a fucking joke.

I had twenty pink nurse passes littering the bottom of my locker. I never went to the nurse except for the one time I was walked down there by the blonde. Luckily, my only friend, Paul, saw them bothering me again and retrieved me quickly afterwards.

Paul was a homosexual man from Thailand who had befriended me in Consumer Education class during our sophomore year of high school. We were partnered as husband and wife in an activity where we had to buy a home, get jobs, and practice balancing a budget. I loved his accent, his round figure, his hair that changed style every day, and his sense of fashion. Paul was the closest, best friend I ever had in high school aside from my younger sister. A lot people were cruel to him because he had a feminine affect and because he was gay and Asian and any other thing a high school bully can find to tease about, but I loved him to pieces. I think because he was gay, he was not a threat to me, and because he didn't judge others, I always felt whole around him.

"Oh my gosh, girl! Where were they taking you?" He said as he grabbed my arm and pulled me towards him. His chubby fingers comforted me as they did not bruise my bony arms.

"They want me to go to the nurse again because I was in the bathroom," I said. He was one of the only people I never lied to during that whole time. I had no need to because there would be no repercussions for my actions and the litany of questioning I was accustomed to from my mother wouldn't be spewing from his soft lips and mouth.

"Girl! Oh, my gosh! They are so crazy. Your hair looks so great today. I absolutely love it!" he said, boosting both my confidence and lessening the anxiety the hall monitors had caused me.

"I love you!" I said and covertly, I think I meant it. I loved Paul. Not romantically, but I loved that he was a friend to me and he gave me a sense of belonging. Without Paul, I don't think I would have made it through my junior or senior year of high school. I loved that he never looked at me in a funny way like the other kids did. I loved that he complimented my thinning hair because he knew I was self-conscious about it. Sometimes, of course, he would still ask how I was doing or why I had lost so much weight, but he never made me feel less than human and he certainly never let me believe I was invisible to him or to others.

"Girl, I love you, too!" He said emphatically while adjusting his white polo shirt and light pink khaki shorts. "You look more beautiful than ever. Don't let those women tell you otherwise. So how was your weekend? Can we get coffee this week? Sit and chat? What are you doing Friday afternoon? I'll buy! And maybe some ice cream, too!" he said. I was supposed to go to counseling Friday afternoon and for the rest of eternity.

"My parents are making me go to therapy again on Friday. I'm sorry," I said.

"They still have you doing that, huh? Is your counselor cute? Ha!" Paul joshed as usual.

He always had a way of bringing light-hearted humor to any situation. "Well the one man I spoke to last week, I guess he sort of is!" I said, sending a sultry wink in his direction.

"411 give him my number! Hot doctor! Ooooh!" He playfully teased.

"We can go out after you're done or sometime on Saturday, okay? You just tell me when and where, girl. I am headed to culinary class. I'll bring you a sample next hour. Love you!" he said as he swayed his round hips while walking down the long hallway.

"Thanks, Paul! Love you, too," I called out after him. I left some books in my locker in exchange for the binders I needed for class and got my backpack organized for first hour. I thought about our impending outing and that drinking acidic coffee would hurt my stomach and how eating ice cream, though I knew the calorie count of ice cream in every shop in town, was beginning to sound kind of good to me. I flipped through my steno notepad quickly. 68 pounds in my last entry. The seventies were good, but the sixties felt better. I would stay the course, some weekend ice cream wouldn't hurt me, would it? Only six more hours left of being at school until another therapy session. I was still in control. I could make it.

10
Mangoes and Shellfish

Later that spring I had started meeting concurrently with Sarah, the psych-therapist and Rosetta, a rotund Indian woman who smelled of cherry blossom perfume that reminded me of the sugar-free Jell-O that had a permanent coating on the back of my throat. She acted as my nutritionist. For being a registered dietician, I quickly learned that she did not have much knowledge of anything related to food or nutrition. Initially, this was disappointing, but when I learned manipulation was a feasible tactic, I readily forgave her lack of professional knowledge.

The first time I met Rosetta was underwhelming at best. I actually felt kind of sorry for her. There she was, this woman with a thick Indian accent, who could not pronounce her 'R's' correctly, who sat in a tiny corner office filled with plants and crates of uneaten, overripe mangoes in some ungodly therapy center in what felt to me like the middle of cornfield country Illinois. At first I actually thought Rosetta was a he, but her long sequined nails, loose floral print blouses, and navy blue trousers assured me 'he' was a she.

There were three other nutritionists that worked in the same building, but none of them smelled like cherries or had

mangoes in their offices. But she did. The strange four foot
tall woman of the cornfields with tanned skin and an
overstuffed figure whose job it was to tell people to manage
their eating behaviors distinctly smelled of floral cherries.
And the longer I was in her presence, the more her smell
brought forth memories of childhood Easter celebrations
and colored plastic eggs full of fruit-flavored jelly beans. Her
hair was short and pinned tightly to her head and I was
mesmerized by the neat curls that she styled it in. There were
a few highlights of red in her jet black hair and I used to
wonder where they manufactured all these red-headed
shrinks. I thought if I got some red color going in my hair
that maybe I would be able to tell people they were mental
freaks, too. Actually, with my waning hair, getting a wig
would not be such a bad idea.

"We are going to begin a food diary together where
you will record everything you eat in a day," Rosetta told me
upon our second meeting. She also told me that my mom
was supposed to stay out of everything. Mom was not
allowed to ask me questions or get in my face or query about
what I was doing. She had to respect and trust me. I was
eager to see how long that would last, but I sure liked the
sound of it. It was a hand-up on my control. The therapists
knew that and so did I. I would have to decide to get healthy
because no one could do that for me. Rosetta and I played
'get-to-know-you' during our second encounter and I lied to
her about my energy levels, my echocardiogram results, and
my growing levels of hunger. To her naivety, she bought
into my monologue because we had easily skipped right past
phase one through five of the supposed mandated therapy
steps. I had become the consummate manipulator and I
quite enjoyed it.

"I already keep a food log," I told her truthfully.

"Oh, good, good. Can I take a look at it?" she asked.

"Well, it's in my backpack at home. Maybe I can bring it next week," I told her.

"In your food log," she began again and my mind wandered to what the last entry of mine said. I think I was still in the sixties or was I? Had I dipped lower than that? She didn't need to know.

"You are going to keep a list of the foods you eat each day and also manage an ongoing hunger scale," she informed.

"A hunger scale?" I queried. I had not known the feeling of hunger for nearly two years. What in the freaking heck was a hunger scale?

"Yes, you will make a notation of your levels of hunger throughout the day. For example if you are feeling very hungry, then you write down a '10,' but if you do not have much of an appetite, you would write down a 'one,'" she explained.

"And what else do you want to see me write down?" I knew there had to be some other part of the equation. I did not want another assignment.

"Well, identify whether a food is a protein or a dairy or a starch. You can look that up and mark it down for me. We will review it next time we are together. We want to create a balanced diet for you each day. Next week we will begin weigh-ins to monitor your progress as well. Would you like a mango for the ride home?" She asked as I got up to depart.

"No, thank you," I said, squinting my eyes in disdain. I grabbed my bag and studied the red streaks in her hair.

"Have a good night," I said and walked out to the car where Dad was waiting for me.

After those mandatory counseling appointments, Dad used to pick me up and we would go to either a McDonald's or a Wendy's drive-thru for shakes or Frosty's. On a special day, or if the counselor told him I was progressing, probably because I'd weight my pockets so strategically for weigh-ins, we would go to Oberweis and get something extra dense and caloric.

I only ordered vanilla because it was a plain option with fewer calories and I had to pretend to drink it the entire way home until I could go upstairs and say I would enjoy it with some educational reading the counselor had instructed me to do. There was never any reading assigned. Food logs, yes, but readings? I amazed myself at how good I had gotten at lying. I felt remorse when I would dump out those shakes, watching the half-melted milky calories plop and splash in the toilet bowl. I made sure to flush several times.

"Gotta fatten you up, kid!" Dad used to playfully say. He was eager to buy those shakes as if he was doing his part to make me better. The soft side of me that was the ever-ready Daddy's girl wanted him to be happy and wanted to drink those shakes for him, but I simply could not do it. However, he certainly drank a lot of shakes that spring even though he wasn't the one in need of the meal replacement.

In the following weeks I kept my personal food diary notated just as it had always been and began a separate food diary for Rosetta. It was fun to create things in the new diary like the elaborate steak dinner I had one night, the waffle-cut, parmesan-sprinkled French fries and the exotic types of fruit I claimed to be eating. She did love mangoes, so maybe I would include some of those if the opportunity arose. A mango smoothie, perhaps? A high calorie, high sugar fruit was sure to please. The hunger scale thing really baffled me. I really, truly did not know what a ten on some arbitrary scale of hunger was supposed to feel like. But was I feeling a one or a five? I played scrabble for those numbers the night before I went to see her again. I had blanks on each page of my food log for the week where I would fill in the numbers. If I wanted higher numbers I rolled two dice. I didn't mind the game. "How hungry are you?" I called it. It was like a mirror to 'Locate the Civ!' – the happy little intermission between the fantasy world of jocularity and the real world of cruel, regulating control.

"Wow!" Rosetta said when she saw my log during our fourth meeting. "You surely are an adventurous eater. How is your stomach holding up? Do you ever feel nauseous? Are there any foods that you are afraid of eating or don't want to eat? Where did you get protein from last Thursday?" She perused each entry in my log carefully.

"Oh, I had fish that night with my family. My mom made salmon," I injected.

"Fish? No protein there," she said. I knew fish had protein, but I did not want to argue with the mango-loving dietician whom I think had a shellfish allergy. She probably did not know what a good source of protein fish provides. I did, though, and my body probably wanted to find out what it would be like to eat it, too.

"Fear foods? No. I don't think so. Tummy ache? No, not really," I said. I mean I was afraid of all foods and my stomach was constantly hurting if I ate anything – let alone a bowl of fruit for breakfast, oatmeal with peanut butter at lunch, and cheesy potatoes with pork for dinner - as I had indicated in my log for her from the prior Saturday.

"That's really great! And you are feeling hungrier too, it appears!"

"Yes! I am truly feeling great," I said.

"And what about your period? Have you had a period recently?" She asked. I could not recall when my last period was. I think I started having them when I turned sixteen and stopped two months later. I had not had another one since then.

"Ummm, I can't recall," I told her. "I think it is normal, but Dad said a lot of times female athletes do not get them," I justified. "The female athlete triad or something of that nature?" Even to myself I sounded like a pretentious snob.

Every other counselor knew exactly what the dangerous 'female athlete triad' was and I said it to sound intelligent and in touch with my own physical state of health more so than anything else, but Rosetta simply said in her thick, gooey, sticky mango voice, "Oh, no I do not know what you are talking about, but do keep me informed when you have a period and I will mark it down in your file. You need to be at a certain weight threshold for that to happen." She scribbled something in her notes. The red highlights of her tightly curled hair flashed their fury at me.

Yeah, I know and that certain weight threshold is baby-making, wide-hips, fatness. I can't let myself get there. I'm better than that. I am stronger than that, I repeated to myself again.

During our regular weigh-in together, Rosetta was displeased that I had not made much progress. She encouraged me to stay the course with my eating and that in time I would put on weight. *Sure, because all I want to do is put on more weight.* I wised up rather quickly though and began devising strategic ways to make myself weigh more. Rosetta always made me remove my shoes before stepping onto the scale backwards – I was never allowed to see the numbers – but she never made me fully undress or remove my sweaters or jeans. I took to filling my pockets with coins and weighted saucer rings from Dad's toolbox. I could fit about ten flat in my pockets that she would not notice and bonus, if I wore a bra, I could fasten it tightly enough to hold pocket hand warmers that looked like incremental breast growth on my chest. I could add ounces with quarters and nickels laid flat on the top of my feet covered by the thick wool socks I wore. She never saw these things, nor suspected I was cheating in any way. God bless her soft mango heart, I was only hurting myself.

When I would get home at night from those appointments and remove my socks I could count all of the indents the coins had made in my thin, bony feet. The imprinted red marks lingered for a few days, reminding me that each foot cost $2.50 for 16 ounces of weight. $5.00 for 32 ounces would be the max in my feet and my disappearing breasts could only grow so big from those hand-warmers and the burns were leaving marks my chest, and after a while I was running out of ways to tack on feigned weight to my shrinking frame. I still have a patchwork quilt of rectangular scars burned into both my right and left breast.

After eight sessions together I still was not showing notable progress. The scale had tipped in my favor, but all other signs of health indicated little to no improvement. I could not conceal everything and my will power for deception was fading.

11
Tatsimou, I Need You

As spring came into full bloom in late April, it was beginning to get warmer outside so I was not feeling as uncomfortably cold anymore as I had all winter. That alone made me feel stronger, healthier, and happier than I had felt in a long while. Maintaining my food logs for Rosetta made me more obsessive about food and calories, but also interested in exploring new recipes. A hobby I began to enjoy was going to the grocery store and studying food labels. I had a photographic memory and I had entire files of food labels stored up in random compartments of my brain. I could access calorie counts with ease, whenever needed. On occasion, I would combine recipes to concoct elaborate meals and then write down each calorie and nutrient I ingested in the fabricated food log I kept for her. I ingested all those meals with my eyes, of course, but Rosetta was impressed that I was such a broad, seemingly voracious eater and had a unique taste for finer foods. Surprisingly, I impressed myself, too!

There was a remarkable turning point for me wherein I started to enjoy going to counseling. I could anticipate what the counselors were going to ask, feed them the answers they wanted to hear, and make them feel encouraged that I was getting better and was on the rebound. It was a tactful game of strategy, amicability, and cunning manipulation. I loved it and I got better at it week by week. They were always astounded by my progress both mentally and physically. I prayed to God in secret to forgive my behaviors, but I was not all that genuine. I figured He was not going to offer me any share of mercy or grace after all I had done.

"Has your period returned?" Rosetta inquired again during our ongoing treatment.

"Yes, it came back a few weeks ago," I assured. I knew to them it was marker of health so I eased into saying anything that would placate. Here and there I was sporadically eating a little more for dinner and the weight I had gained was noticeable. Well, to me at least. I think I was back in the seventies and I did not want to be there. I had to gain some weight to appease the counselors because coins and metal saucers in pockets and socks were not enough to keep me out of in-patient hospitalization anymore, but even an increment of a half-pound gain took at least a week to accomplish. Those weeks of half-pound gains added up though and I did not at all like that some of my underwear felt snugger and that my gums weren't bleeding as much.

We had a forced whole family session with the Christian counselor, Sarah, on a Thursday evening in May and it was one of the worst moments of my life. I had gotten comfortable talking with Sarah as a friend and a safe person to be with, but my lack of notable progress in every regard meant something else had to be done. I assumed everything was fine, that status quo was okay, but when everyone else in the room knows something you don't - perhaps the fact that your heart is slowly atrophying towards cardiac arrest - everything is far from fine.

"Andrea, after we talk for a bit tonight, I have invited your family to join us, okay?" Sarah notified me and there was no way I could back out. There was nowhere to go and nowhere to hide. My mother was my ride home and I was in Sarah's private room with no means for escape.

"I, uh, I…" hesitating I looked down at the sage green pillow I was pressing into my lap and scrunched my legs up further beneath my body.

"I want you to have the opportunity to hear from them. You will also be able to share how you are feeling, too," she explained. I was feeling cold and angry and misguided and alone. I watched as my family gathered in the room around me in anticipation of what was to come next. I liked being in control and knowing what was going on in my surroundings. In a matter of minutes all of that was stripped from me.

As Sarah mediated the joint session I heard Stacey say things like, "I miss my big sis!" and "When will she be better?"

Dad: "Andrea has been routinely defiant, has withdrawn from friends, and she leaves the dinner table early. Andrea – I don't really think you are trying at all to get better."

Mom: "Don't get mad at me, sweetie, but we all want you to get better. We are here to support you."

"No you aren't! You only want to control me and make me perfect. I feel like none of you understand. None of you care. None of you ever listen to me anymore! I am still a person. I still have feelings. I am still me!" I sobbed and I pleaded as Sarah draped my hands with soft, lotion-infused tissues. She knew the normal ones irritated the thin, dry skin on my nose and face.

Dennis stepped into the conversation, "Andrea, what is wrong with you? Look at yourself? Why are you doing this? I thought you just wanted to lose weight, but this? This?! What is this?"

I cried even deeper upon hearing those words from my brother's mouth. I felt betrayed and manipulated and weak, so, so, so very weak. I coiled up hugging that pillow to my chest as each cough and cry hurt to produce.

"None of you love me," I choked again. This was their coup de grâce. My offensive advantage was all but lost.

"Andrea! Andrea!" Mom cried back, tears now in her eyes. Stacey was crying and my brother, smirking. Dad, looking at his watch. He paid for these expensive sessions and this cry fest was not cutting it. He was not seeing results.

"Andrea, your family is here because they love you and they care about you. I would like you to tell your family how they can help you through this. And likewise, Jane, Peter, Stacey, Dennis, please inform Andrea of how you plan to support her moving forward," Sarah instructed. The clock on the wall ticked loudly between my fading sobs into my cupped hands of snot, wet Kleenex, and unsalted tears.

"You can all help me by leaving me alone! Stop asking me so many questions. Stop touching me to feel my the outline of my ribs and spinal vertebrae, stop starting at me, stop forcing me to eat, stop telling me what to do, stop, stop, stop, stop. STOP," I said turning my body into the couch to hide my face from their line of sight. It hurt me too much to watch their suffering. To see them suffering because of me. That cut far too deep for repair.

"Andrea," Dad began. "Andrea, I want as a family that we support you through prayer."

"But Peter, we also need to be making sure that she is…" Mom began. Thankfully, Sarah cut her off before she got any further into dishing out her demands of 'support' for me.

"I think prayer is an excellent idea," Sarah guided. "Can we have a family prayer together before we part ways tonight?" I covered my ears, but my father extended his hands out and my family made a linked circle around me, bowing their heads down and wrapping their arms around one another.

"Heavenly Father," he began. A few finals sobs sneaked out as I listened, and held out for a feeling of warmth, a feeling – of tatsimou. "Tatsimou" (tot-see-moo) was a special word I invented as a young child based off of the sounds of the Greek language and words I was accustomed to hearing growing up. Tatsimou was my own word that I used to describe the wholeness of love when I was in the presence of only my immediate family and I felt safe, protected, and cared for. The word was reserved for special occasions when closeness to my family overwhelmed the fears of life. Usually on long car trips together as a family there would always be moments of intimate closeness that I would call tastimou. Or even better, when Mom and Dad were hugging one another and I would nuzzle my way in between them, I felt tatsimou from their warmth and love around me and I would close my eyes and say, "Mommy, Daddy?! Who turned out the lights?!" Tatsimou time was the quintessence of our familial bond. It was pervasive in that room that night and its warmth gave me a feeling of security and strength I had not known for several months. *Tatsimou, is that you?* I held onto the warm feeling as best I could.

We drove home together that evening in silence and I quietly went to my room and without being questioned, was allowed to go to bed. A lot of things were swirling around in my mind and I was flooded with the emotions of a new pulsation of hunger and the flickering warm comfort of tatsimou. I laid in my bed concealed by my down comforter and heated bedsheets staring at the ceiling. A frigorific wind from outside peeled through my loosely sealed windows. I skimmed my fingers over the goosebumps up and down my body as I felt for fat underneath my skin. It was 8:30 pm. The comments from my family were streaming through my head on repeat. I secretly wished it was noon the next day so I could enjoy two pieces Bubblemint Gum on my dry, parched tongue. I needed to replenish my supply. I only had enough left for three more days. I read in a magazine somewhere that chewing gum on an empty stomach induced higher acid production and could lead to ulcers. A bleeding ulcer sounded like a pain that would take away hunger. Maybe I would be lucky enough to get one.

12
Cotton Mouth, I Can't Swallow: The Zinc Taste Test

<u>Personal Food Log</u>: Week of April 30th –

Wednesday: Current Weight – 68 lbs.

Morning: Juice box (0 calories), Frosted Mini-Wheats Cereal (did not consume, 0 calories)

Lunch: Orbit Bubblemint Gum (2 pieces, 10 calories) (*Note: need to buy more this weekend)

Afternoon Snack: 16 Grapes (45 calories)

Dinner Strategy: Eat late after family dinner or take dinner to room to dispose in toilet or in sink disposal if no one is home when you get there. Leave "used" silverware and plate in the sink for Dad.

Calories Consumed: 215 with dinner (maybe less?)

Exercise Completed: 3 mile walk, 50 sit-ups (had to stop, scabs on my tailbone and spine tore open shirt got too bloody to continue.

Pounds to lose this week: Lose the ½ pound gain from last week. Drop one full pound if possible this week.

Self-Statement: *You have conquered hunger! You are strong! Stay the course and remain in control, Andrea. You are winning!*

> **Daily intake log:**
> **250 Max Cal**
> 10
> 16
> _____
> 224 remaining for dinner

Sitting in the bathroom at school during lunch awaiting my lunchtime redemption of a fresh bottle of water and Orbit gum, I reviewed my personal food log and the food log for Rosetta from the prior week to see where there were gaps and to fill in all of the arbitrary numbers on the hunger scale I was to complete for each day. I wished I had had those scrabble dice with me. I noticed a few days where I could add in a dessert and a couple others where I added a mango coconut smoothie for breakfast. As anticipated, Rosetta always appreciated when I incorporated mangoes into my diet. They smelled strongly enough that I was at least able to describe their taste when she asked how well I liked them. I lied to her about their smooth texture and rich, floral sweetness. I was to meet with Rosetta that evening, but I was nervous because I knew my weight had dipped and my methods of weight additions were becoming limited as the warmer weather outside did not allow for the justification of wearing of multiple layers of under armour, bras, socks, and sweatshirts.

After lunch, the rest of the day my anxiety grew. I knew things were at a tipping point with my parents regarding in-patient treatment. The echocardiogram, the family counseling session, the increased volume of therapy sessions, the

Boost nutrition shakes my Dad kept sticking in the side-pocket of my backpack with constant pleas to try them. It was not looking good for me. If I estimated correctly, I threw away at least $50 worth of food and nutritional shakes each week. My parents were playing every angle to keep me out of the hospital, but I did not expect that they would send me for a three hour meeting with a woman who went by the name of Dr. Diane Barkens. She was a nationally renowned psychologist known for her break-through therapy with patients of anorexia. But Barkens, I kid not, was a friend of Satan; I was sure of it.

"What do you mean I am not seeing Rosetta tonight," I asked Mom on the phone when I called her after school that day. She had sent a text message earlier in the day notifying me that I had an appointment with Dr. Barkens at 8:00 PM that evening and Dad would be driving me there. We were going to leave at 6:00 PM. It was nearly a two hour drive.

"No, you are going to meet with someone else tonight and see if she can offer you any other help or suggestions," Mom replied.

I did not necessarily care for Rosetta, sure, but I did not care to see anyone else. I knew how to play Rosetta and remain in control. I liked that. "Who is Dr. Barkens? Also, I am not going," I instructed.

"We think she can help you. Dad will be there the entire time. Don't worry," Mom said frustrated and unwilling to engage in further discussion.

"Whatever. You win, Mom. You always win," I replied as I hung up the phone to silence her oncoming, long-winded reply.

When I got home after school I was asked to run an errand with her to the drugstore because she did not want me staying home alone since Stacey was at softball practice. After we picked up her prescription, we went through a Wendy's drive-thru to get dinner for the family.

"Do you want anything?" My mom asked already knowing my answer.

"No, I'm not hungry," I said in compliance.

"Anything? What about some hot tea?" she insisted.

"Fine, whatever, you won't be happy until I say, 'Yes,'" I replied. She finished placing the order for the family and pulled up to wait for our food. She was handed my tea first and she gave it to me in the passenger's seat. She looked at me as though waiting for me to say something, but I sat in silence.

"Don't you want it?" She asked impatiently.

"Sure. No. I don't care!" I snipped back. I took a sip of the black Lipton tea to appease her. It burned my tongue on first contact and tasted like tar paper. "Phiishsh!" I spit the tea out all over the dashboard. "This is awful and now I burned my tongue. Thanks a lot, Mom," I seethed. Mom grabbed the rest of the unhealthy, high calorie food from the window attendant and placed it in between us, sneaking a hot fry out of the bag. Nothing could come between my mother and a greasy, hot fry.

"Why do you eat those things, Mom?" I asked.

"The salt tastes good to me," she responded taking a napkin to wipe the dash. "Let's get you home. I am sorry about the tea."

"I hate you for doing this to me, Mom. I hate you! I hate you! I hate you! All these counselors, all this crap you are making me go through. It's not fair," I shouted throwing the tea out the window as we drove home.

"Don't litter like that, Andrea. And watch your mouth," she stated firmly. The car now smelled of greasy fries and caloric meat from slaughtered cows. I wanted to throw up again and I hated her even more for making me ride to the store with her. She did not argue back as I expected her to and she stopped eating fries from the grease-stained bags. "Dad said he will be home by 5:30 PM so you can leave by 6:00 PM. I hope it goes well," she said. I was sorry I wasted my large cup of tar liquid tea on the pavement. I could have thrown it at her face or dumped it on those steaming, salted potato slices in between us.

When we got home, Mom did not say a word to me. Dad and I drove in silence to the appointment. I sat in the far back seat of the van covered in blankets situated next to the heat vent. When we arrived at Dr. Barken's home, which I thought was strange because I presumed we were going to some office, I did not budge from my seat.

"All right, time to go in," Dad said. "Do you have what you need?" He looked tired, worn, completely exhausted. It was Thursday night near the end of a week wherein two of his patients had passed away, he had delivered four babies, he was on call, and a stomach-flu outbreak was keeping everyone in his practice busy. I sympathized with him in a way I was unable to with anyone else in my life. If Mom had driven me, I would have screamed at her the entire way there, told her fries would cause heart disease, and probably would not have gotten out of the car.

"Mom said you were staying for the appointment. Aren't you staying with me the whole time? I'm not going in there alone," I trembled. I creeped up the length of the van towards him and gripped those sturdy hands of his that had brushed the hairs off my face when I rested that morning I missed the state swim meet. He gently guided me out of the car and we walked towards the front door together. His body was warm and I tucked myself under his arm. It was the first time I had let him touch me in long time. I hated being touched because my skin was so sensitive and I knew people were appalled by the skeletal frame they would feel – most especially my dad. It would be alarming to him, so I did not want him to hug or touch me except for that moment standing outside the front entrance to Dr. Barkens' home. I wanted him to hug me, to hold me, and to keep me safe forever.

"I will be waiting outside here after you get settled and after I answer any questions that she has for me. I will not be in the session tonight with you, honey. Barkens does not like to have other people involved," Dad informed.

"You can't make me do this by myself, Dad. This is so unfair. Let's go home, please," I pleaded and pulled his body closer to mine as if a shield for protection. He kissed my forehead and looked into my sunken eyes and up and down at my baggy layers of scarves and clothing.

"You're going, Andrea. We are here and I think she can help you," he said. At that moment I pulled myself away from him and removed his arm from around my shoulder. A few minutes ago I felt sorry for him, but it was clear he was not on my side either. He rang the doorbell again and a light went on in the foyer. Dr. Barken's husband answered the door and welcomed us inside to wait for his wife. Dad picked up a few pamphlets about eating disorders that were on a table in the foyer of their home. The house smelled of day old lasagna, burnt chocolate chip cookies and the Eucalyptus lotion Mom used after her long showers on the weekends. My head was spinning and I felt faint. Normally I ingested at least some tiny amount of food for dinner each day, but in my angry rage of greasy fries and hot tea with my mother, I had not touched anything all day. It was 8:15 PM.

"Sorry, I am running a bit late," Dr. Barkens began as she entered the foyer. "The kids needed dinner and it has been a hectic evening. "You must be Dr. Cladis, and this is your daughter, Andrea, correct? I am glad you could make it," she said.

"Thank you for fitting us in tonight," Dad began, acting the consummate professional as always. "What information do you need from me and how long will the appointment last?" he inquired.

"Usually this type of appointment lasts anywhere from one to three hours. There is a shopping center and a few restaurants about a block from here if you want to stay in the area while you wait," Barkens replied.

Three hours? I thought. *What kind of counseling are we doing? Ask me some questions and let's get out of here.* I was growing dizzier each moment.

"Andrea," Dr. Barkens addressed me in a friendly tone which I knew was only her putting on airs. If there was one thing I was good at, it was reading people and everything about her said manipulative bully. "I would like you to go wait in my study over there while I speak with your dad. I will be with you shortly," she said. Clutching the small cloth bag I had brought inside with me, I looked at Dad with a glare that said get me out of here as fast as you can and you are a most cruel human being if you make me stay here alone.

"I'll be waiting outside, Andrea," was all he said in response as I followed the signs to the nearly barricaded study room of her home. It was past her kitchen and family room, but still faced the front of the home. I lingered outside the door of the study trying to eavesdrop on the conversation she was having with my father, but I could not make out the words other than knowing Dad was doing a lot of the talking in his medical voice and he was firm and passionate about what he was saying. Moments later, Barkens walked towards me and placed her hand on my lower back to invite or rather, to force me into the mostly barren study room where she held her appointments. I heard the front door close and knew I was alone in there. I was so cold and the lasagna Eucalyptus running up my nose was making me feel dizzier.

"Before we begin I need you to swish this solution around in your mouth for one full minute. Let me know when you experience a taste other than that of water," Barkens demanded. She set her stopwatch and glared at me until I sipped the 'test liquid.' I was unsure of whether or not I was supposed to taste something right away or not taste anything at all. I had no clue how to beat the test. At the time I did not even really know what the solution in my mouth was for other than I was so afraid of that woman, I thought the longer I went without mentioning something about the taste, the better.

Hold two teaspoonfuls (10 mL) of Zinc Test in the mouth for at least 10 seconds. A lack of taste or a delayed taste perception in the mouth may indicate a possible zinc insufficiency. If an immediate taste perception occurs, the zinc status may be adequate. Zinc Test can be swallowed after tasting.

Zinc is a vital nutrients for whole body health. It is found in cells throughout the body and assist the immune system in warding off bacteria and viruses. The body needs Zinc for wound healing, protein and DNA production, and supporting strong bones. With an absence of the proper amount of Zinc in the body, it is impossible for the body's organs and systems to function effectively and harmoniously. Dangerously low levels of Zinc means a compromised immune system, inability for the body to synthesize proteins for growth and repair, and finally, an inability to stay alive. Because humans require Zinc intake to remain alive, it is referred to as an "essential" trace element. Present in every cell, organ, bone, tissue, and fluid in our bodies zinc is especially prominent in the male prostate gland and semen as well as female reproductive system functions and libido.

For several seconds, I tasted nothing. I kept swishing it around in my mouth assuming I was supposed to taste something, but I did not. Barkens pointed at her stopwatch and said, "We're at 40 seconds, feel free to swallow."

As she stopped her watch my mouth was whelmed by a dry, metallic taste. I swallowed hard.

"Did you experience an unusual taste at any point?" Barkens inquired.

"Yes, I uh," I paused not knowing whether I was supposed to say I tasted something right away or that the dry, metallic taste did not upset my mouth until right before she said I could swallow. "I think about halfway through I tasted something. It tasted like metal," I said.

She smirked. "I see," she said taking down a notation. "Have a seat here and do not move. I will be back shortly." She directed me to sit down in a plain wooden chair in the center of the stark room. There was only one lantern-style light in the room and it was secured to a beam directly above my head. I learned when talking about the zinc test to Dad later that evening that lasting forty seconds until a taste signal was more than a sure sign of zinc deficiency. It was supposed to be a 10-15 second test. I thought I was proving how long I could last and that was a good thing. Clearly, with Barkens, I had lost battle #1. I would not be getting out of there until she pillaged in conquering victory over me ten more times that night. Ten blows. It was maddening.

Barkens was not kind nor sympathetic. There were no soft, warm fuzzies of building trust or getting-to-know-you happy conversation with Barkens. She was butch-looking female - muscular, with short black hair, beady eyes and a cold, callous heart. Her voice was deep when she spoke and bellowed through lungs of anger and disdain. When she sat me down in the study of her house that she used for counseling I could still taste metal in the back of my throat and I desperately wanted to go back to that ugly sweater-vest, cookie-for-lunch munching redhead I so vividly remembered from my very first counseling encounter. At least that sad, frumpy woman looked friendly, gullible, and heck, even playful.

There was an empty fish tank in the cramped study space, a white board on each of the four gray walls, a small black bookcase near the entrance door, and two folding chairs in the center of the room. I was sitting in one of them and Barkens would eventually sit facing me in the other. I wanted that comfortable couch from Sarah's office or to spot a few crates of spoiled mangoes in the corner. I was frozen in that hard, wooden chair and it was unkind to my bony spine as I leaned back to take pressure off of my tailbone. I looked around for a way to escape, but there was only one covered window on the wall facing the street and the now locked door that led to the rest of the house. My light blue cloth bag was resting near my feet and it had extra coins in it, my food log, and my phone. I wanted to give Dad an SOS text to come get me and say I needed to leave, but just as soon as I went to reach down into my bag, Diane came back through the door to the study room from her lengthy time out with her family and locked the door behind her, further dimming the light. I was still cold, but felt sweat forming in my armpits. It was a warm sensation I had not felt in a while and my heart was beating noticeably in my chest. In her arms she had two notebooks which she set down on the only table in the room right next to the door.

"What do you need?" She inquired as she noticed me reaching towards my bag.

"Oh, nothing. I was just waiting for you to return," I quivered. My chance to contact Dad was all but lost. Blow #2.

"Well, I will get that bag out of your way, we don't need distractions," Barkens said as she grabbed my bag and looked inside. "Oh, a food log – we can definitely have a look at this. What is all this loose change for?" she continued. I could feel heat building through my neck as I was glued to that chair and this brazened woman was rifling through my bag. "Probably for the weigh-in, am I correct?" Blow #3.

Stealing my notebook from the bag and setting it down next to the door and out of my reach, I watched her snag my food log for Rosetta and begin reading it. She had no business doing that. She walked over to the other chair across from me and sat down. I fidgeted, desperately wanting to walk over to my bag, unlatch that deep cherry wood door, leave, and run away from her and from my life for good.

"That's mine," I managed to squeak out. "Can I please have it back?"

She laughed hysterically and faced me while flipping through the pages. "Clever girl you are! Look at all of these things you've been eating. Quite the variety of foods in your diet. You must be gaining weight at a fast pace, huh?" She sneered as she stole a highlighter from her pocket and started highlighting certain foods and calorie counts. "See these?" she asked, shoving my journal back at me. "These are all wrong. You should correct them." *Correct the calorie counts?* I thought. *What the heck is she talking about?* I leaned in to look at what she was highlighting. "First of all, these are incorrect calorie numbers and second of all, I know you never ate any of these things. Take them out. Erase. Delete. Take this notebook for me and cross out everything that is not true. Now. Do it right now." She shoved a pen and my food log in my face and I stared at her. She did not have rosy cheeks nor did she smell like fruity jelly beans. I had worked so hard on those pages for Rosetta; I wanted to share them with her. Not this woman. I sat there obstinately as she grew impatient.

"What are you waiting for? Get started – we don't have all night," she confirmed. Walking over to one of the dry erase boards directly in my line of sight, she wrote down a list of things she perceived I had done or said to "cheat" the counseling system.

And as she did so, I began crossing out nearly everything in that notebook. Blow #4. On the whiteboard she wrote in large, loud, emboldened letters:

YOU ARE SELFISH. YOU ARE NOT WINNING. GET OVER YOURSELF.

"See this, Andrea? This is what you need to hear. You are not winning this one, you get that?" She was malicious. "Look at yourself? Do you see a winner?" she asked. I stopped my scribbling, fighting back tears and the nasty metal taste still lingering in my throat. If I had the strength I would have stood up and thrown my food log at her, unlocked that door and walked out. I was winning still. I had to be. I had to be in control.

"I am… I am," I began, my chin unsteadily dropping in fear, stifling my ability to say anything further.

"Exactly, you're not winning at anything," Barkens mocked. Blow #5. She came and snatched the notebook from my hand and perused the pages. "Lies, all lies here," she repeatedly tapped the cap of the dry erase marker on the white board. She was psychotic. Not me. "That's what I see.

Lies. And who exactly are you lying to, Andrea? Who are you lying for?" She questioned. I had no response. I sat there in a state of trauma. I was trapped. And I was a liar. Blow #5.

"If you are ever going to get better, you are going to have to want to get better for yourself," she explained while making more notations on the white board. Each time the marker made contact with the board, she wrote with an accentuated down-stroke that made it seem like she was punishing the board in place of physically battering me. The white board cowered and warped in its frame. Things about weight and calories and how to gain weight the fastest and steps for progress. I felt like I was sitting through a lecture.

"I'd offer you a blanket or some gum to chew on as I am sure you like gum. As for the blanket, being cold is a reminder to you that you are sick. You should not feel cold all the time. That is because you are losing here. You are not winning anything," she preached at me.

"I am not cold," I lied. "I only like one type of gum," I tried to display a show of strength to her.

"Let me guess. You eat a few pieces a day to avoid mealtime. So creative!" She jeered back at me. Tears were flooding my eyes again and my entire bottom side was numb. That chair was so damn hard to sit in for an extended period of time. I am most certain she knew that. And that gum was a vice for me. Maybe she knew about the sugar-free Jell-O, too. I felt sick. Blow #6.

"Andrea, you have to take ownership of this thing and not be a weak victim to it. You're not controlling it, it is controlling you. Have you named it yet? Have you named your eating disorder yet? Let's call her, 'Rachel.' I want you to repeat after me, please," she said. "Rachel," she began again. Blow #7.

"Rachel," I said.

"Rachel, you are a loser and you are not going to beat me," she said.

"Rachel, you are a ... a loser and you are not going to beat me," I echoed.

"Rachel, I am so much better than you and I will never let you have my life," she said.

"Rachel, I am so much better than you and I will..." I stopped. I did not care if she had my life.

"Finish the statement, please. Finish it, now," she shouted at me coming to sit down in the chair across from me.

"I can't, I can't," I said. I saw my bag by the door and wanted to count the coins and step on the scale and show Rosetta I made progress and that mango smoothies were yummy and that...

"I will never let Rachel have my life," Barkens looked directly into my eyes with her dark cavernous, black-beady eyes that were stuffed into her flattened face. "Finish the phrase," she yelled in tones so shrewd I could not block them out. Blow #8. I was gradually breaking down.

"I will... I can't. I can't say that! Stop it! Please, stop! Leave me alone!"

"Repeat after me: I will never let her have my life. Say it!" she said.

Barkens terrified me in that moment. "I, I, I will never let her have my life. Rachel will not win this!" I screamed back in her face. I saw a smile start in on her face as she knelt down next to my chair. Blow #9. She was winning. Or was she?

"Go get your life back from her and win. Go take it," she said eagerly in my face just below eye level to me. "Say it one more time," she said. "Tell Rachel how you feel."

"Rachel," I began, as if speaking to a friend, but this time with more conviction. "Rachel, you're not better than me. You just don't know that yet. You have been there for me for so long and I am going to miss you if you leave, but I think maybe we can't be together anymore. If you threaten me like this again, I will take you down. Watch me," I said, a degree of self-confidence returning. Barkens patted my knee and stood up.

I closed my eyes and squeezed my hands together. They were as cold as her heart. She was a step ahead of my game the entire time. She knew I should have been admitted to the hospital and that my parents were preventing it. She knew that I was a liar. She knew that I liked gum. She knew that I was strong willed to win. She had me a puppet to her her every word, but somehow I liked her gritty intolerance towards me. Blow #10. Ten blows. She was excellently infuriating.

Before I was allowed to leave that night she told me I needed to add dessert and peanut butter to my diet. A dessert with every single meal to add calories and four tablespoons of peanut butter each night after dinner for additional calories. I was nauseous thinking about all of it. She brought a brownie into the study room with extra creamy peanut butter smeared on the top of it and asked me to taste it.

"You are not leaving until you try this. Unless you want to spend the night with me, of course," she laughed maniacally again. The bold words on the white board diffused my willpower to avoid the chocolate peanut butter lump of fat and calories on the napkin in my lap.

YOU ARE SELFISH. YOU ARE NOT WINNING. GET OVER YOURSELF.

I took a bite. And then another. It was creamy, sweet, rich, and dense. I tasted every last ounce of that 500 plus calorie brownie. I wanted to get out of there and I wanted the metal taste from my throat to go away and I wanted to prove to Barkens that I could win and that I was winning. But by taking that first bite, she won the whole thing. That was the crowning blow.

I became addicted to sugar a few months after I met with her and it led to significant and rapid weight gain. To this day I think it is her fault that I crave sweets and desserts and have a hard time moderating my weight because of that in-bred addiction she caused as I tried to kill off Rachel. Barkens was an evil woman, of that I was most certain. Her voice is still a fixture of my subconscious and I can still taste the iron, cotton, metal, and regurgitated peanut butter bile mix in my mouth when I remember that destructive night.

13
Running to Kill Rachel

Rachel did not leave me as the school year came to a close, but I became more aggravated by her presence. I fidgeted obsessively with my food and adopted new habits to decrease my intake such as avoiding all of the crusts of bread, mainly because the newfound sweet tooth I had, I could not satiate. As I was taking on small amounts of food, only during dinner each day, I felt that I was losing control of everything in my life. Since I was actually consuming small portions of food, I had to combat the calories in another way, so I took to a stringent routine of gym sessions and sit-ups in my room every night. I still barely had the strength for either. I stopped buying Orbit gum because it made my stomach churn every time I chewed it now and I associated that churn with wanting food, a feeling I loathed. There were days where Rachel's presence faded and for short moments, I was able to see life again. It was in those moments wherein I could really take it in – the smell of the perfumed breeze calming the humidity of Chicago's early summer or the bright laughter of children playing at the park, even the daily song performed by the couple of mourning doves who met to sing and groom one another every morning on my parents' veranda.

What I missed the most as I walked by the river near my home one day was the feeling of the wind blowing through my once long, wavy hair. I used to love running by the river with my hair falling loosely and flowing rhythmically down my back. I would not dare do that anymore, for if I did, it would all be lining the muddy riverbank where I now walked. My hair was still falling out and any tension on the strands made it weaker, so I stopped styling and brushing it altogether. Some weeks I did not even wash it because if I put any amount of stress on the strands, they fell right out and I wanted to preserve as much of it as I could. Prior to my illness I had really long, thick hair – the kind that required four to five rubber bands just to hold a ponytail, so fortunately I had a lot to lose, but what was left was thin, wispy, and sparse with patchy spots of complete baldness. I visited a dermatologist who assured me that my hair would grow back and return, but that usually any kind of shock to the system – as occurs with stress, illness, or nutritional deficiencies - can cause severe to rapid hair loss. I was young and he repeatedly affirmed to me that it would grow back. I did not believe that short, pompous doctor. What did he know? Losing my beautiful mane of brunette hair was a source of many tears and left me self-conscious of what I began to classify as my former identity as a woman.

Midsummer came and the warmth of being outdoors infused the soul of my being. I was in love with the sun. Complete and utter adoration. It penetrated deeply into my skin and all through the month of June I consistently got sunburns on my thin, elastic layering of see-through skin. I did not have a realistic gauge on how hot it was outside because internally I still felt a gnawing state of cold. And as for air conditioning indoors, that was nearly unbearable. I wore my winter coat inside my mother's house nearly every day. She loathed the summer heat and did everything she could to prevent sweating on those hot, sticky days. My counseling sessions became icebox freezer sessions too, but my nutrition was improving to some degree.

I replayed the phrase Dr. Barkens had written on the board over and over again in my mind. *You are selfish. You are not winning. Get over yourself.* I did not want to think I was selfish, but maybe I was not winning and maybe I did need to get over myself. Or sure as hell something greater needed to help me get there. Sitting on the floor of my well-air-conditioned bedroom on the evening of the last day of June, huddled in a mass of blankets and towels to stay warm, I wrote down the words, "selfish loser" about nineteen times in my food diary. I wanted to write it down twenty times, but I stopped because I started crying and the negative self-talk was working its magic on my weary mind. Barkens was so deeply embedded in my consciousness that I assumed I would never get rid of her tormenting chokehold on my headspace. She was planted so deeply that my own sense of self-consciousness was beginning to take on a revised shape. I still loathed myself, but the loathing was not the wanting to be perfect and failing to be, the loathing was a self-hatred propped up by a profound guilt. What in the world had I done to myself? I was not just losing. I was a selfish loser. Screw that, I thought. I tucked my food diary into my bedside drawer and instead of ignoring the Bible that stared at me every night from the back of the drawer, the temptation to open it on that humid June night in the igloo that Mom had made of my bedroom, I reached into the drawer and pulled out my Teen Study Bible. Opening it in my lap, I noticed yellow sticky notes from my time in middle school youth group littering the pages of that Bible. I had forgotten how much time I spent every single day with that book in 7th and 8th grade. Some of the yellow sticky notes contained words of wisdom regarding how to seek Christ despite the distractions of society, the immaturity of youth, and the desire of instant gratification. Others spoke of purity and worthiness. My handwritten notes were mostly in cursive, purple ink. I liked that. I thought about the scented purple pen I used to write with in that Bible. It smelled like grape medicine, but wrote with fluidity and specks of silver sparkles. It was my special Bible pen. I made Mom buy it for me when I was in 6th grade and had gotten a new Bible. I told her that God deserved the purple sparkly side of me. She thought it was silly. Maybe it was silly though because that purple sparkly side was long gone from being a part of me. A smattering of hot pink sticky notes marked passages that were of interest to me. Most of those passages were from Philippians, Proverbs, Ephesians, and Romans. It had been a long time since I visited their real estate in the Bible. I rubbed my eyes and sifted through the pages. They were thin, smooth, and lightweight, but their goodness felt warm in my hands. A large, white notecard tucked in the front pocket of my Bible read:

Andrea C. #8 "...just me and God." On the back I had written John 3:16 with the insertion of my name in place the world.' I read it aloud. *"For God so loved Andrea that He gave His one and only son that whoever believes in Him shall not perish, but have eternal life." Below it I had written in cursive, red-lettering: I will not have sexual relations before I am married. I promise. I will stay a virgin because God is my husband. I will only give of my emotion and my body to God and my husband. I will honor my body to honor my God.*

For God so loved Andrea. I will honor my body. I did not know what to think. It was as though God was talking to me in the same forthright nature of my parents and those counselors only He had this unyielding power to stomp out the evil devil of selfish perfectionist desires that plagued me. Even so, "Selfish loser" was still pulsing through my mind. I wondered what the Bible had to say about 'selfish losers.' Maybe those selfish losers were not supposed to own Bibles with purple sparkle ink or have the opportunity to know God. Okay, okay, that was not right and I knew it. God was merciful and He gave the gift of grace. I just felt I did not deserve it. I used the index of my Bible to cross-reference some verses about selfishness. I needed some insight; I think I also secretly wanted the Bible to somehow invalidate my actions. Proverbs 18:1 said, "He who separates himself seeks his own desire, He quarrels against all sound wisdom," something I was clearly doing. Interesting. I continued. Ephesians 4:20-24 read, "That, however, is not the way of life you learned when you heard about Christ and were taught in him in accordance with the truth that is in Jesus. You were taught, with regard to your former way of life, to put off your old self, which is being corrupted by its deceitful desires; to be made new in the attitude of your minds; and to put on the new self, created to be like God in true righteousness and holiness." Corrupted by its deceitful desires. Truth. That was me. No dice, I thought. I furrowed my brow and leaned in to read one more passage and selected a verse that had been listed in the index category about selfishness. Philippians 2:3-4 said, "Do nothing from selfishness or empty conceit, but with humility of mind, regard one another as more important than yourselves; do not merely look out for your own personal interests, but also for the interests of others." I nearly tore out the page from Philippians in a surge of aggravation and oozing guilt. It felt like God was striking blows to break me just as Barkens had done. A bit more gently, I suppose, but at a sharper angle targeted at the fissures in my weakened heart. I had destroyed my body; I had hurt others and lied to them. And in so doing, I was not loving God nor was I honoring him. Guilty as charged.

For God so loved Andrea, I thought again. *For God so loved me! He gave himself for me! He loved me.* I turned the pages in my Bible. More sticky notes and more verses stood out to me. Another notecard in the back of my Bible lured me to read. I pulled it out to put on my bathroom mirror. It was a journal entry I had written after reading the story of Jonah. In my notes I had written about how Jonah cried out to God, God brought him out of the pit, Jonah remembered God, and vowed to make good of what he had done. There was a call and response contained in my entry reflecting the story of Jonah. The call was from me and the response was from God.

My "call" was written in the form of a prayer: *Dear God, I know that I will always be loved by you. Sometimes, I tend to forget you love me. Help me to remember that you are always with me. For the wrongs I have done hurting myself and others, I want to make a vow to try harder and with your help live a better life. In your name I pray. Amen.* My purple cursive writing spoke to me in a frame of innocent admiration for God. It glittered. It made me tingle and the tears that were pooling in my eyes were absorbed into the sunken, sparkle-free skin of my cheeks. "God's response" on the notecard said the following: *Andrea, I am a merciful God of second chances and I won't let you down. I will try to show my love in your life and help you keep your vow to further serve the Kingdom of Christ.* Was I even welcomed into that Kingdom anymore? Eventually I shoved the Bible back into my drawer behind my food diary. Was I still shoving God behind my "selfish loser" ways? It certainly seemed so. I wanted to cry out like Jonah did, but something was still holding me back. It was not just the selfishness though. There was an underlying fear that if I wholly cried out to God He may not want me back after what I had done and if I did give it all up to Him, the control I had worked so hard to acquire would vanish, evaporate. If God was in control again, where would that leave me?

Aside from my unsteady and imperfect faith, the primary impediment to my progress was that I became full very quickly as my stomach had shrunk down in size from being in a state of starvation for so long. And also, when I ate, my body lacked the ability to process foods correctly so my liver worked on overtime and I would regularly pee shortly after food intake and it unapologetically smelled like the last thing I ate. It was entirely acidic urine and I want-ed it to stop coming out of me, but my body remained in a state of shock and hyper-burn. The counselors called it a "re-feeding" process, which I did not understand because I never really stopped eating. Nonetheless, re-feeding was not going all that well.

Each day I would try to consume one mocha coffee or strawberry-flavored BOOST nutrition shake for vitamins and two s'mores or wild berry flavored pop-tarts, mainly because they were sugary and high in calories. It took me over an hour to nibble down one pop-tart and usually two hours for one pre-packaged Otis Spunkemeyer chocolate chip muffin. The kind of muffin so high in trans fats and so densely cholesterol laden that no healthy individual would even consider ingesting. I was still counting calories and logging over 1,000 per day just through eating calorie-dense foods. As the scale began to tick up and I reached the 80s, I could hear Rachel, in her condescending way, smite me and tell me what a failure I was. When my pants felt tighter she would be right there to tell me to flush the pop-tarts down the toilet and to throw away the contents of the nutrition shakes and leave the empty bottles in the recycling bin so Dad would see them and think I drank them. Rachel would taunt me when the mirage of a double chin made its appearance or I felt my thighs touching for too long. She was persistent in each bite I took and each pound I gained.

At the end of July I had had enough. Barkens had gifted me the burden of Rachel. Counseling sessions were growing tiresome, eating was becoming a chore, urinating was excruciatingly painful, Rachel was getting louder and I hated feeling fatter. I was losing control again and I needed to get it back. Hovering around 85 pounds, I committed to taking up running each morning as far and long as I could go until I got back down to the 70s because I felt maybe Rachel would be quiet then. After two weeks of running, I was unable to lose any weight. All that had resulted from my consistent efforts was that I became weaker with each run. Thus, I told myself I needed to go longer and farther and I would grow stronger and I would prevail for Rachel.

On the hottest day of the summer when my family left to attend a Chicago White Sox game, I knew I had my chance. If they were out of town, they could not question where I was or what I was doing. They would be over an hour away busy with the thrill of a summer afternoon ballgame in the company of fatty, caloric hot dogs and sodium infused buttered popcorn. After they were well on their way, I tied up two pairs of neon green running shorts around my waist, put on three pairs of socks to add cushion to my feet and wore a couple of bras to conceal my still sunken rib cage. On top of that, I wore a hot pink sleeveless running tee that said "Run Strong" on the front with a bold, obnoxious white Nike logo on the back. I was ready for action. I laced up my shoes, drank three glasses of water and set out towards the river front path. I had not eaten for 24 hours and consequently, I was feeling strong and empowered once again. I knew Rachel would be pleased with my sly manipulation. I had lied to my parents about not feeling well enough to go to the game with them so that I could stay home and run for as many hours as my body would allow. As I started out my pace was slow, clocking about ten minutes per mile, but as I pinched the 60 minute mark along the wooded riverside trail, I pumped my skeletal arms a little faster and moved up to 9 minutes and 15 seconds per mile. There was going to be no stopping me. Stride for stride I ran and ran and ran unaware of how much I was sweating or of my growing levels of dehydration. I ran only with pride for shrinking thighs and renewed control. After about two hours I was feeling ready to go home, but I wanted to push on further and see how far I could go. I was growing dizzy and nauseous, but mind over matter I told myself again and again. Mind over matter. I was going to do it! About five miles from home my heart sputtered, felt flat in my chest, and I lost control of my breath. I threw up bile on the pavement and staggered to the edge of the riverbank to splash some hot, muddy water on my face. I threw up again – this time staining the entire front of my pink running tee with brown water from the river splotching the front of my bright shorts. I threw up a third time and watery diarrhea came forth and soaked my shorts in the back and spread in a ribbon-like pattern down my legs. My eyes closed and I tried to lower myself to the ground to capture a breath, but no oxygen would enter. My sweat stopped and I felt colder than I had the fateful morning I missed the most important swim meet of my life. I was craving two pieces of Orbit Bubblemint gum. I was praying for an ulcer. I did not know what time it was or when my family would return home. I whispered to Rachel, "Almost there," and passed out.

A few hours later, or perhaps longer, I woke up in the emergency room hooked up to IVs and my family hovering over me. Dad was talking to the on call doctor he knew near the corner of the room.

"Heat stroke," The doctor informed him. "Her heart is extremely weak. The watch on her wrist showed she clocked 15 miles. She is severely dehydrated and when we found her she was in a complete state of shock. Appeared to be four episodes of vomiting and diarrhea. Does she normally run this far alone? Usually we recommend the buddy system for long runs," he informed.

"No, she's not any kind of distance runner and never has been," Dad replied. "How many rounds of fluids has she gotten? Added electrolytes?"

"Seven rounds, one with liquid nutrition. All with added electrolytes. She is stable now. If we had not gotten the call when we did, she might not have made it. A group of cyclists noticed her near the river at the corner of Wilson and Lake," the doctor continued.

"Thank you. Thank you. I'll take it from here," Dad told the other doctor as they shook hands and finished their conversation, something about a medical board meeting coming up. Dad was facilitating it. I think he was embarrassed that I was in the ER. He missed extra innings of a close game. The Sox lost. Apparently, I jinxed it. What a disappointment. My record of failures was strong.

"Thanks a lot, Rachel!" I murmured under my breath. Dad furrowed his brow at me and Mom walked out crying.

"Let's get you home," Dad said. "Enough of this crap. You're smarter than this."

PART II

Breathe. Eat. Sustain. Why Choose Life?

14
The Choice is Yours

Dad was past his threshold of anger and Mom was past the point of patience and sympathy with my continued lies. I went out and ran 15 miles on a day I was too "sick" to sit and watch a baseball game. Forced to the couch again with a three-day Gatorade cleanse, family members hardly spoke to me. Even Rachel had gone silent.

I spent Thursday, Friday, and Saturday night in my Gatorade soaked perch on the family room couch watching sit-coms and reality TV shows that were killing far more brain cells than my starvation diet ever did. When Sunday morning came, Dad stormed through the kitchen at 8:00 AM with two high protein Strawberry BOOST shakes and a glass full of ice in tow.

"Andrea, at 9:00 AM we are leaving for church and you are getting dressed and coming with us. You are going to drink both of these shakes before we go or we will all wait until you finish them and attend the 10:30 AM service together. It's your choice," he said. There was not even a murmur of empathy in his voice.

"I, I, I'm not even hungry. I'll feel sick if I drink anything else," I retorted.

"This is not a negotiation, Andrea. Either you're going to be hospitalized or you're going to make a concerted effort to heal. We've played around far too long, Andrea," he looked me sternly in the eyes slamming the two shakes down on the table next to me. Apparently I appeared to be ignoring him because his shoulders grew wider as he continued, "I trusted you. Enough is enough." As he walked off in wide-shouldered ire to go wake the rest of the family, I stared at those evil, fat-making shakes and tried to cry. Purple Frost Gatorade sealed the back of my throat again and the taste made me cringe. What am I doing to myself? I wondered. Rachel mocked me, but I muted her. I poured the two bottled strawberry shakes over the ice and stared at the frothy light pink liquid. It smelled like white orchids mixed with vanilla and the strawberry powder from the sugar-free Jell-O I never wanted to eat again. I grabbed the frothy pink glass and pulled myself up from the couch as my bony feet penetrated the floor once more. My calves ached, my quads were burning, my hips stiffened with every step. My body was still trying to recover from my 15 mile episodic running failure. It was all Rachel's fault. I took a straw from the drawer and had one sip of the shake. It was cool and refreshing and made the back of my throat feel gummy to top off the layering of three days' worth of Gatorade. I swallowed hard. There was no way this 850 calorie, double BOOST, 50 grams of protein shake was going down in less than an hour. I sat at the kitchen counter and took a sip every thirty seconds. When Dad came back downstairs he looked at me like I was pathetic, but he seemed glad I had gotten off the couch.

"Go get dressed," he said. "Then come back down and finish this. I already drank one this morning. They're pretty good!" I rolled my eyes at him and went to get dressed. He could drink those things faster than Mom could guzzle a 16 oz. passionfruit iced tea from Starbucks. It was an 'I hate you and I also wish I could do that' moment for me. I felt those every time I watched people eat. 'Incredulous' had become the new word of my growing lexicon to describe scenes of food and people eating. It was an anomaly to me. But I polished off every one of those milky nutrients and we attended the 10:30 service as a family. Strawberry calories sloshed around in my stomach, but seemed to settle after I ate the communion cracker. I normally stuffed those crackers into the back crevice of the pew, but my entire family was watching and I was awkwardly well-aware of God watching me, too.

I kept the bulletin from Church that morning and cut out the verse from the bottom of the last page and taped it to my bathroom mirror on a large sheet of yellow paper I had covering the mirror so I would be unable to see my reflection. The verse was Romans 12:12 – "Be joyful in hope, patient in affliction, faithful in prayer." I had written "GOD LOVES YOU" in bold print in the middle of that mirror covering and each day I tried to add a bible verse to it or in the very least, a positive affirmation. I was attempting to teach myself that what I saw in the mirror, physically, was not what God loved, rather it was my heart that he loved and if my heart and reflection was in Him, I knew I would have a much better chance of achieving health. The "patience" part of Romans 12 was what stood out to me. Healing does not happen overnight. It is a daily test of endurance and will. I would need to be patient and I would have to be joyful. I was learning to have faith in each and every one of my prayers. I knew that the God I had pushed away was listening. I just knew it.

15
Fear Foods

As summer came to a close, I was steadily gaining weight and had gotten to a more comfortable place with my personal desire to return to health so that I could excel in college - both in sports and academics. Digestion issues were omnipresent, lethargy from malabsorption was common, and I was terrified of many foods that I used to adore prior to my all-consuming illness. Chocolate milk for a long time had been my favorite treat after a hard workout, I had loved smooth, fluffy buttermilk pancakes, heavily salted food, ice cream, and raw cookie dough. I was also a meat lover, growing up in a Greek family, since lamb was a staple as was beef and different types of pork. However, the 're-feeding' process, as my mango-loving counselor called it, was much more challenging than I thought. Not only did I have a stomach-ache every time after I ingested food, but many foods immediately made me feel the urge to run to the bathroom where I would have been happy if I could have thrown up so the feeling would dissipate. The throwing up food part only happened once though, on account of anxiety the week before I was to leave for my first semester of college. I had gotten a sizeable academic scholarship to attend a private, liberal arts school in Indiana and while I was excited for the new change, I was nervous about the prospect of living alone and away from home in another state. My heightened levels of stress and anxiety surrounding the upcoming transition had negatively impacted my appetite, and to some degree, my ability to cope with Rachel who was always hovering nearby. Sometimes I could see her out of the corner of my eye waiting for the best time to present herself in full view.

"Honey, I think we almost have everything you need, but we can make a few more stops this weekend to Bed, Bath, and Beyond or wherever you'd like to go," Mom said the Friday before the final week of summer break for me.

"I don't want anything else. I don't need anything, Mom. This whole thing is stressful enough," I said. "I never even liked going on sleepovers," I continued. "This is like a forever sleepover."

"It is going to be a great experience and a new adventure! You have to keep a positive attitude and mindset, sweetheart," she said as tears filled my eyes and I burrowed my way about the dining room sorting through my bags, boxes, and new school supplies.

"I am afraid, Mom. I am afraid that I will feel alone all the time. You know how badly I wanted to leave high school and have a fresh start with a new identity, but I am worried about what people will think of me and if I will fit in," I explained.

"Honey," my mom came into the room and sat next to me. It was the first time we had had a genuine and somewhat respectful conversation since the height of my eating disorder. I had not shown her much respect because she had become such an enemy to me against my own selfish desires. It felt good to have Mom back in my corner. A mother that loved me all the same even though I was still less than 90 pounds, had almost lost my life, and had fought with her and treated her poorly for over two long, grueling years. I attempted to organize my feelings, but they merely bubbled into large, salty tears that coated my face and a repetitive cough that made my chest heavy and coarse.

"Honey," she consoled again. "We are here for you as we always have been and we are going to do everything we can to support you. Look how strong you are! And you are getting stronger with each and every passing day. You are a courageous young woman and God will keep you safe. You can do this! Okay?" I desperately wanted to believe her, but even though I might have been successful in putting on some weight I lacked the mental capacity to believe in myself or my worth much past that reality I had attained of being fearful of my own abilities in all areas of life. I felt disabled in many ways and was more afraid of failure than anything else.

"I don't know, Mom. I don't know. But thank you," I said as I let her hug me and I closed my eyes. It felt so warm and safe in her arms. I had missed them so much. I nuzzled my way in closer and I could smell her hairspray and Jean Naté perfume and could feel her hands gently playing with my hair. We sat down in the middle of my mess of things and I rested my head on her shoulder as she caressed my hair and hummed the song, "Rose, Rose," as she used to do when I was little. I was unable to see Rachel lurking about anywhere and I could not even remember what she looked like in that moment. I was at such peace. My head slid down her chest to the place where there were still scars from her double mastectomy. She was such a brave woman. And she loved so deeply my heart could not take it.

"I'm sorry, Mom. I'm really sorry," I cried into her scars for my selfish actions and inconsiderate attitudes. "I love you. Thank you for loving me," I whispered. She held me closer and kissed my forehead.

"Andrea, I will always and forever love you no matter what. Nothing will ever come between me and my love for you," she replied with an affirmation that I knew would never leave me.

I went up to my room as she prepared dinner and laid down on my bed. In the stillness, I squeezed my eyes closed while my tears dried on my cheeks and I let memory whelm my thoughts as I reflected on my Greek grandmother's (Yia-Yia) instruction about love and Mom's valiant fight with Breast Cancer.

"S'agapo!" (sah-gah-po), my Greek grandmother says to me, "S'agapo!" In Greek, s'agapo means, "I love you," and it comes from the Greek word for love which is agape (ah-gah-pey). Agape love is considered to be equivalent to the love of God or Christ for mankind. Agape love transcends all understanding and has been defined as unconditional, divine and self-sacrificing love. It is the kind of love that first Corinthians discusses and is the highest and purest form of love – one that surpasses any other type of affection.

In 2001, my mother was first diagnosed with breast cancer. At the time, she had a biopsy and a lumpectomy, and proceeded with medication for treatment. We thought she was doing well, though she had been monitoring a benign cyst in one of her breasts. Dad, a doctor of nearly 30 years, did not suspect anything had changed, but one day, a few years after her initial diagnosis, Mom felt an immediate change in the cyst so Dad took Mom for what we all assumed would be a few routine tests. Dennis and I waited at home while they went for the tests. We attempted to build a snowman, we played with our dogs, we shared stories, and caught up on life. A few hours passed and our parents were yet to come home. We waited, and waited. Finally, impatience getting the best of us, we called Dad.

"Everything's fine," he said. "Mom just needs a few more tests." Though we were confused, we all felt relatively certain that everything was indeed, fine. Then, nearly five hours after my parents had left for the check-up, my mother walked in through the door, her eyes wet and teary, her face red and her entire spirit deflated. My father followed her in with a stern look on his face – the same face I had witnessed many times growing up when he forced himself to mask his emotions so we wouldn't ask questions about what he had to deal with at work that day.

"What's wrong, Mom?" Stacey asked. "What happened?" Still crying and speechless, dabbing her eyes, my mother went to lie on the couch.

"She's going to be okay," Dad said trying to comfort us. "But her cancer is back. There are small spots in both breasts." At that moment, just hearing those words, my chest felt heavy, I sunk to the ground and my mind went numb.

"What a great Christmas present," I thought. "I cannot handle anything else this year," I mumbled to God. God was entirely silent, offering no ready answer.

Later that night, Dad spent time explaining everything to me and my siblings – the tests Mom had, where they found the cancer, what Mom's options for treatment were, and how we were going to proceed. Mom was the one who held the family together. She was the one who did everything for everyone. She never put herself first and she never complained. Now, it was our turn to show her just how much we loved her and appreciated all she had done for us.

The decision to undergo a double mastectomy, followed by an oophorectomy, hysterectomy and more chemotherapy medication was an unsettling one for Mom, but she was confident that it was the right thing to do. We were informed that the mastectomy would take place right after Christmas. At the beginning of January, my older brother left to spend his college's January term doing a service-learning trip in Guatemala. He was reassured by Mom that everything with the surgery would go well. She didn't want him to worry, and I was amazed at how well she held it together as we said our goodbyes in the airport.

My mom lost her mother to breast cancer in 1995 and I was not at all prepared to lose my mother. Each day as the surgery approached, we prayed together as a family. Our nerves were mounting, sleepless nights endured and fear, overcome with worry was our biggest burden. Mom worked hard to ready herself for the surgery and Dad, who knew too much about her exact type of breast cancer, survival rates, complications with surgery, etc., kept relatively quiet, but he did not stop encouraging, loving and praying for her.

When surgery day came, the culmination of fear, anxiety and stress came to a head. Through Dad's actions and reactions during the day, I finally came to fully understand the meaning of love. Though Dad had considered working on the day of Mom's surgery probably to distract himself from the reality of her surgery, and because he's never missed a day of work in his life, all of the other doctors and nurses he worked with counseled him to take the day off. He needed to get some distance from the hospital and not be confronted by people he knew all day. Dad knew the surgeon performing the double mastectomy well and he was told he'd be updated as the surgery progressed. The most important piece of information Dad was waiting for was whether or not my Mom's cancer had spread into her lymph nodes and into her body. If the cancer, which was present in both breasts, had not spread, mom would have a much better chance of survival. But if the cancer had spread to the lymph nodes, we all knew what that meant.

With Stacey at school and Dennis in Guatemala, it was just Dad and I playing the waiting game that day. My mom's brother joined us for part of the day, but every minute seemed to last forever. I had never seen my father act the way he did that day. For as long as I had known him, he was always the epitome of the calm, cool and collected cliché. He dealt with patients in surgery, he managed tragedy, he witnessed hardship, stress and triumph every single day in his job. But January 10th was a different day. All of a sudden, his entire world had shifted. His wife was the patient. His wife had cancer. There was the possibility that his wife of nearly 30 years would not be around much longer.

All day, Dad seemed to be trembling. He kept looking at his pager, his watch; he clutched his phone tightly in case someone called. We decided to go eat some breakfast at a café near the hospital, but neither of us had much of an appetite.

"You have to eat something, Andrea," Dad said. Though he was right, we both stared blankly at each other and our plates of steaming eggs and glossy strawberry-covered pancakes. We prayed, held hands and a few tears snuck out of the corners of Dad's eyes. Eventually, we managed to eat a little and then returned to the hospital. Dad fielded updates regarding Mom's surgery every half hour. He continued to wait for the report about the lymph nodes. The surgery was only supposed to take a few hours, but it ended up taking over six hours in total.

By early afternoon, Dad's hopes were beginning to fall. He hadn't heard anything in a few hours about how the surgery was moving along. I told him we needed to go home for a while to try process things and calm down. Our home is only about a five minute drive from the hospital, so we could quickly return, if necessary.

So, we went home, took our dogs out, who also sensed our tension, and continued to wait. Pacing back and forth in our kitchen, shaking, crying, holding hands with me and not knowing how to handle himself, my Dad finally got the call he'd been waiting for all day. A call he should've received by 12 pm and it was now late afternoon. He picked up the phone. His face looked as though it had aged ten years in one day.

"Yes. Okay. Thank you," he said. "When will she be done?" Tears immediately began streaming down my father's face as the disjointed conversation continued. I feared the worst. I thought the dreaded news was now official. Dad hung up the phone in silence. He didn't say a word. My eyes started watering and I sat motionless looking at him to move his lips. I wanted him to say something, anything! After taking a few wobbly steps forward, he fell to his knees in the middle of our kitchen and sobbed uncontrollably. I didn't know if the news was good or bad, but I had only seen my father really cry that way one other time in my life, which was when he lost his father. I couldn't help but cry when I looked at him, and it felt good to relieve all of the pent up emotions I had experienced that day.

Through teary eyes my Dad finally looked up at me and said almost in a whimper, "The cancer has not spread. There was only a microscopic amount in the lymph nodes on the right side, but it had not spread to her body." I wept with joy as my Dad kept saying, "Thank you, God, thank you, God, thank you God! He pulled himself from the ground and with a surge of adrenaline flowing through his body, he literally started jumping for joy. He bounded about the kitchen, picked me up and swung me around, smiling and repeating, "Yes! Yes! Yes! Woo!" He filled the house with shrieks of joy, passion and sheer, untempered emotion. He couldn't contain himself. A few fist pumps later, he ran out the front door of our house and started doing laps around our home. He was overwhelmed by elation, relief and the deep love and devotion he felt towards my mother. I had never seen him respond to anything in such an emotive way and I was incredulous. I cried for my mother. I cried just watching my father and knowing how much he loved and cherished his wife. Seeing him react that day, I did not just feel love or have the experience of love – I actually came to fully understand what love is.

Agape love or tatsimou love is not just the warm, fuzzy feeling you get when your dog lies by your feet, love is not just the simple hug from a friend at the end of a long day – love is not just pancakes in bed on your birthday. Love is an indescribable emotion that transcends feeling. It is the quintessence of compassion and the utmost desire of the human spirit to be connected to others. On that cold, January day, I learned just how much my father loves my mother. I learned just how much he needs, respects, admires and cares for her. She is everything to him – a part of his world he cannot imagine being without. That was the day I came to fully understand their love for each other. And also that love is life-changing. And in the spectrum of human emotions, love is the most powerful and zealous one of all.

As I sat up and regrouped from my dreamlike state of past recollection, I went downstairs and joined my family for dinner. After thinking about her scars, her bravery, and how much she needed to be reminded she was loved, I knew I wanted to reward Mom in a special way or show validation or gratitude to her. Or in the very least, make her happy. She had prepared a beautiful pesto chicken dish with vegetables and rice pilaf along with homemade honey wheat bread. While I did not have an appetite coming to the table and I still had not yet eaten any meat during the re-feeding phase, I wanted to have some. And since my mother takes great pride in serving food to people and those people enjoying the food and themselves in her presence, I understood what it would mean to her if I did not play with my food on my plate or leave it for the dog to eat or spit it out in my napkin. As I cut into my chicken she looked up at me and smiled. Dad's jaw dropped. "Are you going to eat that?!" he inquired, energy building in his voice.

"Yes, Mom made this for us and I think I should have some!" I said.

"Thank you, sweetheart," Mom said. "It means the world to me that you are willing to try it."

As our dinner table conversation drifted to Stacey's fall softball league and talk of the chemistry award Dennis was to receive, I put my best effort towards that full six ounce piece of well-lathered pesto chicken on my plate. It smelled of garlic salt and parmesan cheese. I knew it had to taste good, right? And I had not eaten anything all day, mainly on account of feeling uneasy about going to college, but I knew I could afford the protein and calories in my day. Of course the lingering thought in my head was if I could adequately burn it off through exercise. I knew chicken of that kind would have roughly 350-400 calories, but I was going to show my mother my courage and strength in my healing. I cut the boneless breast into ten even pieces. The first two I chewed quickly and hardly tasted. But as I got the third and fourth bite my chewing slowed and my stomach began to feel heavy and my mouth held a tingling sensation as though I was sucking on some kind of electrical current. It was unpleasant and I could feel remnants of the zinc test and I was unable to swallow. Rachel was standing near the refrigerator in full view. The meat was sinewy and hard to chew. I wanted to spit everything out, but I kept my mouth closed and shut my eyes. I hoped it would all disintegrate and I would figure out what to do with the rest that remained on my plate. Nausea was setting in and I saw my mom look over the table at me as she asked me to pass the butter. I knew she saw my full cheeks, too, so I swallowed hard – the full, golf ball-sized chunk of saliva-worn pesto chicken that had been slopping around in my mouth. I drank my entire glass of water and asked for another one. My gums were still bleeding periodically and the salt of the meat grinded against them. I winced and forced my back teeth together so I would not be able to feel if anything was about to come up or if I was going to throw up.

"Did you like the chicken, Andrea? How was it?" Dad asked.

"It was fine," I said. "My fork was cold though." I was not even sure what my "cold fork" phrase even meant, but I wanted to say that it was horribly disgusting and chewy and impossible to swallow and I sensed no flavor other than salt and cheese and the blood from my gums and the horrible cotton mouth feel from the Zinc test I was forced to do.

"Have some more, meat! You need it!" He said. It was annoying always being told to eat more and the second helping I was going to have of pesto chicken that evening came out in the form of a large vomit pile of chicken and bile not too far from the kitchen table as I failed to make it to the sink or bathroom.

"My stomach wasn't ready. I am sorry, Mom," I said. "I really did want to have some for you." She looked at me with that face of disappointment I hated so much and told me to put my shirt in the laundry room so she could wash it because I had gotten some vomit on it. She cried that night about me and Dad argued with her about my well-being, in my defense, as always. Four bites of chicken was four bites too many. I went to bed feeling hungry and never wanting to see, touch, or taste meat again – let alone pesto chicken. To this day I am a Vegetarian, but not for the ethical reason of saving the lives of animals. I am a vegetarian because the week before my first semester at college I failed to prove my strength to my mother in eating the pesto chicken she had prepared and I failed myself because Rachel told me never to eat meat again because it would make me sick, and in my weakness, I have believed her since then and I refuse to touch, cook, or eat meat. In the twisted irony of the darkened places within my mind, refusing to eat meat makes me feel stronger than giving in, getting sick, and being reminded of the lingering disappointment I have been to my parents.

16
Homesick No More

My hair was finally starting to grow back and the next week when my parents and I packed the van and began the four and a half hour drive to the college I was to attend near Indianapolis, where I was going to join the honors program and try out for the tennis team, despite my less that fit figure, I realized that I was leaving tatsimou behind forever. Suddenly, I was terrified. Maybe there were times wherein I had despised home and my parents, but I was leaving tatsimou; I was leaving home; and I was still struggling every day to leave Rachel and my desire for control behind. I was fearful I would never be successful in anything. I reminded myself of the verse on my mirror, Romans 12:12 - "Be joyful in hope, patient in affliction, faithful in prayer." I had to keep my heart and mind set on that goal. It was a battle every single day to keep my chin up and be hopeful not just for my physical health, but for everything else in life.

After excessive crying on the drive, and the long process of getting settled into my first ten foot by ten foot dorm room, my parents and I had to say our goodbyes. The early fall air made me uneasy and my stomach felt as raw as it did during all those lunch time indulgences of two pieces of Orbit Bubblemint gum. I felt hollow and alone; I felt weak and small. I buried myself in between the warmth of their bodies and felt them hover over me, their arms wrapped around me as I listened to them pray. Mom prayed for my strength and resilience, while Dad for my confident belief in myself as a woman of God. They both prayed for my courage and for me to use my academic gifts to excel and to grow. In that slice of time as they prayed, I nudged my long, thin arms around both of them; I wanted to return to the beginning of high school, to get a second chance, to see my family as they were and how they loved me. I wanted to feel whole again and to know what it meant to be me again. Not to be Rachel's victim, but to be healthy and loving, and nurturing and strong like they were. I did not want them to leave me there. I wanted them to take me back home and be there and nag me to eat food and help me with my laundry and tease me and love me and be there. They stayed with me as long into the evening as they could and when they finally peeled me off of them and drove away, I saw Mom had tears in her eyes, too. They knew what I had been through and what I was still going through. I felt they were at last sympathetic to my struggle and they worried for my well-being. As for me, my separation anxiety was far worse than anticipated and a dark depression sunk in before the first week of classes officially began. My zest for life waned once more and I knew I needed to hold on for tatsimou because it was not gone from my life, but I did not know if I could.

Freshman orientation was a three-day event that I hated full of ice-breaker activities and get-to-know-you games and over-zealous student-leaders, and way too much free food. I had to watch a lot of people I had never met before eat and participate in team-building activities and talk about how swell their high school experiences were. It was the apex of torture for the introverted 85 pound, anorexic, nerdy, former athlete from Chicago. The orientation concluded with a huge party for new students to mix and mingle with each other, enjoy some alcohol-free beverages, however long that trend lasted, and learn about different clubs and activities the university had to offer. In my growing social anxiety, I avoided talking to people unless they came up and talked to me. I was badgered by a group of international students because I was so "white" and I was going to be living with an Asian roommate, and some black girl teased me because I did not have an ass, and a bunch of tennis players from team tryouts chided me about how I was not fast enough or strong enough and would probably not make the team. The word 'bitch' came to mind when they spoke to me, but I didn't need them anyhow. I wanted to get away from all of it and in the student union a few buildings over, I heard they had a lot of maple cake with cream cheese frosting for after the celebration and I was craving sugar like a crack addict. I had not eaten since my parents had dropped me off several days prior, aside from coffee and a few mushy, overripe apples, and at that point I urgently believed Rachel would have approved of me eating some cake.

It was an unseasonably cold September evening and I ran from the freshman orientation party across campus to the Student Union where I found, as reported, a lot of cake! Not many people were around so I filled a large plate with several thick pieces of maple walnut cake. It smelled sweetly

148

tantalizing and I had not remembered the last time I was so eager to eat something. I would have marked a 10 on that hunger scale for Rosetta. Even cruel Barkens would have been proud of me.

I found a place near the open fireplace, pulled up my maroon hoodie, zipped my dark navy blue winter vest, and sat there, alone, for nearly an hour licking the sweet, granular icing off of more than ten pieces of cake and then disposing of the rest. It was horribly disgusting and if anyone had witnessed it, I would have had a solid reason to not have friends again. After a while my taste buds became numb to the sugary delicacy and each subsequent lick was like collecting waxy, white sandpaper on my tongue. As the ball of frosting in my stomach grew like the golf ball pesto chicken Mom made just over a week ago, I began to feel sick and nauseated. I did not throw up though. I secretly wanted to, but I could not induce that. Not for the hall monitors at Park Ridge High and not for myself the first week of college. I could not fathom all of the calories I just ate and I could not place a number on the scale of how miserable I felt.

I got rid of my final plate full of naked pieces of cake and felt my calves, my thighs, my stomach, and my chin as though checking for immediately pooling pockets of fat. I convinced myself they were there and they were growing exponentially beyond my control. I threw away the plastic fork I had used to swipe out the frosting coatings in the layered cake I could not reach with my tongue, looked at my phone for a text from Mom with any indication of validation or love, and I was deterred from hope when there was nothing there to read. It was an hour later for me than them, me being in Indiana, while they were in Chicago, but for some reason I still thought maybe they were already in bed. I guess it would make sense. Mom did sleep a lot when she was stressed and worried and I knew she was feeling all of those things about me. I did not wish that on her, but I was not naïve in that regard either.

I felt lethargic, fat, and cold. I did not want to return to the orientation party with the stress of the people there and all that would entail in trying to act like I cared or wanted to meet the people in my incoming class. My priority was not friendship, it was getting back in control and getting rid of all that frosting I ate. I thought of the birthday when Mom looked into the sprinkles from my cake with hollowed red eyes because of the distress my eating disorder had caused her and the fact that my grandfather had just died. Cake was sweet, but life sure could be emotionally hostile and unremitting. Mom was proof of that. She is the strongest woman I know.

Leaving the student union with a growing glob of frosting bloating my stomach, I proceeded to make my way to the gym where I did 200 sit-ups and walked on the treadmill for three miles. But when the gym closed at 12:00 AM, I still checked and felt fat everywhere seeping into my skin folds from the maple frosting of temptation I had indulged in and I had to, I just had to get rid of it. I stepped outside shivering, removed my coat so I could move faster and began jogging around my dorm room facility after most people inside had gone to bed for the night. From 1:00 AM to 5:00 AM I ran in the crisp, cold, autumn air trying to burn off all of the maple syrup pounds of cream cheese frosting I had consumed. I never did throw up from that torturous, self-inflicted cake binge, but the following week I was bedridden with the flu and I have permanent frostbite on my left ear and right index finger from that night. I will forever hold a slight affinity for frosting, but never will I ever eat maple flavored cake or waxy cream cheese frosting again.

As the weeks passed and I became all the more insular at school, it was more apparent each and every day that Rachel was alive and well. And she was engaged in constant battle against my own internal drive to take in food for survival. College made it easy to entertain her friendship. No one followed me to the bathroom and there were no hall monitors distributing pink passes to the nurse or sulfuric bathroom stalls or people telling me to take care of myself. It was on me and my terms and that meant control. My newfound realization of control in that setting gave me power, but it did not make the homesickness go away. Perhaps in my compulsion to organize everything to levels of perfection, it actually became worse.

I did not make any friends. I quit tennis even though I made the second string team. I ate alone, if I ever did, and I poured myself into getting an A in every class. I was studying English and French and taking all honors classes, which academically I thrived within. I met people in classes, but the only true friend I had had four legs and I affectionately named her, Butterscotch. Butterscotch was a stray cat that wandered to campus looking for food and affection. I provided her with both, as well as a name, because her markings reminded me of Werther's sugar-free butterscotch candy. She was fluffy with white fur and dark red-orange stripes similar to the cartoon, Garfield, in exterior appearance and I grew to love her. She greeted me outside my dorm each morning and we walked to my classes together. In the afternoon and evening she would be waiting outside my dorm, too. I even asked Mom what kind of cat food I could afford to get for dear Butterscotch. I wanted to provide for her and care for her properly. I also liked that she would sit outside with me while I studied or did homework. I had never liked cats much, but that silly cat made a world of difference for me. The more time I spent with her, the less I heard from Rachel and knowing that I mattered to something, meant everything.

Despite Butterscotch's best efforts, as I settled into the first quarter at school, homesickness rapidly took its toll on me as did my thinness and inability to maintain a healthy state with my weight and emotional anxiety. My parents came to visit me every Friday afternoon and I started going home every weekend. They drove four hours to get me and four hours back home on Fridays and then followed the same pattern to drop me off on Sundays – an additional eight hours on the road. 16 hours every weekend to keep their daughter alive. 16 hours and that was if traffic was good. Sometimes it took 20. They alternated those weekend drives for an entire semester. And in between those long hours of driving, I spoke with Mom for at least two hours on the phone each day. She had a faulty cell phone at the time and those long talks led to permanent hearing loss in her right ear as a result. She has suffered so much on my behalf, but it is also because of her that I am still here today. They feared a relapse for me – rightfully so, the potential of a suicide attempt, and I was beyond homesick.

I was excelling in classes, but not socially. I lived with a roommate from China that posed its own cultural problems that I was unable to navigate in a mature fashion. I knew I was failing to live up to my own expectations when I decided that at the semester break I was going to transfer to a college closer to home. It was the right decision, but I felt utterly disgusted with myself that I was not strong enough to let go of home, to shun away tatsimou, or to stand on my own two feet as a confident, independent young woman. My last week at school before Christmas break, my family came to pack up my things and take me home. Even though my dad hated cats, I was planning to bring Butterscotch home with me, but she was claimed by her rightful owners the day before they came to get me and I had to say a penitent, 'goodbye.' The drive home was long and quiet. My mother nor father said a word. It was nearly Christmas and I was quitting school after only one semester. I was failing yet again, but at least their 16 hour drives on the weekends were coming to an end. My head felt cramped and my body felt an ephemerality of cold sinking in again.

When we arrived home with all of my things I was on a slippery slope riding the weighted wave of continued failure in my life. I didn't really have any friends. Butterscotch was now a furry friend of the past, I had quit school, though I had plans to attend a college closer to home for the rest of the year, and my fight against disordered eating, stomach pain, and health remained. I wrote Ephesians 6:10 in even bigger print than the verse from Romans on the yellow sheet covering my mirror. "Finally, be strong in the Lord and His mighty power." I knew that strength to continue fighting through my life as it was sure as heck was not going to come from me.

17

Humming, Merry Christmas!

Christmas morning came and those pesky bells jangled on my door as Dad came in my room to wake me up and invite me downstairs for breakfast and to open presents.

"Merry Christmas, sweetheart!" he said as he gave me a kiss on the forehead.

"Merry Christmas, Dad," I said holding back the tears welling at the surface. I heard Mom downstairs cooking bacon and making broiled grapefruit with sugared cherries on top and a special almond sweetbread that I was tempted enough to eat without once considering a calorie count. I feared a lot of foods, but I could not hold down the argument against my mother being an incredible cook. I sunk down further beneath my covers as I became woozy with the sweet salty savor filling my nasal cavity as the food smells, the chiming bells, and the chatter of dogs barking, my siblings arousing for the day, and the warm hustle that Christmas morning was for my family. I shivered again and felt my body for skin folds and massaged the bruise on my left hip, the ever enduring bed sore I could not get rid of. I closed my eyes again to avoid the mistletoe madness of my home and to shut out the cold bedroom air.

What an absolute failure I am. I'll bet that bitch, Rachel, is having a good laugh about all this. Andrea, you're back home taciturn (your English professor liked that word), unable to get out of bed. Andrea, you are pathetic. I told myself. I was completely devastated and felt just as dejected as I had the morning of the championship swim meet about a year prior when I laid in bed feeling nearly the same both emotionally and physically. Cold, alone, and entirely useless. I was still sick, had quit college after one semester of whelming homesickness and my favorite holiday now felt like the worst of chores to attend and be excited for.

"Andrea! Andrea! Are you coming down to open presents? It's Christmas," Stacey shouted up the stairs to me. I turned over in my bed to mumble something at her, but the pine and bacon aroma made me too queasy to think of how to respond.

"Honey, we are waiting for you," Mom said. I tossed and turned spreading the wealth of my tears onto my pre-stained, permanently salted pillowcase.

"Go ahead and start without me. I'll be down in a minute," I replied.

"Are you sure?" I heard Dennis question me with a level of concern in his voice I was not accustomed to hearing from him. I was still bitter about his choice words towards me during the family counseling session with Sarah the previous year. I thought of Rosetta and tasted mangoes on my breath. I pictured Barkens and my mouth filled with cotton. I thought of pink hall passes and sulfuric bathrooms and Orbit Bubblemint gum and how hungry I was not for food, but for life and for purpose. To feel warm again, to feel in charge of my life again. To be strong. To be so strong that those cotton water mango gum covered headaches would forever be displaced from my mind.

"I am sure," I called back. "I'll make it down in time for stockings. I promise." I heard them proceed with laughter and photo clicks and joy for the prideful moments of giving and receiving. I burrowed down into my bed and created an igloo underneath my heavy covers. My fleece polar bear print pajamas and heated blankets were at long last providing enough warmth to allow me to think clearly. I sat up inside my igloo, tucking my knees into my chest and prayed like I had never prayed before.

Heavenly Father, please give me strength to love. To love my family as they have loved me. Give me strength to fulfill your purpose for my life. Lord God, please heal me. Please give me courage and the will to continue on in this life. Thank you for the life you have given me. Thank you for my family and the few remaining friends I have and for a warm bed to numb a bit of the cold that penetrates my skin. Thank you for giving me life. Forgive me, Lord, for my selfish ways and for participating in behaviors that do not honor my body as a temple of your holy spirit. Lord, I am so sorry. I am so sorry for what I have become. Please forgive me. Help me to serve you and not any other idols or masters, including food and the vanity of appearance. And since it is Christmas, thank you God for sending your son, Jesus Christ, to die for me and my sins. I do not deserve grace or mercy and you have given me both. I'll try to talk to you more from here on out, okay? In your Holy name I pray. Amen.

It had been a long time since I really prayed for healing or even believed God had the power to heal me, but somewhere in the caverns of my skeletal body and the sprouting re-growths of hair on the top of my head, I felt God's presence. He was saying to me as His child that He

156

had not given up on me and that He had great plans for my life. As the Ephesians verse on my mirror reminded me – I had to be strong in His mighty power. God was still speaking and by His grace, I was still breathing.

I went back to that Teen Study Bible and perused its gems of yellow sticky notes, notecards, highlighted passages, and worksheets from youth group Bible study classes. I discovered a worksheet nestled in the middle of 1 John that seemed to answer a lot of the probing questions my faith-dwindling selfish-self had been having. It was about confession – how and why we need to confess our sins to God. In my notes I had written that we have to confess our sins so we can be forgiven and we confess our sins by telling God about them and repenting. Repentance, I wrote, meant to admit that you are wrong, tell God you are sorry, and promise to Him that you won't sin again. My actions were not just selfish and self-destructive, they were sinful. Realizing this, I had a renewed frame of mind in thinking about my self-inflicted illness. If I framed it as a sin, that meant I could be forgiven. I was sinning against God and my sinful ways needed to stop. But if I did not cry out and seek His forgiveness, Satan's grasp would suck more life out of me and deteriorate my will and ability to see God through the storm that had intensified in its magnitude of perpetual cancellation of sun and rainbows. I continued reading through my notes about sin and confession. I had highlighted the following phrase: "Sin is a wall between God and ourselves. We need to continually break down the wall and confess our sins to God so that we can truly know Him better and fulfill His purpose for our lives." If I confessed my sins, I would be forgiven. If I repented and promised to abstain from my sinful ways, I trusted God would provide redemption for my weeping spirit and my waning life.

I searched for the accompanying Bible passage to the highlight statement about sin being a wall. When I found it, I wrote it down in bold print on the front of my food diary. "If we confess our sins, He is faithful and just and will forgive us our sins and purify us from all sin" – 1 John 1:9.

I pushed my food diary to the back of my bedside drawer and laid my Bible to rest in front of it for ease of access. Then, I set a new challenge for myself. I was going to cry out like Jonah, and every day for the next month, I was going to write down my prayer of confession for God. I wanted to discover if I would be able to turn away from my sins on an everyday basis. I wanted the rain to clear and the sun to shine. I wanted to be covered in rainbows of His forgiveness.

I joined my family to open stockings and I ate three pieces of Santa-shaped, foil-wrapped chocolates without thinking about sugar or calories. I even enjoyed breakfast. I mean, I actually enjoyed it. The scrambled eggs with grape jam tasted heavenly and the broiled grapefruit danced on my tongue with sour tang and sweet juice. Mom's almond bread was warm and creamy and I lathered it up with real, full-fat butter. I had forgotten how good food tasted.

"You're eating?!" Stacey commented as we confabulated at the table. I was wrapped in three blankets, still not warm, but somehow not made stoic by her comment either.

"And you're humming!" Mom said, her eyes lighting up brighter than I had seen in years. "You know you always used to hum when you liked what you were eating growing up. I knew if you were humming at the dinner table I had prepared something you enjoyed! I am so happy to hear you hum again," she said, honestly, and I noticed a camouflaged tear of relief and sadness pooled in the corner of her right eye.

I managed to send a smile and a proud hum in her direction. "Mom, this meal is wonderful. I wish I was not feeling full or I would have more. The almond bread is the best it's ever been. Thank you," I told her with a sincere nod. There were no napkins in my lap filled with food, the dog was not eating half of my meal, and for the most part, my plate was clean aside from a few crumbly remnants of almond bread and grape jam. My stomach felt enlarged, but I did not feel sick as I expected I would from all of that food. And suddenly, as it was, Christmas morning was not about food or presents or chocolates in over-stuffed stockings. Christmas was about renewing hope in the gift of Christ and His presence over that table and over our lives.

I continued humming as I ate the last bites of bread on my plate and soon the rest of my family joined in on a special feature hummed version medley of "Carol of the Bells" and "We Wish You a Merry Christmas."

I hummed louder and a tender smile teased the corners of my face. My mouth was full of cinnamon almond sugar and velvety butter. I felt a wave of warmth envelop my body and I knew it had no intention of leaving.

"Merry Christmas," I said as I threw my empty napkin in the air. "Merry Christmas!"

18
Shark Fins & New Year's Resolutions

The New Year came and I was finally beginning to feel a little bit stronger. My thoughts were more streamlined and I could focus on tasks for longer periods of time. Perhaps I was most emboldened by the new growth of hair on my head. I had lost 75% of my hair and what remained was still falling out, but the erratic patches of new growth was a good sign.

"It looks like little shark fins coming out of your head!" Stacey would tell me. Sometimes I let her touch them because they were so spikey and it felt like a massage if you patted them down with your palms. Every day there were new shark hairs popping out of my head. They were of a much lighter brown coloration than the dark brunette mane of hair I had before I got sick, but it was a sign of life that gave me hope. My hair gradually filled in and the patchwork shark-fin quilt that covered my head with all different lengths of hair was not at all flattering. But – it gave me enough confidence to take the yellow paper off of my mirror and study the new growth. I was coming back! I was still thin and gaunt looking, but my hair, that visible sign of lively womanhood, was growing back!

I went to visit Sarah one final time to talk about management for staying on a path towards health and she was undoubtedly proud of the progress I had made since the last time I had seen her the summer before.

"It was a difficult semester and I fell back into old habits," I explained. "I was very homesick, but I think if I commute to a local college for a while I will be able to have my family as a support system and that will help me to continue to heal," I said.

"I admire your maturity in assessing this situation and responding to what you need to do for yourself. That is most important," Sarah confided to me.

"Do you think I will ever be 100% again? Will I ever be me again?" I asked.

"Andrea, you are still you! You will continue to grow as you heal. With your diligence and stubborn mindset, you can do anything!" She assuaged.

"I will try my very best!" I told her.

"I know you will. Keep in touch if you need anything," she said. I was grateful she cared about me and I was beginning to see her as not only a therapist, but as a disciple of Christ. She served Him through caring for me. Where I was once sinister, I was able to see beauty in the power of healing and God's work in our lives even when we are unable to see it.

That January I began taking classes at Elmhurst College, a private school West of Chicago and about an hour from home. I commuted by train or by car to campus each day. This alleviated the stress of having to sleep away somewhere and the added responsibility that independent living brings. I plugged myself into my academic schedule and worked hard to get to know other students and my professors. It was a fresh start for me and I was relieved when on my very first day on campus, someone looked me in the eyes and addressed me by name as I was walking towards the student center. "How are you, Andrea? It was great meeting you in class. Would you like to grab coffee together?" I was too shocked to even respond because in that very moment I was again given an identity, a personhood, a feeling of living again. *Someone saw me. Someone called me out by name!* I had felt invisible, except to Rachel, since the end of my junior year in high school, but that, "How are you?" indicated to me that I existed again. I felt like I mattered. I had an identity. I was getting an opportunity re-create the "me" I had always aspired to be.

It was during my first semester at Elmhurst College wherein I began to blossom as an individual again. I became the Executive Chair of the Honors Program, I became a tutor in the writing center, campus tour guide, and a student ambassador for the school. I declared a double major in English and French with a minor in Interdisciplinary Communications; I helped to found a new sorority on campus and became a leader within that organization. And most importantly, I believed in myself again. I believed in who I was and all that I could be. I also recognized how important it is to validate other people in our lives. The simple act of calling someone by name, saying, "thank you," and acknowledging the existence of another means more than I ever realized. A "How are you?" changed the trajectory of my entire life. I will never forget the girl who said that to me. Ironically, her name was Rachel, and we became study buddies and lab partners in a meteorology class we took together. She became a real, live friend who never once commented on what I ate or how thin I was.

There were intermittent periods of food struggles, body shaming, and anxiety when eating with others that semester, but I was not journaling or counting calories or worrying too much other than doing my best to maintain a healthy vegetarian diet, complimented with nutrition shakes and yes, Barkens approved, peanut butter brownies!

The only part of the equation that I was unable to control was the endless stomach pain that I had and the pain and discomfort that I felt not just after eating, but consistently throughout the day. On occasion, I had hyper burn bouts of urine or bloody diarrhea and I did not have a clear explanation as to why. I knew I was still healing and my body was adjusting to a more normalized food intake again, but the stomach pain was lending itself to me slowly easing into starvation periods in order to avoid it. Consequently, my weight stagnated. I was concerned something else was wrong. I confided in the nurse on campus about my stomach complications. Something had to be done.

19
Farts of Laughter

During a weekend home following a long week of exams at school, I had a candid discussion with Dad about symptoms I was experiencing and how my stomach pain affecting my ability to eat. He was rightly concerned so we went to see a specialist who ordered tests to see if anything internally was going on other than residual effects of my eating disorder. The doctor ordered a colonoscopy and Dennis and Stacey both thought this was the greatest gem of medical news since the incarnation of the polio vaccine.

"You have to get what?! Oh, my gosh, a colonscopy? That's like what 50 year-olds get. You do know they are going to stick a camera up your butt, right?" Dennis gibed me in good humor. My sister howled with delight. Somehow I did not see their humor, but I played along.

"I told the doctor that is an out hole, not an in hole!" I said.

"They better knock you out or there is no way that is happening!" Stacey said.

"I know. I know," I said bemused, but also nervous for the procedure.

"Have fun fasting and drinking that make-you-poop juice the day before," Dennis taunted.

"Thanks a lot," I said.

"Hey! Clear the pipes," he laughed with Stacey and then farted the stench of brotherly love.

"You are so gross! That smells! Dear Lord, have mercy!" I held my breath making a twisted face of squeamish disgust.

"You'll be having a lot of gas after you get a roto-root of your colon. Then who will be farting?" He said. "I mean a least we don't have to strap kid-sized suction cups to your chest again. I mean you do have a real heartbeat now, right?"

"Yeah, yeah. I think I am alive. Who knows?" I snapped back. He raised his eyebrows, farted proudly, and walked off.

I was snarky and mad, but also glad. It was the first time since I was in high school that we had shared that convivial sibling connection I had thrived on as a child. Yes, I was going to be clearing the pipes and someone was going to stick a camera up my butt. That was not attractive or desirable and I was far from colonoscopy age. But, nonetheless, it was worth a good laugh. Flatulence brings out the best in all of us.

The following week I completed the colonoscopy test as well as few other probes and internal diagnostic tests. My brother was right; I had gas for days afterwards! If only he had still been in town for me to share with him and return the favor for surviving 19 years of his stinky farts! He would have been impressed beyond measure. Out-farting your brother is no small feat for a 90 pound girl. The results of the tests showed that nothing dramatic was found other than some patchy irritation in my intestinal track as well as a narrowing of the valve connecting my large intestine to my colon. There was also a prominent display of ileocecal valve disorder. Both of which created sharp pain, bowel malfunction, and caused a host of other nervous system problems I am still dealing with today. The doctor informed me that there was a high probability that I had been living with intestinal malformations long before my eating disorder, but the illness made them more pronounced and unfortunately caused them to worsen and become harder to effectively manage and treat.

I started taking a fussy regimen of medications, none of which worked well aside from making me tired and causing frequent trips to the bathroom. I set about to do my best nutritionally to manage the pain and discomfort. But depending on stress levels, foods eaten, and time of year, I still have days where the pain keeps me up at night or bent over during the day. I am aptly reminded by the doctor and my brother that I can get another colonoscopy anytime to check on how things are doing. Yet, if I can postpone the fart-producing procedure as long as possible, that would be ideal. Unless, of course, if my brother is in town. Then, and only then, I might have to reconsider.

20

*A Spotted Skirt &
A Resolute Racquet*

The relentless, gnawing pain and inflammation in my stomach did not subside, but neither did my willpower to continue living and gaining strength. Throughout the summer after completing my first full semester at Elmhurst College, managing to pull off a 4.0, maintaining my grade point average from my first, otherwise failed semester in Indiana, I decided to follow an intensive training regimen so I would be able to try-out for women's tennis in the fall. It had been nearly three years since I had played, not counting my measly efforts in Indiana and the last time I picked up a regulation sized racquet I was so frail that I could not lift the eight ounces of carbon fiber weight over my head to pick off a serve or control a forehand shot. I was still a shadow of my former self, but I was convinced that if I was able to put on enough muscle to at least hit the ball again, the other skills in game play would come back with enough practice. I informed Dad of my plan and he was, as expected, excited for me. He offered to help by going to volley with me in the evenings, shag balls from my practice serves, and pay for private lessons. He believed in me and that gave me reason to believe in myself. I did not want to be mollycoddled, but I would have been a fool to turn away his attentiveness towards helping me achieve my goal that summer. Mom thought that it was a foolish idea to go out and begin exercising because I would be burning more calories and thus, in her perspective, be unable to maintain the weight gain I had already achieved. I was hopeful that more exercise would equate to more strength and possibly a heightened appetite, which would only be a good thing for me as time wore on.

I had a long journey ahead, but with the right focus and discipline I knew I had a chance. At least I wanted to give myself the best possible opportunity to be successful that I could. Even if I failed I wanted to prove to myself that I was strong enough to try out. I prayed that maybe I could be granted at least one more season of tennis in my career. Swimming was all but futile and I had not yet overcome the symbolism of the neon shirt that solemnly hung in the back of my closet as a reminder of my letdown. An unremoved token from the swim meet that I bailed on and the weight I still shouldered nearly two and a half years later from letting the whole school down. Yet with tennis, I knew I had a reasonable chance of making something work for me. Perhaps it was because I loved the sport so much or maybe because a tennis skirt stuffed with tennis balls would make me look physically more intimidating than I was. Moreover, I knew I would have Dad's help. And with his sideline support, the competitive sports fanatic in him would coach me along to make it a reality if I was willing to work for it.

"Honey, are you sure you want to go through with this?" Mom asked as Dad and I got home from the sporting goods store in late June with a new racket and a large bucket of 200 new tennis balls. I had just over a month to prepare for August tryouts.

"She can do it; you need to trust her," Dad defended me. She glared at him in that unmistakable fashion of hers that said she wanted to blurt out one thousand words of argument, fear, and worry, but she would accept the silent defeat of being overruled by her husband. It was a relational sacrifice she rarely allowed for.

"Mom, I can do this, okay? I know I can," I persuaded. I knew she was not convinced and no amount of my calculating rhetoric would get her to think otherwise. While visions of Bubblemint gum in bathroom stalls had dissipated and the voice of Rachel had grown less frequent, the internal raging control between Mom and I feuded on. Our relationship, the cyclical catalyst for my abysmal mental health craved healing. But wounds fester. Even on warm summer nights when hope glimmers on the face of a freshly uncovered tennis racquet.

Eating was still a daily battle for me. Fending off an upset stomach was nearly impossible, and diarrhea was common at least four times a day. Adding the elements of heat and increased exercise did not ease symptoms, only worsened them. I elected to take the rest of the summer off of my part time jobs tutoring and working odd hours at a local smoothie bar in town. Working with food aggravated my disordered eating and tutoring was taking time away from my focus on training. I woke up each morning at 5:00 AM to go outdoors to run, bike, or if it was warm enough, to swim about 50 laps at the local pool. Any form of cardio was beyond exhaustive to me so I knew I had to attempt at least one session before ingesting food for the day which would serve to complicate intestinal levels of bloating and discomfort. At first I could only run about half a mile and my goal was to be able to run three steady miles by the end of summer. Cycling was easier, but after about thirty minutes of steady-state, slow, flat riding, I had to take a break and rest. My heart often fluttered in my chest if I did anything for a duration longer than twenty to thirty minutes and my breaths indicated the development of a shrunken lung capacity and asthma. Following my morning sessions, I usually spent a good deal of time going to the bathroom and would then prepare a chocolate protein shake with bananas, ice, vegan protein powder, and almond milk. As a side, I would have a piece of fruit, usually a cold apple without the skins as well as four tablespoons of freshly ground peanut butter. My goal for those eating sessions was 500 calories. I was not always able to finish it all, but it was not for lack of trying.

Over the course of the entire summer only two shakes met the fate of being dumped in the sink. Sometimes eating was just too much to bear. After my stomach settled, my afternoon consisted of as many hours as I could withstand out on the tennis court practicing serves and hitting forehand and backhand volley shots against the practice wall on the far end of the court. On Tuesdays and Fridays, I would have one hour lessons with Brian Connor, who was one of the best coaches known in the region. After those lessons I could not do anything other than drink copious amounts of water and sleep away fatigue. On the evenings when I did not have lessons, Dad came out to the court to volley with me. We hit until well past dusk nearly every night, but we always made it home for dinner and I showed Mom each night that I was eating. I was thankful for the meals after those gruesome days of training. I did not want to admit that she was right in the fact that I was not ready for so much activity so fast and that it was hard to keep weight on. I was working hard, but between my queasy stomach, dehydration, and growing fatigue, the idea of even being remotely ready for an entire tennis season seemed to dim in possibility. I hated that she was right so I never told her how weak, tired, and drained I was feeling.

"Tennis training was great today!" I would lie to her. "I am getting faster and stronger with every session of practice!"

"That's wonderful! But be careful. I hope you can continue to improve," she said warily wanting to give support, but also wanting to protect my health.

"I will," I said. "You'll see." I hardly believed myself. I felt alone in my struggle and I was discouraged enough by watching other adults play six or seven matches of intensive tennis on the courts where I practiced each day. I could not consume enough food or drink enough water to keep up with the needs of my body, but nevertheless I kept trying day after day after sweltering heat, draining day.

I continued my morning cardio sessions and tried to add calories to my diet in every last crevice that I could. I had gone up a size in shorts, but not yet in shirts. I was still an XXS, but I was starting to see slivered outlines of muscle contouring beneath my translucent, yet sun-tanned skin. Tryouts would contain a profusion of suicide sprint endurance tests and that was what I feared the most. When I ran at my fastest it resembled nothing more than a bony legged power jog. I was like a galloping pony, wannabe racehorse. The ability to run with the strength and power I had growing up was a warped hallucination malformed by an ego that once believed it was greater than the need for the electrolytes Purple Frost Gatorade had to offer and the caloric nutrition of BOOST high protein strawberry shakes. I wanted to run like a gazelle. But I walked like a mangled young giraffe unaware of his dangling limbs.

With three weeks remaining until tryouts, nearing the end of one of the hottest, most humid Julys on record for Chicago, I sat on the burning tennis courts after my Friday morning lesson and cried. I worked so hard for Coach Connor to show him strength that I physically did not have. He did not get impatient with me, but he had noted that progress was slow.

"When you are hitting the forehand and backhand volleys you really need to engage the muscles in the lower half of your body. You have to power those shots with everything you've got," he coached me. Little did he know, I was giving everything I had. There simply was not much of it to give. My serves were getting faster and more targeted, but I could only serve about ten in any given stretch of time before my right arm gave out. The motion of service for a volley put strain through my back, forearms, and chest. A given match of six games requires at least 24 serves and that was if you aced every one. Not a chance in hell to ace every serve unless you're a seasoned professional.

Sweat lathered my back and slid down my legs as a sunburned glow appeared on my bony shoulders and collarbone making them dry and raw to the touch. My aqua blue, sleeveless tank, which was supposed to be a fitted tee, remained to dangle loosely over my body. Sitting down, I tested my fat levels by creating a circle with my thumb and index finger and wrapping it around my wrist and sliding the ring I created with my fingers as far up my sticky arm as possible with my thumb and index finger still intact. During high school I could go all the way up my arm without having to move the gauge to my thumb and middle finger. I was still able to go past my elbow joint but I could not make it all the way up to my armpit. I did not care either way. It meant I was somewhat fatter, but still not much stronger. There was no way I was going to make it through those tryouts physically or mentally. I regretted ever thinking it was possible. As I baked in the sun on the court, only content not to be shivering, the tears I tasted were not salty like my sweat and I knew I was past dehydration. If I drank Gatorade the taste and smell sensation would incite memory relapse and my stomach would tighten up and all appetite would dissipate. I crumpled my pony-giraffe legs into my chest to stand up and noticed small blood splotches on my skirt. I thought I might have cut myself somehow, but I quickly realized where they were coming from.

That explained the fatigue and distempered mood swings. I bled tiny dots for two days; it was not all that significant. My body was trying to work though. Its systems were trying on their functionality of vitality. I had a period. I wanted to tell that mango-loving therapist in truth that it happened as though somehow that would delete my former lies. I was beginning to realize how right everyone was about everything that was happening to me and had happened to me. It was an unpleasant feeling as was the sweat, blood, and

Sitting down again in the corner of the courts I opened my legs and slid a finger down into my skirt and touched the warm crevice between my legs. The slimy heat of blood in the penetrating heartbeat I felt there told me I was still alive and I was indeed a woman and not a little girl, but I wanted that oozing blood my body needed so much to stop coming out of me. I stopped crying and applied the pressure of three fingers to the small opening. I inhaled deeply, fully grabbing oxygen through my nose as my chin rose towards the cloudless sky. An upsurge of cool relaxation pulsed through my body and the heartbeat between my legs throbbed of satisfaction. Coach Connor had left and besides me still on the court from my earlier lesson, no one else was playing on those courts that day so I held that position until my bloodied fingers slipped from their massaging grip on a part of my body I had not even known still existed. I walked back to my car with a freshly painted, blood-stained skirt, sticky fingers, and a craving for some kind of savory food. I kept my chin towards the sky where the oxygen was. Win or lose, I was not giving up on making that damn tennis team.

21
Stand in the Rain

After my bloody escapades renewed my drive to carry forth my goal to be successful in my pursuit of tennis team tryouts, I completed the most epic run of my entire life since my lapse into illness and my last long run the prior fall when I was trying to terminate the onslaught of maple cake calories of body shaming hate. Okay, so maybe it was not an epic run by any other scale than my own, but it was fast, it was strong, it was not for the purpose of burning calories, and it lasted an entire 4.3 miles. I laced up my black and pink lightweight running shoes coordinated with my pink and yellow running shorts, two bras, and my black and teal Nike running tee. My clothing hung loosely from my well-tanned body. The abundance of sun that summer made my skin appear a little less translucent than usual; the blue veins in my arms less conspicuous. I adjusted my purple Garmin watch on my wrist and took my pulse on my neck. It registered around 45 beats per minute. Still slow, but an improvement from the 25 beats I was logging my senior year of high school. I wanted to go run by the river, but after my collapse on that path and subsequent visit to the ER, I decided that a loop around the golf course in my neighborhood would be a safer bet. It was 5:30 AM and the sun was on the cusp of making its appearance in the early morning sky. Still cool enough to cause goosebumps up and down the length of my arms, I rubbed my hands together to create friction and warmth as I stood in my driveway, earbuds in ears, iPod around my waist, cell phone tucked into my double-layered sports bra in case something happened, and my Garmin watch ready to track my progress. My goal was three miles. During my athletic sporting days, three miles was considered a warm-up. But today, it was considered a quest of self-worth and identity. Three miles. I could do it. I rolled my shoulders back and alternated knee raises into my chest to warm-up. I bounced in place on my toes and started my watch timer and my music. My song of choice at the start of every run, walk, or jog that summer had been, "Stand in the Rain" by SuperChick (2006). Its message was an empowering reminder to stand, not sit, not crawl, but stand even when everything else in life falls down.

As I started down my street, the rocky pavement caused pressure up through my knees and calves as my steps ate away at the unchartered distance before me and my heart began to beat in rhythmic cadence. I could see the shadow of each breath expelled from my lungs as I turned right at the end of the street. I had already completed a quarter mile of running. My heels swelled and my toes gripped the earth to propel my body swiftly forward. I was chilled by the early morning air, and the dewy mist from the grass made my toes wet and cold as I ran through it crossing the connecting path from the main subdivision roads to the circular loop around the golf course. I pictured the first day of tennis tryouts and playing a complete match, holding my new racquet proudly and sprinting faster than any of the other girls on the court. My breath was growing more steady and my legs felt sturdy as my earbuds rang out, "So stand in the rain, stand your ground, stand up when it's all crashing down, you stand through the pain, you won't drown, and one day what's lost can be found…" I looked at my Garmin watch as the lyrics of the first song I had put on repeat rang out, "the only way out is through everything she's running from," and to my surprise noticed I had run over half a mile. *I can do it!* I thought. *I can do this!*

As the song ended I could feel sweat beat droplets down the sides of my face bringing forth pseudo dundrearies of my earnest work. The pulse in my temples tickled my cheeks as I looked out over the expansive rolling hills of the serene golf course observing the careful work of the ground crew to maintain the perfectly manicured course for each of the men and women who would come to play after Church that Sunday afternoon. I used to think they were lazy, but watching them go about their work, I admired them for their dedication. Another thin river of sweat came down my face adding salt to my lips as I was absorbed in thoughts of service-based jobs and the dignity that accompanies them. It made me feel selfish for wanting an independent career rather than one of the servant-leader. Sweat danced in the creased lid of my left eye until I blinked away the smooth, cool tear and looked down at my watch. I had lost track of distance and had already finished two miles at about a 9:15 pace. That was the farthest I had run without stopping for a walking break all summer. My hands were clammy and my legs lacked full feeling, but I pressed on. I knew that I was running. I was not walking. I was not jogging. I was running. Running to live, to think, to be, to create, to do. I was running for me.

The sun was gradually creeping into being bringing light upon the path before me as I circled the 14th hole of the course. *Only one more mile,* I thought. *But what if I can go farther, should I try?* My shorts rubbed abrasively against the skin of my inner thighs, later causing chaffing and a bleeding rash, but I was okay with that. Any sort of pain aside from the physicality that I had been perpetrated by my years of starvation was a most welcomed pain. My knees buckled as I passed the 15th green, but I stayed upright. The marching tempo of my black and pink shoes droned on and the tantalizing chill of the morning breeze with its surrounding halo of warmth enveloped my body in the perfection of the peaceful world around me. The last crickets from the night chirped and the blades of bright green, well-watered grass multiplied their dissipating echoes. A few bright neon insects flashed their ambient glow close to the ground. My horizon of sight from the 16th hole showed the quiet slumber of beautiful, custom homes, burgeoning trees, and the growing glow of the rising blood orange sun. For some reason the churn of my thoughts took me to something I had remembered hearing in a sermon one day about the "ABCs of prayer." A was for "Admit" sins and ask for forgiveness. B was for "Believe" Jesus is Lord and God raised Him from the dead. C was for "Commit" to follow Jesus for the rest of your life. I could say my ABCs and pray while running! How neat was that? Jesus even showed up in my wobbly knees and weary sneakers. I was convinced it was God who had been knocking at the door of my heart all along.

A faster run tempo song played in my ears and I picked up my pace checking my watch that clocked me in at 3.1 miles. I pumped my skinny little arms in the air indulging in the achieved moment and kept going. I completed the golf course loop and ran back towards the neighborhood streets that would link up with my street. The stealth silver boomerangs on the side panels of my scruffy shoes deflected light as the cars of the morning work or Church commute cruised by humming mellow music emblematic of the complexion of that inimitable summer morning. Their movement and presence revived my efforts fueling my final steps towards the top of my street. My tired, scraggly pony tail mercilessly flopped on the top of my back wiping off the layering of sweat that had formed. I kept moving. One foot in front of the other, I pressed on barely able to feel my legs. My heart, depleted of oxygen, worked to recover. *Only a few more blocks and I'll be there. Only a few more blocks.* The sun was slightly higher in the sky and neighbors in bathrobes trickled out of their homes to facilitate the alleviation of their dog's need to go to the bathroom. *Just a few more steps. A few more steps.* I closed my eyes and exhaled. A whisk of cold air overwhelmed my shoulders and neck in the placidity of the morning as I reached the top of my street. I slowed my steps and walked the quarter mile down my street and my sand heavy filled shoes tugged on my shaky, Jell-O pony -giraffe legs. The tingling sensation did not cease, but the smile across my face grew as wide as the rising sun across the horizon. It was just past 6:30 in the morning and God was in the clouds watching me, hearing and holding onto my breaths with each and every step. God's earth was swollen with joy.

Breathe in; Breathe out. As my right foot crossed the Rubicon of my driveway, I checked my Garmin watch. 4.3 miles. I shuddered in disbelief and rubbed my sweat-soaked eyes. *4.3 miles?! 4.3 miles?! Take that, Rachel!* I snickered in a stealthy wave of self-satisfaction. I removed the poly-chromatic rubber bands from my hair and let the wisps of thin, but still growing, soft, light brown hair cloak my neck and shoulders. My bliss-filled breath was silent within the captive calm that came over my body. I reached my arms up towards the sky and held them there as I allowed my lungs to fill to capacity with a fully oxygenated breath. I whispered a 'thank you' towards the sky and turned off my music. I heard a few lawn mowers start their hum, dogs bark in conversation, and birds sing their delicate songs. The temperature was rising, but a cool morning respite from Chicago's summer heat was not quickly forgotten. 4.3 miles. I was thirsty, but I did not collapse. I was tired, but I was not weak. I went inside, wrapped myself in a fleece jacket, as the piercing air conditioned cold rapidly hibernated my skin, and proceeded to peel, slice, and consume two whole, ripened mangoes. It was a juicy, smoothly succulent, and most wondrous post-run treat.

22
Tennis Team Tryouts

Women's Tennis Team tryouts lasted for two weeks in August and my body was beaten and sore from nearly six hour practices full of matches, conditioning, and strength training. I did not make many friends during those two weeks and I struggled to keep up with the suicide sprints and ongoing sessions of strength and endurance tests. I threw up from exhaustion almost every night when I got back to my dorm room, but somehow I pushed through the arduous days of tryouts and on the final day of training, I drove the hour back home thinking there was no chance I could have made the team. The other girls were bigger, stronger, faster, and highly skilled in everything from ball placement to speed of serve and net play. My skill set was not necessarily the problem, but I was slower, smaller, and despite my desperate attempts to mask my inferior physicality, it was discernably evident I was far weaker than all of the other girls who tried out.

When I arrived home, Dad helped me bring my bags and tennis gear into the house. "How did it go, honey?!" He asked with anticipation mounting in his voice. "You look pretty darn beat up, kid."

"I am, Dad," I admitted as I heaved a deep breath and plopped myself down on the cool tile in the center of the kitchen floor. I slid off my tennis shoes to reveal my blood-soaked socks. "I have blisters and bruises everywhere, Dad. I gave it my all," I said, legs outstretched, reaching towards my toes to massage my feet.

"I'm proud of you! And you should be proud of yourself no matter what happens," he said.

"We find out who made the team tomorrow night. I am nervous because it will secure my track record as a failure and likely set me back in terms of healing if I don't make it. You know, I am not that strong yet, but I sure got a lot stronger over the summer," I looked at Dad through tired, glazed eyes.

"Give yourself some more credit, Andrea," Dad justified my reasoning. "Only you know how far you have come and I want you to be proud of that no matter what the outcome. You know I will always be here to practice and play ball with you!" Lightening the mood, his commentary made me smile.

"Dad, can you help me off the ground here? I can hardly feel my legs," I said.

"Couch time, ice, and Gatorade?" He asked. The image stirred up foul memories.

"No. How about a big dinner, and savory dessert!" I called back. He helped get me into a standing position and wrapped fresh socks over my bleeding feet. I held onto his shoulders for support as he kissed my bruised right knee-cap still swollen from the chaffing abrasion I had gotten when I clumsily fell and skidded across the hot courts attempting to return a volley the second day of tryouts.

"That's my girl!" He said as he effortlessly lifted me up and swung my sweaty, lanky body around. I did not reject the attention even though his grip underneath my arms still hurt as his strong hands pressed into my body and rubbed firmly against my sensitive skin.

"Daddy! Daddy! Put me down, please!" I laughed slightly, but breathed heavily as he set me back down and moved my bags towards the stairs. "Let's find Mom and get some food, okay?" I said.

"You got it. She will be happy for the invite and to share a meal with you," Dad went off to locate Mom who was doing yardwork by moonlight outside. When he said the phrase, 'meal time,' I knew how important that was to our family. Dinners as a family were the most important thing we did together growing up and sometimes the only thing we did together as a whole family when schedules were scattered and evening time was limited. To Mom, meal time meant family connection time and that was the most cherished time of all. The food association of the act of breaking bread together at dinner was the part I had to get past, but once I did, I could see the spontaneous connectivity of all of my favorite people in one place as a most beautiful gift.

Coach Griffith called me late on Saturday night and I let the first call go to voicemail because I did not have my script prepared for the likely chances I was going to be cut from the team. He called two more times though and on the third time, I finally answered the phone and sat down on my bed.

"Hi! Is this Andrea?" Coach Griffith asked.

"Yes, this is she," I said in muted tones fearful for the next words out of his mouth. Dad was waiting patiently in the room next to mine.

"I'd like you to be a part of our team," he stated with confidence. "I would like to officially welcome you on as a Bluejay! You will not be a starter, but I am placing you at fourth doubles. You have great mental clarity on the court and ball awareness. Your raquet skills are strong and as for the rest your game's development, we will pair you with our strength and conditioning coach twice a week to catch you up to the rest of the girls in that category. You have great potential and showed excellence in all areas of perseverance both on and off the court the last couple weeks. Practice on Monday starts at 6:00 AM, South Courts. Looking forward to seeing you then!"

"Thank you! Thank you! I will see you there, Coach! Thank you for giving me this opportunity!" I said as my muted tones quickly elevated towards exhilaration.

"Have a wonderful evening," he said. I nearly shrieked into the phone, but held back until I heard the receiver click on the other end.

Dad had overheard the conversation and snuck into my room with a beaming smile across his face and wetness dampening the corners of his eyes. "You did it, sweetheart! I am so proud of you! I knew you had it in you!" He picked me up and swung me around and I knew he could still feel the outline of my bony ribcage, but I did not care or asked to be put down. I knew he saw a girl who still had a low heart rate, was underweight, and could barely stomach 1,500 calories a day. But he also saw a young woman who was more determined than ever to prove to the rest of the world she was strong enough to keep up. "Still need to put some meat on those bones little lady," he said affirmatively placing me back on the ground.

"I know, I know, Dad. I will. I am trying every day. Where's Mom? Don't tell her just yet, okay? I don't want her to worry I am going to kill myself with an entire season of sport." I paused and looked at myself in the mirror. Dad came and stood behind me, kissing the back of my head still covered with fuzzy hairs of regrowth. "One day at a time. That's all I can muster. One day at a time," I told him.

"You will get there, honey. You will! Keep up the hard work and I will be here for you every step of the way!" He said. "How about we go out and find you a swell, new racquet for the fall season tomorrow?"

"That would be great! And can you spare an hour or so to hit with me, too? First practice is Monday," I asked gently, ever wishful for his positive response.

"Of course. And I will go ahead and set up a few more lessons with Brad. I am sure he will be thrilled for you as well.

I grinned. "Dad, you're the best! Let's do this!" I wanted to jump up and down and frolic about in delightful pride and aspirant thoughts, but it was to no avail. My legs, arms, abs, back, and knees were achy and throbbing from the last two weeks of workouts. One day at a time, I thought.

My first tennis season as a Bluejay was a challenging one indeed. I struggled with energy levels throughout the season and whenever it was even the slightest bit cold outside, my sensitivities to temperature changes would disrupt my physical abilities to the point wherein I was unable to grip the racquet well enough to play a controlled or effective game. I played third and fourth doubles most of the season.

It was mostly a quell of one disappointment after another and the discouragement I felt was only magnified by Dad's face in the bleachers at matches. It was the same face he wore when I struck out playing softball as a kid. Fortunately, I did see some improvements in my stamina through the assistance of the strength and conditioning coach, but as the season wore on I stagnated at the same plateau of weight, strength, and skill level for much of the season. Nevertheless, I stuck with it and win or lose, I was proud to be a part of that team.

Dad and I practiced every weekend after Saturday matches that season despite the time constraint on his busy schedule as his medical practice continued to thrive and new technology was complicating basic charting procedures. Not to mention, time with me took away from time with others in the family. He willingly made the sacrifice, but in looking back I am not entirely sure why. I don't think he believed I was going to go on and become a star tennis player of any kind, but because he was determined for me to be the best I could be in the given time I had, he made me feel worth his time and his efforts. It was quite remarkable.

By the end of the season I was intermittently playing second and third doubles and saw small improvements in my game, but not necessarily my physical health. Regardless, I finished that tennis season with pride and went on to complete my sophomore year of college maintaining the 4.0 GPA precedent I had set the year before. It was not until the fall of my junior year, when I once again made the tennis team through determination and hard work that, at last, I found victory in sport again. It was victory that would make my father euphoric, bring my mother to tears, and bring peace and contentment to my world again.

23
The Winning Match

In fairness, I had a less than remarkable junior year tennis season, but I was stronger than I had been the year prior and I had moved to a new spot in the line-up at second doubles. On occasion, I was given the opportunity to play third singles, of course, depending on the skill level of the opposing team or if we were in tournament play or not. All in all, as the tennis season neared its end the fall of my junior year of college, I had won a measly five matches, three of which were decided by tiebreaker sets, which to me, made them seem illegitimate. So basically two matches as clear victories and those were won against weak opponents who essentially gave away the game in service fault errors. I had racked up a solid fifteen losses. My teammates remained encouraging to me even though I was a drag on our ability to win at nearly every match that season. My doubles partner, Carly, kept me sane through my frequent ball placement errors, and made me want to be a better player with each passing match. She worked double time on the court to make up for my shortcomings. I was fortunate to have her as a partner. Carly never judged me or got in the way when I made a mistake. She encouraged with a sense of genuine care for me and we developed effective court sharing strategies. She became a friend and at the time, I still did not have many. Tall in stature and of a sturdy build, her head of long, thick, dirty blonde curly hair made me jealous most of the time. My hair was still a mossy mess of fuzzy undergrowth, regrowth, and mixed lengths of shiny and dull strands. My ponytail was small and unkempt. The extra strength, glittery hairbands I used to break on a daily basis growing up were a thing of the past. But, from a more assenting perspective, the tennis team uniform skirt I wore was an XS that season meaning I had graduated from the XXXS sizes that were baggy on my bony legs the season prior. Muscle development had minimally set in and I was at last able to fill out my XS skirt that season – well, at least hold it up without cumbersome pins.

Fortunately, on no account of my personal performance, our flock of Bluejays ranked as the best team in conference that year. That ranking translated to the opportunity for the first time in the team's history to play in the Division III College Women's Tennis Championship. When we got the news as a team, all of the girls cheered and hugged while I sat on the bleachers listening to Coach with the sudden quell of chilled numbness as the first thing that came to my mind was a flashback to the sectional championships for swimming in high school.

"Girls, you rocked it! We've made it!" Coach reported. "We're headed to the Championships! And after we win that, off to Hilton Head!" More shrieks rang out from my teammates as failure echoed through my mind. I could hear Jeannie, Katy, and Captain J mocking me in the hallway and throwing a neon tee in my face. I was the one at fault for my former swim team's forfeit in the main relay event which would have gained the most points for our swimming team and the secured placement in Nationals. The team did not make it to Nationals and I was the reason why. The last thing I wanted was to be a repeat failure. High school memories remained an ingrained horror. I would forever wear that burden.

"Tomorrow at practice I will announce the line-up for the championship tournament match," Coach reported. "We will have some play-offs for spots as needed. Get some rest tonight, ladies. Let's go win this championship!" He said. I lagged behind the team as they marched towards the dining hall after practice. It was a cool evening in late October and I was secretly hopeful I would not get placed on the line-up for the Championships. I would gladly go along to cheer on my teammates, but the pressure of impending loss against some of the best regional female tennis stars frightened the Orbit Bubblemint gum out of me. Championships were the first week of November. Playing or not, I was already feeling queasy.

The following afternoon at practice Coach announced the line-up and the scrimmage matches that were going to be set-up at practice that day to vet for spots. It was hot as hell that day and in my nervous escapades and flashbacks the day prior I had barely managed to eat anything other than an apple and a handful of almonds. It was announced that I was going to play fourth doubles – exhibition as an alternate – but also was being given the opportunity to participate in play-offs during practice that day for third singles.

"Third singles? Coach, are you serious?" I looked at him in disbelief. "I don't think you want me in that spot. Beth can have it," I said attempting to dismiss myself from having to be a part of the play-offs and potentially getting out of practice that day.

"Andi, you're perfect for the spot. Your speed and accuracy have greatly improved as has your intuition on the court," Coach persuaded.

"You may be right, but I do not have the record to prove it and I also do not have the experience of playing under pressure as the other girls do. I am happy to go along as a cheerleader and sub if needed. Thank you for considering me!" I tried to convince him of his faulty bet on me.

"Andi, grab your racquet and stop trying to finagle your way out of this. I want you playing in our mini-matches today and I want you playing to win," Coach Griffith said.

"I don't want to be humiliated and I don't want to let anyone down. Please understand that. I feel lucky enough just to be a part of the team," I explained.

"Andi, what don't you understand? You're a wildcard! You're a secret weapon yet to be unleashed. Precisely because you have not played much at singles this year and because you are relatively unknown with these teams and players, you have every opportunity to throw off their strategy and their game. Those other teams out there have studied our ace players and they are strategizing right now against the game play of every girl on our team. You're an unexpected. You're an unknown. You're exactly what we need in our line-up to secure those crucial points for a whole team victory. We need you, Andi!" Coach exclaimed as he grabbed his racquet indicating he wanted to volley on the court with me.

"So I'm the low expectations 'baller,'" I teased as I went to the nearest court and we began a volley. My stomach rumbled with hunger.

"Well, something like that. But that right there can be lethal. Mess with their mental game and you've all but won the match," he said.

"Okay, fine. Fine. I'm in. I'll go for the shock and awe effect best I can. Whom am I playing today?" I asked dazed by my ego and aptitude to exude such a sure sense of self-confidence. Who was this woman? I wondered. A fearless 90 pound dynamite! Let's see how long this lasts…I can always intentionally lose today…but what if I deserve to win?

"You'll be playing against Courtney. I moved Beth to second singles. Six games, win by two," he said. "Warm-up your serve with me here and then get off to court eight and you can start your match," Coach instructed.

My navy blue cotton and spandex sleeveless shirt was nearly drenched after only ten serves to my coach. My black tennis skirt was soaking up sun like its livelihood depended on it. The fierce sun pelted down on my back as the late afternoon heat swelled the courts, but I aced every single serve against Coach. Who is this woman? I wondered time and again throughout practice that day. When it came time to play Courtney, our usual number three singles player, somehow beat her in four games. It was not even that hard and I did not even ace any serves against her. When we finished the match, I could tell she was pissed. I felt no need to apologize. I was hungry, thirsty, and as things stood, I was going to be playing at the Championships.

"Good luck at the Championships," Courtney stabbed at me, sarcasm rising in her voice. "Any other day I would have beaten you. Fucking bitch," she threw her racquet down cracking the frame of it, grabbed her bag, and dramatically gave Coach Griffith the middle finger as she left practice. I had a healthy urge to chase after her, to tell her to take the third singles spot, and to admit how she deserved it over me. However, her most histrionic exit made other team members laugh and the ever-bullied 'fat' kid in me did not want to position myself to become a target, too. Carly threw a subtle wink my way and clinked two racquets overhead to cheer in my favor. I smiled wholeheartedly. Beth, who was close with Courtney, threw down some tasteless language in my direction and I was not about to become jaded by it or back down.

"Coach, let's do this! I don't want to let you down!" I raised my voice in his direction.

"You won't," he said without hesitation. The team rallied around me and built the final huddle of practice around me.

"One, two, three, we've got Andi! Four, five, six, let's go win this!" The girls shouted, and cheered in my direction. I had forgotten what it was like to feel needed, wanted, valued, included in such a meaningful way. I mattered, and for some strange reason, Courtney's vicious comments did not stay with me for long. I had some serious work to do.

Eager to inform my parents, I drove home that weekend and announced to Dad that we had two weeks to prep and prep we did. Nearly every moment we could find outside of work, practice, and my studies, we served, volleyed, did wind sprints, and loaded me up on BOOST high-protein nutrition shakes. I did not skimp on drinking them, nor did I employ the toilet bowl as a vehicle for their consumption. As the championships approached, I was nervous, but ready. Even though Courtney had intentionally tripped me at our final practice resulting in a sprained knee for me, I was still ready. Nothing was going to stop me – not even a malevolent teammate. The night before championships I scribbled nonsensically into my former eating journal and asked God to give me strength, to calm my anxiety, to get me through the match, and to guide me, win or lose. I knew that a loss would be devastating for me and the weight of failure could send me on a long spiral backwards from whence I came. I had to think positively. I had to believe that I could do it. By the grace of God, I woke up the following morning for the match and was weak in nervous anxiety, but not in physical strength. Make it happen, Andrea. Make it happen.

On November 6th, 2010, we loaded the buses and headed north to Carthage College for the weekend-long championship event. It was a warmer day with a dry heat and rain in the forecast. I was grateful the weather was not dipping below 50 degrees otherwise that would have presented its own set of problems for me. We took our team warm-ups with the other four teams present for the finals and then we waited for announcements and the National Anthem. I darted to the bathroom around the second stanza of the enticingly patriotic rendition of the anthem and let go of everything inside of me. My bottom side stung, but it alleviated some of that nervous churning. For the first few hours of match play courts were full of first and second singles players as well as first, second, and third string doubles teams from each school competing.

Finally, around 10:30 AM, I heard my name over the loudspeaker as the next wave of matches was getting set to begin.

"Cladis/Hoffstra, Court Four. Third singles," the announcer said. I pulled in a short, quick breath followed by a slow exhale. This is it. This is my chance. I sucked on oxygen once again. Lord, help me, I pleaded as my pulse beat at my temples. It was no 30 BPMs.

"You've got this, kiddo. Remember what we practiced, but don't think too much," Dad counseled. "And don't worry about that knee. Plenty of time to heal after all is said and done." I was worried about that knee. It was swollen and throbbing and the Advil I took earlier that day had worn off, but taking more would only serve to upset my stomach, gnawing at the acidic hole I already felt burning through its walls.

There was a dry heat clouding the air that day and plenty of rain scheduled in the forecast. Dad was there for me and Mom was coming. Their presence made me nervous, but also gave me a reason to dig even deeper to prove my worth on the court that day. As I walked towards Court four, my head was wrought with thoughts of every possible "what if" scenario the match could possibly entail. What if I lose and let my team down? What if I do not have enough stamina to get through the match? What if this other chick has an ace serve that I cannot return? What if Dad is disappointed by my efforts? What if I don't have what it takes? What if Rachel shows up to psyche me out? What if…what if… what if…

The Court Four scorekeeper and purveyor asked for our names and signatures before the match to make sure we were the ones to be playing. Claire Hoffstra and Andrea Cladis. Third singles. First to six games, win by two. Nothing scary about that. Claire and I set our bags near the bench on the side of the court, and prepped our gear to begin warm-ups. My knee was wobbly and the piercing pain in my stomach wanted to remind me of its presence. I reached out my right hand to shake Claire's before the match, but she did not reciprocate. She scowled with her eyes and I scowled back the same way Barkens had at me. We began a warm-up volley across the court without speaking a single word to each other as Claire's coach came up to the fence to give her some pointers and advice. Her coach was a large, stocky female, who looked at me as though I were some scrawny good-for-nothing piece of shit. I'd show her. I shuffled back and forth on the court and did high-knee kickers to keep my body warm while I waited for her brawny coach to tell her all the ways she could kick my ass. Coach Griffith noticed the psyche-out tactic and called me aside. At least he was young, tan, fit, and handsome. Not that it mattered, but I was going to take any confidence points that I could. As I huddled near the fence, Coach counseled me in a rather unexpected way.

"Cladis, what do you want from this match? And don't just say to win," he began.

"Well, yeah I want to win. I want to rack up points for the team!" I replied as though that was the obvious response that he should have known all along.

"No, Cladis – what do you want from this match? The team wants you to win, but you have an opportunity here. You've worked harder than any other girl on our team. I know you have some physical limitations, but that's never held you back. What do you stand to gain? Look at that girl over there." He pointed as she strategized with her creepy ass, butch coach. "She's probably 60 pounds heavier than you, she has tattoos and bleach blonde hair with a skirt showing far too much of her backside. She's beatable. You can win this, but I want you to dig deep. Why do you want this so bad?" He probed further. Here I thought he was going to outline my point by point strategy or if I was to go hard on forehands or overhead shots, or focus on net play, or go for my strengths on the baseline and focus on ball placement. But instead, he wanted to know what was in it for me. Third singles and a huge opportunity not just for the team, but for me.

I pinged the center strings of my Wilson tennis racquet repeatedly against the base of my left hand as I prepared to respond. "Coach, I want to prove to my parents that I am strong enough to do this. I want to prove to my teammates that I can hold my own, and I want to prove to myself that I am not a failure. Once and for all to show that I can overcome and be victorious. I want to be a winner. If only for this one day and this one moment, I want to win. I want carry that torch and hold my racquet up high," I said.

Coach smiled and those devilish dimples made their presence known. It's no wonder all the girls on our team thought he was hot. I was so intimidated by him most of the time that I had failed to notice how unmistakably sexy and good-looking he was. I blushed and smiled forgetting the pain in my stomach and knees. He winked at me and crossed his arms. "This Hoffstra chick has nothing on you.

Go take her, Cladis. Show her who's boss. I'll be here. Come talk to me when you switch sides between sets," he said.

"You got it, Coach!" I smiled and sprung back towards the court wearing nothing but confidence and a willingness to win. I heard Dad whistle at me as we finished our volley and took our warm-up serves. She had a strong serve that was going to be hard to return. But I would prevail, somehow. All I needed to do was get the ball in play. Just keep the damn ball in play against the tattooed blonde snickering at me. 'Claire's' don't snicker, I thought.

We spun racquets at center court to see who would serve first.

"M or W," I said, indicating which way the Wilson logo on my racquet would fall.

"M," Claire said.

"It's W. My serve," I said. She huffed her way to the baseline and the court master gave us the green light to commence the match.

"Cladis, Game One – service," he said.

My watch read 11:15 PM and I felt the sun reflecting heat through my feet and up my body. My hair was pulled back in a tight pony tail and my eyes were shielded from the sun by a mesh navy and white official Bluejays tennis visor. My skirt was short, snug, and filled with three extra balls for the match.

"LOVE-all," I said as I threw the first ball of the game overhead, reached towards extension of my right arm through the service motion and came down hard and fast on top of the ball.

"Out!" Claire called.

"Second serve," the court master said looking down at me. In routine fashion I bounced a new tennis ball at the baseline eight times before taking it into my hand to prepare for the serve. I rocked back and forth four times, reached my right arm back behind my body, threw the ball up with my left hand, and with all the force within my body, the sweet spot in the center frame of my racquet smashed down hard onto the ball. I heard the ball die on Claire's racquet as she tried to return the serve. She hit the ball into the net and nearly dropped her racquet. That ball had some wicked topspin on it. I glanced at Dad. Even he seemed a little unnerved.

I moved to the other side of the baseline and announced the score. "15 – LOVE," I said. I bounced the tennis ball eight times, rocked back and fourth for four and hit my motion. The wind of Claire's racquet was loud as she swung and missed my ball. The court master motioned that the serve was good. I narrowed my focus. "30 – LOVE," I announced. Another ace. "Forty – LOVE," she returned the ball with a high lob back to my side of the court. I had plenty of time to follow the ball as it descended and was able slice a nasty overhead shot to the far back left corner of the court. "Game," I said.

"1-0, Cladis," the court master announced. We proceeded to switch sides of the court. I noticed Mom arrive and she waved at me, but Dad got her settled and told her not to fuss. I had just won a game with only one volley. Claire stood at the baseline and I felt those stomach pangs return as I swayed back and forth on the balls of my feet in ready position to receive her serve.

"LOVE – LOVE," she announced as she threw the ball up and sent forth a wailing, fast serve. I did not react quickly enough to return it, but luckily the serve was out. She took her second. It went into the net. "LOVE – 15," she called as she readied her next serve. It was a slow serve to ensure we could start a volley and she would not lose the point through a service fault. I returned the serve with a forehand and we started a long volley back and forth, testing each other's backhands and movement on the court. She was slower than I was and I used that to my advantage. Once she crowded the net, I lobbed the ball over her head and she was unable to get to the baseline fast enough to return it. LOVE – 30. She served again. Another fault. I was feeling lucky. LOVE – 40. On my toes and ready, she served the ball hard and fast and I returned it with a hard forehand shot right back at her that surprised her so much she moved out of the way. Game over.

"2-0, Cladis – service," the court master guided. I walked to the baseline in a heightened state of focus. I was winning two games to none, but that could change quickly. We were heading into game three and Claire was giving me her best tattooed bitch scowl. I was not going to let her psyche me out.

"LOVE – LOVE," I called out at the baseline. I went through my routine and faulted on my first two serves, giving her the advantage in the game. "LOVE – 15," I said as I threw up my next serve. It was a conservative serve and she easily returned the volley. I played baseline for the entire point because I knew if I came to the net she would try to return the lob favor that I had played on her. She also tired quickly when I made her run the baseline. Forehand, backhand, forehand, backhand, we volleyed on. Finally, I made a move towards hitting a backhand with loaded topspin – a shot I had been practicing all season, but had never tried in game play. The ball soared over the net, almost appearing to move sideways as it neared Claire. It hit the court just inside the baseline and bounced awkwardly in a shooting direction opposite Claire's racquet. The point was mine. We were tied. 15 – ALL. Feeling a bit cocky, I went for the slow, slice serve. Ace. 30 – 15. Ace. 40 – 15. Claire looked pissed. I loved it. I took to a normal serve for the last point and she volleyed back, but on her second hit she dented the net with both the ball and her racquet. She was mentally shaken and I could see it. "Game," I said.

As we went to switch sides of the court, we both stopped to receive counsel from our coaches. I don't know what her coach was saying, but it did not seem pleasant. I honed in on what my handsome Coach was telling me as I glanced over at my parents nervously pacing the sidelines. "Hit her corners," Coach instructed. "And run the hell out of her. Don't get cocky on your serves. Just put the ball in play. Don't be afraid of the net either. If she lobs it, you can get there. Her accuracy is not all that great. Cover the baseline, but charge the net when the opportunity comes. More than two volleys and you're moving in. Close out the point. Kick her ass, Cladis," Coach said as he gave me a fist pump and a cold cup of water. The sun was higher in the sky, but clouds were rolling in. "Finish this before the storm comes in. You've got it," he said.

I did have it; I knew I had it. Well, I had to have it! No stopping me. We swapped sides of the court. "3-0, Cladis," the court master announced our standing. I only need three more games. Claire had a new racquet in her hand as she scuffled to the baseline. Her blonde hair was down sloshing about her shoulders and trailing her back. As I was watching it fall, she served the ball. I whiffed entirely at the shot.

"15 – LOVE," she snapped. Damn, fucking blonde hair was the only thought that came to mind. I chastised myself as she served again. It was hard, fast, and untouchable. "30 – LOVE," she called out waltzing to the other side of the baseline. Two more shots like that and she had won the game. I had not even touched the ball.

"3-1, Cladis," the court master shouted over the gusty winds that were picking up and the thunder now being heard in a far distant echo. I kicked the center of my racket with the toe box of my shoe. My turn to serve. I had to get this game. Firing up again I bounced the ball, rocked, and swayed, served, and we volleyed. I was not feeling confident enough to move into the net, but I did anyway and on the third volley, Claire set me up for a solid put-away.

"15 – LOVE," I said. Just like that, I told myself. Just like that. The brace on my knee was growing itchy and the wind was making it difficult to place the ball. I faulted on my first serve of the point. On the second, I decided to go against my coach's better advice. I aced the heavy topspin serve. He nodded in my direction, subtly acknowledging what I had done. "30 – LOVE." Claire fumbled to return the next serve, but her loss was my gain. "40 – LOVE." I only needed one more point and I would be up four games to one. Pressure was mounting. As I took to my serve, I heard Claire call out, "Hit me, punk. Hit me with your best shot, you anorexic bitch!" I let the ball fall to the ground without going through the service motion. I was tempted to respond, but kept my cool.

The court master blew his whistle loudly. "Unsportsmanlike conduct! Hoffstra, this is your first warning. Cladis, point in your favor. Game set score: 4-1, Cladis."

Claire snuffed her way to the comfort of her burly Coach and I retreated to mine. Dad was pacing with reckless abandon and Mom was biting her nails. I took a sip of apple juice because the taste association of Gatorade was off-limits in this sort of event, but I spit it out.

"Don't let her ride you and shake you up," Coach said. "She's got nothing else left. She is chalking up several errors and she wants to throw you off of your game. Don't let her. Keep the mental edge. And don't mess with those fancy serves unless you know she's going to go for it. Don't waste those shots," he said.

"Got it, Coach. I bent the visor on my head so it had more of a curve and wiped the sweat off of my hands on my skirt so I could better grip my racquet. Claire had yet another new one. It must have been a really rough day for her. Switching out racquets mid match poses a risk all its own. Salty sweat was dripping into my eyes and the taste of warm apple juice coated the sides of my mouth and under cavity of my tongue. It was a stupid decision of mine to drink that. Whatever. Focus, Andrea. Focus. She called you a bitch! Don't let her have this.

It was Claire's serve and she again aced the first two points. "30 – LOVE," she called out. My blood was boiling.

"Come on, kid. Let's go," I heard Dad call out from the stands even though he was supposed to stay quiet during the point play. Hearing his voice, however, was all the panacea I needed to win that game. I fended off the rest of her serves and crushed her in baseline running and two shut-out points at the net. Boom!

"5-1," the court master announced. Game to win – Cladis, service." This was it. Fatigue was setting in for both of us. My watch read 1:25. We were past the two hour mark, but if I won, this would be our last game. *Cladis, let's go!* I thought. *Cladis, let's freaking do this!* As I approached the baseline, I squeezed the fuzzy neon tennis ball in my right hand and briefly closed my eyes. This. Was. It. I saw that neon swimming t-shirt from high school in a heap near my locker and I heard the echoed taunts of those swimmers mocking my failure. Not this time, I thought. Not this time. The game wore on and we played out nearly ten minute volleys for each point. I ran her inked arms and legs down and won every single one of them.

"40 – LOVE. Game point," I announced I could taste fresh mangoes in the back of my throat and I thought of Rosetta and coins in my pockets and atop bony feet. I watched my cup of hot tea flailing out the window after Mom and I argued at that Wendy's drive-thru. I witnessed tears on Stacey's face and 'what's wrong with you?' come from Dennis's mouth. I saw frothy, sloshed milkshakes line our bathroom toilet and I felt the echocardiogram test suctioned tightly to my chest. I saw Mom and her apron of purple frosting and the pink passes to the nurse carpeting my locker. I squeezed my lips together as I had during that Zinc test and I felt the resounding urge to devour an entire package of Bubblemint gum. I had to win this. I just had to.

I opened my eyes as rain started to sprinkle the court and threw the ball high into the air. I let it fall without hitting it. *Focus, Andrea. Focus. Gosh darn it. Get it done!* I bounced the ball eight times, rocked and swayed for four, and threw the ball up into the air once more. With every last ounce of anorexic overcoming bitch in my being I jumped and slammed my racquet down on the ball as hard as I possibly could. I heard the air move past me as I followed through on the serve. I lost my balance and fell down on the court. I watched Claire move towards the ball and lost track of it as the rain poured down faster. Claire did not return the serve.

"Match point. Game goes to Cladis. 6-1, final," the court master announced. I could not believe it. Claire threw her racquet down and stomped off the court as the rain picked up and thunder bellowed loudly. Dad, Mom, Coach, and my teammates rushed onto the court. They picked me up, shouted, and chanted, "Cladis! Cladis! Cladis! We did this!" Eventually I shook hands with Claire and she congratulated me on the match. Soaking wet from head to toe my team surrounding me in prideful glee, it was one of the happiest moments of my life.

The rain delay made for a longer day, and we did not end up getting first place, but at least it was not on account of my botched efforts. However, my win did secure our spot as second place champions and I had proven to Dad, Mom, Coach, my family, and even myself that I was a strong woman of dignity and purpose. I was in fact, a winner, and no one could take that away from me.

Our team went out for pizza afterwards and I ate four large pieces – cheese and all, grease and all, sweaty smiles and all. We ordered brownie sundaes for dessert and I got a Reese's cup on top of mine. I thought of Barkens for the last time in the restaurant, momentarily, as the swirl of creamy peanut butter and smooth chocolate decorated the sides of my mouth, but I was not mad. The dessert was absolutely delicious – rich, velvety, and decadent. I had earned every single calorie of it. And even if I hadn't, who cared?

I was astounded I did not get a miserable stomach ache that night from eating so much food, but I know now that the reason for the lack of a stomach ache was as simple as I did not will myself to have one. That night I was not focused on victory over food, but rather on victory for the team, for myself, and for the pride of earned accomplishment. I praised God for His steady hand on my disciplined mind, my rejoicing heart, my cross-court competition, and my war -torn, red Wilson racquet.

I have not turned down a tennis challenge since that winning match and Dad's affirming smile is what comes to mind each time I lace up my shoes and head out to bike or run. In bringing him joy, I, in turn learned to grow that in myself as I became more confident and proud of who I was and the strength evolving within me with each passing day. Winning was sweet, but eating hot fudge lathered brownies with vanilla ice cream and peanut butter cups without fear, was indeed far sweeter!

24
Predisposed to Discontentment

How could I top courage over chocolate calories and a victorious tennis team win? Perhaps not by holding myself to the standard that I could achieve those things again. Maybe by learning to accept less than my best. Or by learning to live with failure. And by growing to understand that what makes life perfect is all that makes it not so. So what happens when we learn to overcome? What happens in the shadows of triumph over tribulation? What is it that keeps us motivated to keep going? We have to keep growing, learning, and changing. However, there is always going to be an element of our past selves that lives on within us. And in some way that past fights as an anchor against our renewed selves as it morphs about our being in a newly evolved way.

As I entered my final semester of college, my life had normalized to a certain degree. The ebb and flow of eating and exercising had become less of an obsession, and the concern over my physical appearance dwindled to only random night time body checks for expanding fat particles. I avoided the scale at all costs and did not chew on gum at lunchtime. I did not make mango smoothies or drink BOOST shakes. I had ruthlessly shredded the personal food log I kept while browsing presidential history archives in the basement of the library one night. *Our country had rarely learned from its woeful history, so why should I?* However, my control of food from past experience did not bother me in the same way anymore and the fierce self-loathing that had consumed me was tranquilized by the perfectionism and obsessive-compulsive tendencies that took over other parts of my day-to-day life.

Next to prayer, order became the most important thing in daily existence. I could not go to bed without mindfully setting my outfits out in order of how they would be placed on my body the following morning. I never let more than six items of clothing crumple in the bottom of my laundry basket before washing and neatly folding them. The shoelaces in my closest were neatly tied in bows on top of each of my shoes so the bottom of my closet would not appear messy. My trinkets and belongings had to be placed evenly apart from one another on my bookcase and dresser and I was anal about every aspect of my personal space. My desk always appeared untouched without a trace of dust. My school-papers, books, and binders were color-coordinated by subject, alphabetized by topic, and my coursework for each individual class was organized and lined up on my bookshelves in immaculate ways. When I loaded my backpack to go to class or to the library I sometimes became aggravated by the removal of books or binders from my shelves and desk as it would bollix up my strictly maintained order. I cleaned my dorm room two times per day at exactly 6:00 AM and 8:30 PM. I lined up my hair bands, make-up, and jewelry as if creating an army in formation for action. I often left my dorm room for class only to turn around before I made it to the main exit to go back up three flights of stairs to revisit my room and fix the angle of the lock on the outside door knob or straighten out my comforter to avoid encroaching wrinkles, situate the eight pillows on my bed that I put in the same balanced place each day when I made my bed, or replace or discard a loose piece of paper from my desk. I also had six stacks of sticky notes on my desk that were a source of annoying time consupmtion. Three stacks of azure blue and three stacks of indigo purple. I alternated using a note from each stack so by the end of each day the stacks remained even. When that habitual task became too cumbersome to manage, I took two hours one night after cleaning my dorm room and created a new stack – a mega stack – in which I combined all six stacks. Delicately I placed one purple note atop a blue, atop a purple, atop a blue. Purple, blue, purple, blue, I kept the pattern of sticky notes consistent. No more uneven sticky note towers would upset my workspace. Or so I thought. I had one to contend with, but that, too became frustrating because on Monday, Wednesday, and Friday I wanted the day to end with a blue note ready to be used and on Tuesday, Thursday, and Saturday, I wanted to end the day with a purple note ready for use. It was ridiculously maddening. No matter what I did to control a space, something else had to be done. Some other thing had to be put in some other special place and neatness was a virtue I worshipped. It was a lot of effort and an unnecessary amount of time to keep everything in its place. It is one thing to be organized, as most college students are not. It is quite another to do nothing but fixate about organizational procedures. I got weirdly obsessive about hand sanitizer and germs. Third quarter was when I started trying to have a bowel movement at the same time each day and if I did not I would take laxatives and worry. I had a set workout routine and gym time each day that I followed without exception. I once missed a class on account of having to 'stick to the schedule.' It was lunacy and certainly a psychosis all its own. Food restraint was no longer my target, but everything else and I mean, *everything,* else was.

Under no circumstances do I think I will be free from the grasp of the past and the mental and physical strain that anorexia put on my incapacitated sense of being. Strength would return, hair would grow back, but what about the me underneath it all? Will she ever be the same? Experiences challenge us and they tempt us and they teach about all it is that we are. If we are to come out alive, we learn resiliency. And if we are to come out stronger than we were before, we learn a sense of cynicism for all that we once believed to be truth. I was a resilient cynic.

During my senior year of college I was a finalist for "Senior of the Year," a prestigious award given out to only the highest achieving students in academics who were dedicated in service to community, campus engagement, and showed the most promise and readiness for success in graduate school and future careers. It was an honor even to be nominated and I had grown to be a consummated magnate whom everyone on campus knew. I deserved it. I had positioned myself as a straight 'A' student with a double major, a minor, and a host of campus involvements and affiliations. People knew my name and I was a spokesperson for the school. In a little over two years I had reached a peak of success in the venue of academia, but I still was not satisfied. I wanted to do more and to be better. I wanted to win that "Senior of the Year" award and write it on my growing resume of achievements and accomplishments, but instead, a young African-American female won the award. I think she won it because she was a first generation college student and she had a service-oriented background with a winning personality. She was also a minority, the cynic in me justified my loss. I was bitter I did not win. But why? Why was I bitter? She was just as deserving as all of the other ten nominees. What was it that that award was going to do for me besides boost my ego or tell me I was great based on some organized set of stipulations, not even of my own accord? And when I further thought about it, even if I had won the award, the resilient cynic would have found a reason to be discontented with that specific accolade, as well as with the trajectory of my life in general.

Senior year taught me a lot about discontentment. Becoming comfortable with the uncertainty the future holds is more than enough to breed a malcontent. The same discontentment I felt senior year of college was what originally caused my eating disorder - whether I blame it on the desire for control or my mother's pressure towards perfectionism, at the end of it all, I was the only one putting the rules, regulations, and standards on my own life. Yes, I was unhappy with Mom's desires for me and yes, I was discontent with my physical appearance. I wanted to be in control and be the best. End of story. And even when I achieved the lowest numbers on the scale and the highest marks on my transcripts, I remained unhappy and wanting more. I still want more. I work several jobs, am constantly moving in tangential directions, and while I am not flawless in anything I do, I work to fill the gaps of time in my schedule or imperfections in my life to ease the open spaces that make me feel empty inside. I think that vacuum of emptiness will perpetually be there and nothing, except for my faith, will ever rightly be enough to keep me content. The verse about contentment on my dorm room wall read as follows: "And He has said to me, "My grace is sufficient for you, for power is perfected in weakness" ...Therefore I am well content with weaknesses, with insults, with distresses, with persecutions, with difficulties, for Christ's sake; for when I am weak, then I am strong" (2 Corinthians 12:9-10). I stared at it every day in my neurotic cleaning rituals, but was I really listening?

Three weeks before I graduated from Elmhurst, top of my class, I learned that I was going to earn a 'B' in my 400-level English course, "Writing Fiction." I chastised myself quite often about not being a great fiction writer, but syllabus-wise, I did everything possible to earn an 'A' in that course. I spent long nights doing research at the library, writing copious essays, participating extensively in short story revisions to please my professor, and spending hours upon hours performing peer reviews. But, as the professor warned early on in the semester, she did not award high marks to anyone and no one ever got an 'A' in her writing classes. Writing is subjective and ripe with rejection; she made sure we knew that. That was her lesson to teach and ours to learn. We were warned to drop out if a grade lower than an 'A' was not acceptable for us. I did not heed the warning as I believed it was an empty threat and that I could go forth, demonstrate my hard work ethic, and earn an 'A.' That was not the case. Everyone else in my class got C's or D's for the semester. I think they were all better writers than me. Actually, I read the works they produced. I can say with great confidence their abilities far surpassed my own. They were more creative in every way, but I still got the highest grade. I was not proud of that 'B.' It was not an 'A.' I had never gotten less than an 'A' throughout all of my schooling. It was damning to me. I was becoming my mother more and more with each passing day. That realization was terrifying and troubling especially because there was no way to stop it. There is no way to stop the quest for perfection because perfection is a machinating fallacy.

My final college GPA was a 3.98. When I got my final transcript it was like seeing 98 pounds on the scale when I hoped to see 95. It was an arbitrary number, but it was a weighted discouragement that bred discontentment. Sometimes I tell people I got a 4.0 in college because I was only one course short of attaining that perfect mark. It makes me feel good to mention my hard work of the past. It is an impressive feat that I think most people take into account as either seeing me as naturally intelligent or a superfluous library nerd. I like to think I was and still am, both. But I know I am more the latter. My work ethic is my strength, the intelligence then I hope grows in consequence. I missed out on getting into my top choice for graduate school because one professor and one class docked my 4.0 GPA to a 3.9. It was another indelible indication that I was not perfect.

My GPA forced me to accept less than perfection. I did not want to do that then and I still do not want to now. It is underwhelming and upsetting. We are all less than perfect, but I liked to think if I could attain the closest thing to perfection, I would have the highest chance of realizing happiness. But a 3.9 did not make me happy. Nothing did. The shifting of compulsion from dieting behaviors mirrored themselves in my vain efforts to be the best version of me I possibly could. Yet in the process of becoming the best, I lost more of me than I had throughout the duration of high school. Whose standards was I living up to? This was not on Mom anymore. This was on me. My shoulders were wilting beneath the weight of my own anxiety for productive action in all parts of my life.

I graduated from college wearing more honor society cords than anyone else in my graduating class. Alas, I looked like Harry Potter! I had maintained a low weight while still indulging in desserts each day, and that made me feel empowered. I was an athlete with a record and a student with proven success. I was the highest-grossing marketing tool for the school. I was it. I had a job lined up if I chose to follow-through with that venture, and the prospect of graduate school awaited me as well. I thought I had it all, but in reality, I had nothing that makes life worth living. Authentic friendships remained sparse, I was not in a loving, doting, gushing relationship on course for marriage, like many of my peer, and I did not know what I wanted out of life. I had pleased and surpassed the Dean's mandated school rules and script for success. What more could I want to do? I was no longer anorexic in the physicality of having 'loss of appetite.' Rather, I was hungrier than ever before to achieve, to be, to do, more and more and more. Nothing would satisfy. As I walked across that stage, a Summa Cum Laude graduate, I was proud of myself, but numb to the moment and numb to all I had achieved. I smiled next to the President of the College with my parents standing on either side of me. I had that photograph of me in my decorated robe standing next to my weary, but pleased parents, framed with my gold, "Summa Cum Laude" tassel and it sits next to my shiny diploma exhaling achievement and success when others walk by. But when I see that slivered image in time, I count the honor society cords and see the hollow loneliness in my eyes that says, "Andrea, you did not get a 4.0. Try harder next time." The past can be a most cruel mistress. And its tentacles only widen their reach in time.

PART III

Transcendence and Resolution:
Keeping the Light On

25
The Mother. The Matriarch. My Yia-Yia.

Being ever fearful of failure, ever ready to fill time with diligent, productive efforts, and desiring of order and perfection to conceal unhappiness, I wasted hours of energy trying to keep myself moving forward. If I was not going forward, I feared I would go backwards. Or worse, I would waltz in a side leaning, grapevine-step of imprisoning lateral motion. I was not only re-learning to eat and take care of my body. I was learning how to live again. And living takes far more mental and physical energy than I had anticipated. Slowly re-gaining my grip on life, setbacks were common, and the tenuous state of my mentality quivered when things outside of my control undulated against my efforts to maintain equilibrium.

Seven months after my college graduation when my Greek grandmother, the family matriarch passed away, my world stopped entirely as perfectionism, order, and productivity were put on pause. I did not know if I felt hungry or if I felt full. I did not know if I had friends or if I was alone. I did not know how I would live without the matriarch, the true north, and the family compass. On one hand, attention was removed from me and that was a relief, but the grief was heavy and the tears the Greek priest described at her funeral service as oceans were real. There was a far more pressing concern on our hands in the face of her death, and that concern was not something anyone could "fix." Its magnitude weighed heavily upon us all. Would the family unit crumble in the wake of her loss?

Yia-Yia reminded that family is the imitable standard in Greek culture and life. Family, to a guilt-ridden fault, always comes first and takes precedence over all other things. When I was a child, I remember going to Yia-Yia and Papou's house for extended weekend visits. Yia-Yia was a plate collector — they adorned every wall of her home—and for that matter, her small abode in the world. I remember the magic I felt when I walked into her home and observed the panoply of plates from all different states, provinces, and parts of the world delicately hanging from every single pale pink wall of her home. For a while, I thought "plates" was the thing Greek people did as wallpaper instead of the traditional wallpaper I had seen in other non-Greek homes. I assumed, as with many other strange phenomenon in her home, that it was a cultural custom with an intriguingly rich history. But I learned it was not some fancy 'Greek' thing. It was just a "Yia-Yia" thing and that made it even more satisfying to me. I hope to have a similar pattern of plated wallpaper in my home one day, too. I plan to make a trendy statement with it and call my interior design: "Yia-Yia-deco." It will be grand for Yia-Yia will be prideful, looking down upon me and blessing my home.

I remember that as I would admire the breakable souvenir plates, she would fidget in the kitchen preparing delicious Greek foods. I heard her golden charm bracelets with the birthdates of her grandchildren engraved on them wriggle and chime on her wrists suctioned off by unforgiving rubber bands she kept there "just in case" the entire time she cooked. I remember the smell of Kalamata olives, feta cheese, and salty Greek meats. The coffee table in her living room was covered with a faux marble top to replicate Greek monuments. It was not functional, but rather she kept it covered with grandiose religious icons she kissed and ornately framed pictures of her grandchildren. The glass-door china cabinets, plastic-covered couches, and raspy radio and television were the cheerful things to the child-visitor of her home. To me, Yia-Yia's house was like some grand museum where we'd get to go and play if we were good. There were stale saltine crackers, pillow mints, sweet nuts, and break-your-teeth mystery candies always waiting for us just within our the range of our reach on the silver carousel display near the front door.

Yia-Yia was a special kind of crazy and her home I most adored. She had a picture downstairs on the far back wall next to the board games, half of them missing elemental pieces, the other half soggy cardboard remains of her own childhood memories. In one of the hidden dark crevices of the low-ceilinged basement in their tri-level home was a portrait of my grandmother as a young woman – an elegant, proud, confident, Greek woman. She was beautiful. I was mesmerized by the portrait because when I looked at it I saw myself in her image. And the older I became the more and more my own personal resemblance matched the portrait. It became a mirror for me in her home and I secretly felt as though I was growing into her being. The cycle of life mystified me.

Because my grandmother was the matriarch of purple, of course, because purple is the color of royalty, I assumed that in her likeness, I shared that vein of royalty, too. She had a presence that warranted attention and the purple accents that filled her home made me happy to be there. To Yia-Yia's pleasure, purple became my favorite color at a very young age. Sometimes as I stared at that photo and tried to drown out the noise of cousins, aunts, and uncles filtering through their home, the museum overwhelmed and the heavily salted meat and odor of Papou's cigarette smoke outweighed my desire to be there.

It was December 31, 2011, New Year's Eve, when she passed away. My Uncle Mark, one of Dad's two brothers, found Yia-Yia lying motionless in her bed at home. It appeared as though when she had tried to get up to go to the bathroom in the middle of the night that her heart stopped, forcing her to fall back onto her bed, where it was likely that she peacefully passed away. Congestive heart failure. Uncle Mark had gone over that day to have breakfast with her as he had every morning for over a year as her health and ability to function independently declined. Yia-Yia needed additional help with day to day living, but dignity prevailed against her being placed in a nursing home or another care facility. She did not want to leave the place she called home. With its Grecian splendor, lemon and oregano perspiring from the walls, pictures of her family and dinnerware China plates from all over the world covering every last inch of her walls. Discussions were ongoing about her taking turns living at the homes of her sons in the coming year if she needed. But pride kept her home. And in the same fashion as I, she always wanted to do things in her way and on her terms. I know my stubbornness and feisty personality very much came from my grandmother. She always used to tell me I was the "most Greek" of all the grandchildren and I would be the one to keep the heritage of our family alive. I boasted of this and to this day I wish to honor the cultural significance my family holds. I wish to be the proud woman in that basement portrait.

Yia-Yia had been wearing a silken purple robe when Uncle Mark found her. The night prior, Dennis had washed her feet and placed fresh stockings and new support hose on her legs to assist with blood flow and swelling as she slept. He and his wife were driving by her home in Chicago Heights on their return to Indiana. Dennis was the last member of our family who got to see her and speak to her, but I am infinitely thankful that he did. At the end of a long tributary poem I constructed the day I learned of Yia-Yia's death, I wrote of this most remarkable scene. As with many times of tragedy that befell my life, I knew not what else to do to cope or attain catharsis other than to write:

My tributary poem to my grandmother concluded with the following reflective stanzas:

To me, Yia-Yia meant many things, but most importantly,
Yia-Yia simply equated just one thing:

FAMILY.

When I was young I never really understood why
Family had to be number one,
But Yia-Yia was persistent in reminding me that
a strong family
was not something that you won.

A family was something that you work for,
to which you devote your heart and soul.
And as such, your family does not leave or abandon you,
They'll keep you grounded and in control.
Your family consists of the people who are without
question by your side,
They're an indelible stamp upon your life,
And they give you joy and pride.

No matter what the circumstance,
No matter how far you roam,
Your family are the ones who gently call you home.

Our presence was demanded – holidays, weddings, birthdays,
And now here our entire family stands unbroken,
giving JOY for her life this day.

Purple was Yia-Yia's treasured color; she cherished its royalty,
Though whenever she spoke of family, she called for steadfast loyalty.
Renascent and creative, Yia-Yia was marked by her aplomb,
But now in striving to be like her;
failure comes and my memories leave me numb.

I told her I got another 'A' in college during
one of our beloved weekly chats,
And she said, "Of course you did, I expect no less,
you're an intelligent woman,
I've never questioned that."
"Andrea, I know you'll go places, my dear.
You work very hard just like your father and Papou and for that,
I guarantee the reward will one day come near."

When I graduated college with honors and a 4.0,
there was no big congratulations from
Yia-Yia, she just modestly said, "See. I told you so."

She never allowed me to feel sorry for myself,
She'd tell me straight and she refused to let me fear:
"Believe in yourself. I know you'll be great," she said.
"You're my granddaughter and there's absolutely
nothing that a Cladis can't conquer."

TATSIMOU, HOLD ON!

I will not erase the memories.
I will not ignore the past.
Though Yia-Yia's compassion, her dedication,
her prescient ways
may slowly fade, I assure you, they will last.

When informed of Yia-Yia's passing,
I was completely bewildered and
lugubrious tones overwhelmed my ears,
but now in the slow days after,
God's plan has become more clear.

For on the night she died, just before she went to sleep,
My brother, the eldest male grandchild,
knelt down to wash her feet.
He showed her that he loved her,
He demonstrated grace -
And of this I am certain, he handled her with care.

This image has stuck with me as tears flood
my days and nights – I see that God has blessed our family
at all times – through triumphs, tribulations and
the occasional, undue fights.

Yia-Yia's first grandchild and his wife were there,
They stopped to visit as they were passing through,
Selfless and kneeling at her feet,
preparing her with alacrity and mercy, too.

Visions of this evening have brought a calming peace
to my mind,
and in such memories my faith is renewed,
for it's only God's love which defies time.

Yia-Yia's feet were sparkling as she entered Heaven's gates.
Clean, crisp and ready for the glorious eternity that awaits.

Reunited with her husband, and other family members, too.
Someday, we all shall join her, our spirits will reign anew.

Yia-Yia can never be forgotten, though it's difficult to part,
I know that I will keep her forever within my heart.

I cannot change reality.
I cannot question God's plan.
Yet through the strength of family and a fiduciary faith;
Trust in God, I can.

And so we thank God for Yia-Yia,
We thank him for her beautiful life.
We GLORIFY His name
For in His time, all things are right.

In dedication to a life most resplendently lived –
One that extended far beyond our reach:

Tassie Tafilos Cladis
ΑΙΩΝΕΙΑ ΤΗΣ Η ΜΝΗΜΗ
[MAY HER MEMORY BE ETERNAL]

Christmas Day, the week prior, was hosted by my parents in our home. The most boisterous Greek family celebration of the year preceding Epiphany, Yia-Yia looked tired, sallow, and extremely thin. She was not smiling as much or singing, "The Twelve Days of Christmas" in the way she used to. She sat near Dad most of the evening nibbling on whatever appetizers she could gum down, mostly some pieces of feta cheese and mashed up Grecian meatballs while adjusting her oxygen tank as it made her uncomfortable and was obviously more than a nuisance to her. Occasionally she swore in Greek about that damn machine but even then her face looked gaunt and ashen. I think that Christmas, the only thing that made her smile was our young dog, Kody. She loathed all animals, but that Tibetan Terrier ball of fluffy caramel and white hair had somehow won her heart. She even bought him an entire bag of winter-themed squeaker toys for his stocking. A couple years later, when he passed unexpectedly at just four years old from cancer, it just so happened that those were the only toys we wished to have surrounding him in the last days of his illness. Death has a strange way of reminding us how delicate time is.

As Dad blessed and cut into the Roditis red wine and Colavita extra virgin olive-oil-drenched Greek Christmas bread called Christopsomo, Yia-Yia sat and watched gracefully upon her family from a distant corner of the kitchen. "Christopsomo" in Greek means "Christ's Bread," which is why the bread is decorated with a cross that is curled at the edges. Traditionally the head of the house makes a sign of the cross on the bread with a knife while saying, "In the name of the Father, the Son, and the Holy Spirit," and then cuts a piece for each person with a wish of "Kala Christouyenna" ("Good Christmas") or "Chronia Polla" ("Many Years"). The bread is fragrant in clove, nutmeg, and rich in cinnamon accents with a slight hint of sugary goodness. Made with anise, mastic, nutmeg, wine, and brandy, this bread is considered very sacred in Greek households, which is why whomever prepares it usually does a cross over themselves before beginning to bake it. Yia-Yia eagerly awaited the person who would receive the special piece of bread from the round Christopsomo loaf that contained a foiled-wrapped silver coin. The silver coin indicated to the winner that their year ahead would be a lucky, blessed one filled with great prosperity. Even as she watched wide-eyed, it was evident that Yia-Yia was in a great deal of pain. She wretched about in her wheelchair and her feet and ankles were more swollen than they had ever been. The bunions on her feet were pressing through the edges of her orthotic shoes. During one the most beloved Christmas traditions, she barely broke apart the piece of bread that was selected for her. The round loaf was traditionally cut into enough pieces for each member of the family with one symbolic piece remaining for the beggar. The piece for the beggar was to remind of Grecian hospitality and that as a Greek, you must always have bread and food available to invite the stranger in for a meal. Ceremonially, we each walked up to the table to select a piece of bread and we followed an ordering from youngest to oldest. The youngest were to be given the highest probability of winning good fortune. As my turn came in line of my aunts, uncles, and cousins, I felt my piece of bread and knew almost immediately that the wine-soaked piece I had selected contained the coin. I concealed it under a napkin on my plate as to not spoil the fun and watched as the rest of my family grabbed their pieces of bread, doused them in more wine, and searched for the foil-wrapped coin.

After a few short minutes passed, Yia-Yia queried in frustration from her wheelchair, bread crumbs decorating her lap, "Who forgot to put the coin in the bread? Who made this loaf? No winner? Did the beggar get the coin this year?" She became impatient and pushy, just the way she had always been and the kitchen of our home was immediately filled with noise and laughter and Christmas carols and bread crumbs and wine splashing and people spitting on one another, singing in Greek cantors! The frenzy was worth the pause until at last I held up the coin from my bread. I announced to everyone that I had won the coin, but in the cacophony that had overtaken the kitchen, no one heard me. I walked through the moving bodies towards Yia-Yia and showed her I had won the coin. I knelt down towards her and she grabbed my face to kiss me. Her lips were dry and her chin was covered in olive oil and a few random whiskers – the kind only old Greek ladies get. They tickled my chin and lips, but I kissed her back. She smelled like stale bread, and potent medicines. We did not exchange many words, but she made enough of a fuss to garner the entire attention of the family. Stray whiskers, oxygen tank and all, that was my Yia-Yia! "Andrea has won! Andrea, you will have the most blessed year, my couclamou (μικρή κούκλα, Little Doll)," she beamed with pride.

"No way!" Came the chants from my cousins. "Not fair! You have won so many times, Andrea! Let someone else have a turn!" It was true I had won so many times. At least five times growing up and that was a lot when there were a lot of cousins and family members with which to share the foiled wealth. I kept all the foil wrapped coins I had won in a special place in the back of my bedside drawer near the purple leather Bible, all written in Greek, Yia-Yia had once gifted me. I never read it because for one, I couldn't read Greek, but for some reason I loved that I had it. Each Christmas wherein I had received the coin, a good year came ahead. I grew in sports, academics, won trophies, found love, or made friends. I was not one for superstition or mysticism, but if you got the coin, the Greek Gods were going to be on your side. That 2011 Christmas coin was an omen of what came ahead in finding a job, getting into graduate school, and finding love. Years later, the 2016 coin I won turned me into a fiancé. Yia-Yia was right. God was good. As were the Greeks.

Other than being the recipient of the coin and sharing the good news with Yia-Yia, for whatever reason, I did not spend much time talking to Yia-Yia that Christmas, which was rather uncharacteristic of me as we could talk for hours about anything from politics to her childhood to my desire to become a writer one day. I was fond of our conversations, but that Christmas our intentional time got lost in the swell of food and carols, traditions, and sumptuous honey cinnamon and buttery powdered sugar desserts. When Yia-Yia left for home with my Uncle Mark and his family that evening I promised her we would talk the following week at the family celebration on New Year's Day. She told me she was most looking forward to that and asked if I would make some scones and bring some chocolates, too. "Of course, Yia -Yia! Of course!" I called out as she left. I never said I love you that night and I don't know why. It was a snowy evening, but she made it home safely. I missed her each time that she left our home. She did not make it to New Year's Day and I always regret never getting that last conversation with her.

Suddenly with Yia-Yia's death the notion of time became all the more understandable to me. As I looked at the moving rays of sunlight beaming down onto the purple casket she requested to be buried in and I saw her perfectly coiffed hair as it always had been, I could not understand what her loss meant. I could not understand that there would be no more phone calls to Yia-Yia each week, there would be no more guilt trips, but perhaps those that magically came from the grave, and that they did as time went on. There would be no more kourambiethes, rice pudding or Grecian potatoes with extra rosemary. No more secret recipe salad dressing that made me a forever salad-eater, or spanakopita, avgolemono or aromatic vegetable soups. As the water in my eyes obstructed my view of her body at rest, I listened intently as the Greek priest chanted on in mourning of her loss and her new home in heaven. I longed to talk to her one more time, to tell her in Greek that I loved her. To show her how much she mattered to me. She was an intelligent woman who had given her life to her community and to her family. She was stridently assertive, but she cared more than anyone I had ever met. I loved her and will forever love her with every last Greek cell in my being.

Greeks believe in the eternity of memory and that those who pass must never be forgotten. Yia-Yia would never be forgotten and I would do everything in my power to honor and bring forth the gifts she brought to my life. Yia-Yia was there when I learned to dance, to sing, and to cry. She was there when Papou died and she kept the family together at all cost. I looked up to her, admired her strength, her dignity, and her undying loyalty to her family.

What is strange in thinking about my grandparents is that my Papou was content to be in the background. He was there, but constantly told what to do by Yia-Yia or else he was gambling or playing card games. When I was little I never reached up for the obligatory greeting kiss because he smelled of smoke and it hurt my throat. His coke-bottle glasses looked like goobers to be devoured and his facial hair cruelly scratched the delicate skin on my face.

Yia-Yia you could not avoid because she'd suffocate you with kisses and her strong perfume – a robust mix of lilac, Greek vegetable soup, and lemon chicken, heavy on oregano and seasoning. I truly was never really fond of their embrace as a young child, but enjoyed playing in that lovely home of theirs. They were my father's parents, but I struggled to love them when I was really little in the same way I loved my parents even though without them I understood I would not be here. But now I see my Papou in my father's aging eyes and my heart lurches towards my grandparent's grave. I tell myself age stops time because I am not brave enough to swallow the reality that it does not. My Papou passed and it left me empty —he moved out the day of my birth. But when my Yia-Yia died on the eve of a new year, the purple casket left voids I'll never unearth.

I still want to go back to that home. To those china plates and plastic couches and stale crackers, and egg lemon soup. To the overflowing coffee table with photo frames, and the cloudy front windows she never opened. I want to go back to the tiny basement of the museum so I can see my reflection in her picture on the wall to remind me who I am and that I am them. That home and the people it held was the heartbeat of my tatsimou.

Surpassing everything else that fell in the aftermath of her passing was what death taught me was that in death, what matters most is what people remember. As lines and lines of people for two days poured out to say farewell to this woman who had changed their lives, touched their hearts, or laid down the most feudal of Greek guilt trips upon them, what was remembered was not the robust nature of her life's resume. What was remembered was her presence in shaping and impacting the lives of those around her. What was remembered was the character of her heart and the involvement of her life in the world around her.

Thousands of people for one woman who was never allowed to go to college and taught herself English, music, and became a wife through arranged marriage, a store owner, a librarian, a piano teacher, an influential church and city member, and a most beloved grandmother. I wondered in the most troubled ways for weeks after her funeral, what would people remember me for? Would it be for my failure in high school? Would it be for chasing everything under the sun and only having time for selfish desires? Or would people remember me as a woman with a compassionate heart who loved her family and friends and wanted to do the best by them? The discontentment I experienced in this reality morphed into Obsessive Compulsive Disorder, but in my grief I stopped chasing so hard after what I did not need to have and the multitude of trivial things I did not need to do.

Each Friday beginning during my junior year in college I had written Yia-Yia a letter on purple stationary and sent it to her. It was the most cherished time in my week. I worked in the writing center at college and would arrive early on Fridays before my shift to write to her. Sometimes I shared recipes or ideas for future books or told her about the people I spent time with and how my classes were going. I would ask her about Church and how she was doing and what Greek dish she would make for me to eat the next time I came over to visit. I loved writing those letters and I loved the return letters that would always arrive on Wednesday of the succeeding week. On occasion the outer envelope on the letters she sent to me would read: "Photos: Do Not Bend" and I knew that on the inside I would find a five or ten or sometimes twenty dollar bill wrapped in foil. I later learned that the foil wrapping was what they normally did when they sent cash money back home to family in Greece. The foil concealed the money when it would go through customs at the post office. The hope was that it would not be stolen and would make it safely to their relatives who desperately needed it. Foil envelopes were certainly my favorites even though I did not deserve them. We exchanged letters up until a few months before she passed away when her tired hands became too weary to write them or she would forget to check her mailbox to receive them and a neighbor would deliver her a whole a stack of purple letters to her when he visited. At one point the letters confused her and she was disillusioned because the outside of all of them looked the same. But when we cleaned out the museum, we found every single one, opened, and with her scribbles in the margins.

After she passed away the stationary mocked me in a most sinister and haunting way. I only ever used that stationary for her and there were still hundreds of lavender cards that remained to be used. So I wrote to Yia-Yia and I sent the letters to an address that was to be taken by another. After a while, logic told me to stop mailing the letters, but I never stopped writing them. Each Friday on Lilac stationary I still write to my grandmother, hoping, knowing, and believing she is listening. I don't get calls or letters back in the mail anymore. There is an absence of foil envelopes. But I know she is there as I write her the letters of my heart. It has been my way to keep her memory eternal and to mend the hollow feeling that lingers from the promised New Year's Day conversation that was stolen to time.

26
A Testimony towards Health

Yia-Yia's passing sucked every last ounce of joy from my life for months, but in the aftermath, her death also gifted me a renewed sense of purpose for living my own life. Yia-Yia wanted me to be healthy and to live life with passion and the full intensity of my spirit. Post eating disorder, I did not know how to live with passion or even where to find it. Anorexic was the label and persona that had ruled my life. I did not really know who I was. I knew I was a fighter and I knew by the grace of God, I was still alive to offer something to the world, but I had no idea what that something was.

When sporadic and far from lucrative jobs in journalism did not pan out as expected immediately after college graduation, Mom and Dad said I would make an excellent teacher, despite the fact that I never wanted to chart that course for my life. Nevertheless, I heeded their advice and the fall after I graduated college I began freelance writing while going back to school to obtain a teaching license to become a secondary education English teacher. My justification in returning to school for teaching was that education was essential to success in life and since I was already a steadfast proponent of its transformative power, why not become a teacher? I could make a difference in the lives of students as many others had before me. I had a natural affinity for English and linguistics, so I knew the teaching component would fall into place with proper training. Though coursework for an education degree and teaching license were easier than anything I had done during my undergraduate experience, I was exposed to math and kinesiology courses that I had not experienced during undergrad. The math classes were remedial, which made my apparent struggle with basic concepts all the more humiliating. Math was an arch nemesis of mine. Whether high school math or advanced calculus, it was not for me. If two plus two was to equal four, I was the one to find a way to make it equal five. Yes, it was that bad. I wrote a book of "Andrea's Original – Tested and Proven Theorems" in Geometry class. Dennis, the math whiz, snickered at my illogical efforts to bring nonsensical creativity to a math classroom. None of the ones we learned made any sense at all to me and of course, my logic and authority was of utmost superiority. If all goes as planned, I'll make it big when I publish that title one day.

However, the kinesiology course, a requirement for completion of an education degree, was robust and challenging in a unique way. As a science course, it fascinated me. I was eager to learn about anatomy of the body, movement studies, nutrition, exercise, and how all of the systems of our bodies must work together in harmony in order to obtain optimum health. My professor was a young, tall, post-collegiate athlete who was beyond dreamy. He only made my engagement level in the class higher. Each two hour class began with thirty minutes of active cardio or weight training, after which we would delve into small group work or lectures. As the semester progressed I could not help but think if I had only learned all of the valuable health information from that class instead of the useless information from Rosetta or the drab insights from Sarah, I might have better understood the harm of my habits and the damage I had inflicted upon my body. In that class, I learned of how unhealthy I was by every measure of physical wellness. When assessed, I saw how painfully low my BMI still remained. I also learned about the obesity epidemic and the mounting evidence supporting a balanced lifestyle that supports a healthy weight. On the other end of the spectrum, we studied eating disorders, malnourishment, and its cumulative negative effects which further convinced me that I would never allow myself to fall back into that state of both musculoskeletal and cardiovascular system bodily shock.

Our semester term project, with the ever-handsome, tan and muscular, Professor Bradley Richards, was to set forth a health plan for our lives, follow it for six weeks, track progress, and then write a research-based analysis of our experience. We had to include specific details for categories such as diet, sleep, work, standing and sitting time, physical exertion and set specific daily and weekly goals to improve our overall health. It was a detailed and tedious assignment, but if there was one thing I could do well, it was log and track food and activity. But this time I was doing it authentically and I was not basing it off of any pre-conceived notions of my own accord about diet, exercise, and weight loss. We all know how that ended. As I progressed into week two and showed progress in nutritional gains, exercise expenditure as well as organizational structuring of sleeping patterns that led to better rest, I began to feel better than I had remembered in a long time and I wanted to maintain a course of action in that way. As the assignment came to a close I spent hours upon hours doing research for the final assignment. I was absolutely hooked on learning about health and wellness. Professor Richards winked at me and my physical improvements, impressed by my progress and the studious nature of my discourse in that class.

When I gave my presentation to the class as part of our final exam I remember looking out at my classmates, all of whom were younger than I, most fit athletes, and thinking that all of those jocks whom I thought were useless tools for most of my college experience, actually had knowledge that was beneficial to fundamental needs that everyone shares. As I spoke, I transmitted my personal experiences of mental trauma and relayed how developing strength through exercise was a determining factor in my journey back into health. Exercise lifted my depression by releasing a constant stream of endorphins and taking care of my body nutritionally became paramount to my recovery. Following my in-depth analysis and research in exercise science, I concluded my presentation as follows:

"We are only given one body in this life. We must honor it, nurture it, and take care of it. Self-care is not selfish. I willingly destroyed my body, shrunk my heart, and nearly passed on from this life without any bother to care about the consequences of my unhealthy choices. In retrospect I can now see how destructive my behaviors were and also what a high value good health has. The past six weeks taught me how to properly care for my body and I want to become an ambassador to share this knowledge with others. Remember: A body in motion stays in motion. And a body fit for Christ, seeks to serve." I could not talk a lot about my faith in our secular classroom, but being fit for Christ was the overarching aim I had set my sights on. Eventually, I would fully discover my measure of worth did not rest in calories, the haunted scale, or my personal victories in achieved grades or mortal accolades. My victory was in living for Him. At the end of my project write-up, I wrote the following verse, to which my professor highlighted and commentated fondly upon.

"But do not forget this one thing, dear friends: With the Lord a day is like a thousand years, and a thousand years are like a day. The Lord is not slow in keeping his promise, as some understand slowness. Instead he is patient with you, not wanting anyone to perish, but everyone to come to repentance"
(2 Peter 3:8-9).

My presentation served as a public confession in its testimony and it was a stride towards permanence of my progress towards ongoing health in every facet of my life. If I had not gone after a teaching degree, I would not have taken a kinesiology course that in due time, transformed the course of my life. God does everything for a reason.

I obtained my teaching license shortly after completing that course and applied to teaching jobs in Illinois and Indiana. However, even as I became engrossed in the world of teaching, I continued to pursue the path of fitness for my life. It was perhaps oxymoronic in some ways. An anorexic, mostly failed athlete, was to go about dictating to others how to live their lives. But with the proper training I knew with my newfound personal passion for health, I could help others and in turn, help myself. I did my research and decided that I would study and obtain my license to become a certified group exercise instructor and personal trainer. The process for that would require several hands-on workshops as well as over 500 hours of self-study and then sitting for a five hour exam, with a 40% pass rate. A couple years prior I had obtained my license to teach Zumba Dance Fitness and I had found the group exercise setting to be a natural fit and great outlet for me. It combined my leadership skills as well as my love of dance and movement. Acquiring my group exercise license would allow me to teach different types of fitness classes and it would also prepare me to be a certified resource in the professional realm of health and wellness.

In late June, I passed the exam and completed all of the practicums to become a Group Fitness Instructor and Personal Trainer through the American Council on Exercise. It was the summer immediately succeeding my success in that Kinesiology course and before my first full-time job began. I was proud, affirmed, and ready.

27

God Affirms His Presence

While I was hopeful to go directly into full-time fitness, I had just invested two years and a lot of tuition dollars into becoming a certified English and French teacher. I had common sense enough to follow-through with what I had started, at least until I could better substantiate fitness as a career choice. I had several offers for teaching positions in the Chicago area, but ultimately accepted a position at a private, all-girls suburban school as I thought it would provide the most freedom in teaching outside of the public school system. I could not have been further from being right about that assumption and my first full-time experience teaching was a miserable one. I hated working for nuns and being scolded for teaching classes that were "too hard." I disliked how conservative the school was and how bland, dry, and dull things were. My creative mind was being swallowed, suffocated, and deteriorated each passing day. The girls there looked like uniformed Zombies and it made me depressed beyond reason. Most of the teachers there did not have any credentials for teaching, but somehow earned the same salary as me. As for the curriculum? Well, that was non-existent.

So for my first time in a full-time job I was being critiqued by nuns who knew nothing about teaching, had never attended college, and were downright thieves embezzling funds from the school into private accounts, all while I was writing a curriculum on the fly and trying to sift through the classrooms of catty, estrogen-laden freshman-girl teenage angst. On the bright side, I was given the opportunity to nurture young adults in the way of Christ, as it was a Catholic school. But outside of prayer time and spiritual counseling, the whole thing turned out to be a most wretched, mind-sucking job for me.

I taught Bootcamp fitness classes on Monday nights and taught Zumba every Tuesday night at different gyms near my home after school. Those became the most beloved nights of my week. Fitness had given me the outlet I needed not to turn to food restriction or to attempt to unearth Rachel in the height of anxiety and stress that fall term. My atrophied heart muscle was pained from the mind-numbing work my first teaching job caused, but it was growing physically through my daily sessions of exercise via the group exercise classes I taught and others regularly attended.

The first day of classes that semester I gave all of the girls pale yellow, laminated bookmarks that I created as a first day of school gesture of welcome. On one side of the bookmark was a quote from Shakespeare or C.S. Lewis, and on the reverse side was one of two significant verses from the book of Romans and James, respectively. As it turned out, the girls used iPads for their notebook and textbook access, so the bookmarks served no functional purpose other than to litter their hallways or for the less attitude prone girls, to hang up in their lockers. 175 bookmarks swarmed halls and backpacks that semester. Sister Marie Catherine, the head nun, threated to suspend my job for a week because I had given the girls bookmarks. It was not protocol to do what I did. That was only one of the many puzzling quandaries I experienced teaching in that school.

But amazingly, God still finds a way to speak to us through the muffled chatter and judgement all around us. Maybe my grand idea of bookmarks and team building activities was not acceptable in a private school that did not take a glimpse of time to care about the individuals who walked its halls, but God makes His presence known and He fulfills His purpose in all things. A week before we went on recess for the Christmas holiday I was sitting at my desk in my classroom well past 6:00 PM crying over ungraded assessments and wondering why in the heck I ever became a teacher. My desk that once held pictures of me and my family and my boyfriend was now mostly empty. The nuns had stolen my precious memory-framed photos the first week of school, broken them, and thrown them away all as I watched. The lesson I learned from that first formative event was that as a teacher we were not supposed to highlight our personal lives in the classroom. The classroom was a place to learn and the teacher was the teacher – nothing more, nothing less. A purveyor of information. Not a girlfriend, not a sister, not a friend. I think we still got to be daughters of Christ. But not the kind of daughters that can give out bookmarks with Biblical scripture or hang posters with inspirational quotes on the wall. Even by that late point in the semester, I was still struggling to recite the words of the Rosary prayer. *I'm not cut out for this teaching thing*, I thought. As I sat there in despair, the sophomore Chemistry teacher came into my classroom, also with tears in her eyes.

"Ms. Cladis," she began.

"Hi there, Ms. Finley," I said. "What should I call you? I know we have not really gotten to interact much even though there are not that many of us teachers here on staff."

"Oh, call me Carol. Sorry to interrupt, but I just have to tell you something," she continued as more tears showed in her eyes and reddened face.

"What is it? Sorry, just been trying to grade here and get through the rest of this week somehow. I can't stand being here. Is Sister Mary Catherine gone yet?" I asked.

"Yes, she left about an hour ago. I only saw the light on in your classroom and was hopeful I would catch you before you left for home."

"I'll be here for a while; I have a lot of grading and lesson prep to do. I get anxious during the day when the sisters are marching through the hallways. I always try to appear engaged with the students and I don't get much work done even on test days," I said.

"Oh, I completely understand. I have been so stressed working here that I have been putting on a lot of weight and losing hair. This is one of the unhappiest places I have ever worked. Not to mention, we are always being chastised for trying to do our jobs and care about students!" Carol explained.

"I am happy to hear you share some of the same feelings as I do. It has been a rough semester. I can't wait until break," I enforced.

"Same here. Break is much needed. I am sorry we have not connected more this semester, but I have been meaning to thank you for something you did that has gotten me through the past several months," Carol stated.

"Something I did? For you? I have barely reached out to any of the teachers here. I have been so focused on the students, writing curriculum, and trying to finagle my way around the whims of the Sister Mary Catherine and Sister Beth," I replied. As I looked over at Carol, her ill-fitted khakis, frumpy gray sweater and frayed, thin, shoulder-length wavy brown hair held back only by half-bent red-framed reading glasses, I realized I was not the only one at that school struggling to get through each day. She reached into her back pocket and pulled out one of the bookmarks that I had given to the students back in August. She placed it on my desk and smiled as water started to fill her eyes again.

"You made these, right? I saw your name on the back so I presumed it was you who gave these out?" she asked.

"Ah, yes," I remembered well. "I got in trouble for handing these out all have you know. I was informed that it was unorthodox to do something like that on the first day and then when they were littering the halls the second week of classes, I heard about the consequences of my malicious decision again," I said.

"Seriously? I thought that was such an innovative thing to do as a way to welcome students on the first day," she said, somewhat shocked by the fact that such a simple thing had caused so much drama for me.

"I learned my lesson, I guess. Where did you find this one?" I asked picking up the bookmark she had set on my desk.

"Well, long story short, I found it in the bathroom on October 7th. It was the day after I learned that my father had passed away and I was a complete wreck. Sister Mary

Catherine said that I could not have any time off following his death. She was ruthless about it. The students were kind to me, but Sister said 'death is part of life and he probably did not take care of himself anyway.' He was not ill or very old. He was killed by a drunk driver," she said tears streaming from her face, her red glasses falling from her crooked head. I handed her a tissue. Her pain was tangible and I stood up to approach her, embracing her in my arms as she sobbed.

"Carol, oh Carol. I am so sorry. I did not know that happened. I am incredibly sorry for your loss. I pulled a couple desks together and we sat down next to one another. Carol told me about the incident and the ordeal that her family was going through, how they were strapped financially, and how the school had done nothing to allay the trauma of her situation. "Carol, is there anything I can do to help?" I asked, immediately feeling selfish and ignorant for crying over a stack of unfinished papers.

"That is actually why I stopped by. You have helped me in the most unspeakable way and I wanted to thank you for that," she said.

"How so? How have I helped? I did not even know that this happened. Again, Carol, I am so, so very sorry," I bowed my head in reverence to her as she spoke.

"You see this bookmark here? The verse on this bookmark: 'Blessed is the one who perseveres under trial because, having stood the test, that person will receive the crown of life that the Lord has promised to those who love him' – James 1:12 is what has gotten me through. When I picked it up that day in the bathroom I felt the wholeness of

God's presence and I knew he was guiding me through that scripture. And when I saw your name on the back, I meant to come talk to you and ask you for more of them, but I never got around to doing so. I kept that bookmark in my pocket the rest of the day after I found it and it has remained there every day since then. It a reminder that through trials we build character, and through character, we grow closer to Christ. At my father's funeral, we distributed yellow slips of laminated paper, in the same way as you created, with this verse on the front, which just so happened to be my father's life verse. When we went through his belongings and his will we discovered this verse was listed several times throughout all of his paperwork. He wrote in a journal that it was a verse given to him by his great-grandfather. We were moved to learn of that history. Whether you knew it or not, you gave hope and new life to me and my family this past fall. God works in us and through us with intentionality of purpose and I know that he planted you here to lead me to listen closely to Him as I struggled through that most trying day after Dad's death and this most difficult year for my family," Carol finished her story and grasped both of my hands into hers. "Thank you. Thank you," she said with the greatest sense of sincerity in her voice.

I held onto her hands, both in awe of her story and troubled by the tragic loss her family had been subjected to. "Carol, please. If there is anything I can do for you, let me know. I am so thankful you found that abandoned bookmark and God spoke to you through it. I am glad that I made those! Even if they ended up on the bathroom floor, I am grateful that verse was a source of comfort for you."

"Yes, yes, thank you again," Carol said. "It meant so much to me to find. I don't know you all that well, but I can already tell that you have a beautiful heart," she said with smiling eyes. We hugged and cried for hours that evening in my classroom, holding each other as we talked about the memory of her father and complained about the life-sapping environment of that school. I found a friend in work and an even greater friend in Christ.

I ultimately quit that job, but I had far greater things to set my sights on. The summer prior, I had finally gotten up the courage to date again and after a few months, had met a handsome, chivalrous gentleman named Matthew, who was head over heels in love with me. Being in a relationship was a new struggle all its own as I had to learn how to be loved again, but it grew me in the most unexpected, phenomenal ways. Growing in tandem to my relationship with Matthew was my passion for fitness. And as that passion grew, I began to take on the responsibility of teaching more classes and attained several specialty certifications in class formats such as Barre, Kickboxing, Yoga, Spin, Pilates, Metabolic Conditioning, and High Intensity Interval Training. Teaching a fitness class beat teaching a high school class any dam day of the week. The spring of that year my competitive side was beginning to surface and I began researching recreational racing events such as 5Ks, 10Ks and even triathlons. I needed an outlet to temper the sparky edge of my newfound energy. Tennis leagues for adults required expensive memberships and my brief time dabbling into that arena left me feeling an outcast amongst the wealthy housewives with whom I was paired to play against. I wondered if I would be able to complete an endurance event in running. I thought that maybe if I started with shorter events and trained diligently, I could build myself to have the strength and stamina to finish a longer race. I set a year-long goal timeline for myself with a few short running events and cycling events scattered throughout. The ultimate goal was for the following summer to compete in my first triathlon. Nothing was going to stop me.

Exactly a year and three weeks later I completed my first Sprint Distance Triathlon on Lakeshore Drive in Chicago. It was a steamy July day and while not vainglorious in my feat, I was proud, wobbly-legged at the end, and surrounded by Mom and Dad. I stood on the podium stand for my age-group wearing white, size extra small, but not XXXS spandex bike shorts over a form fitting blue azure and black TYR racing suit with the horizon line of the sandy beach and Lake behind me, Mom and Dad looking up at my lean, tanned, strong, protein-fueled body. I keep that snapshot safely framed at the head of my bed. I am looking with revivified deep hazel eyes into the distance while Mom and Dad are in the bottom of the frame looking up at me holding my wetsuit over my right arm and my third place medal high in the air above my head with my left. Their faces are glowing in the early morning sunlight with drifting tears and budding smiles. That first triathlon, podium moment was self-reincarnation at its very finest.

Life experience is how we learn. It might be unkind at times and if we do anything right it will not be easy. But experience gives us great hope and immeasurable courage. God puts us through trials to build our faith, grow our resilience, and develop our character. I did not know all that

God wanted me to be – a teacher, a fitness instructor, a ministry leader, but I knew that His plans were far greater than my own and in my surrender I was not awarded fame, wealth, or riches. I was awarded the happiness that comes in finding purpose in life. In the pursuit of His will, He unveiled the passions on my heart that I would use to serve Him and further His kingdom. Through my redemption and renewed salvation, I could breathe God's love into others. By the time 2016 began, I had become all that I thought was impossible. I was strong and I was confident. I had muscles on my suntanned arms and I could eat three pieces of pizza, albeit without cheese, but three pieces, crusts and all, without flinching. I could eat brownies and peanut butter without thinking about calories. I was a leader in a High School English classroom and a fitness studio instructor with a voice of courage and encouragement – determination and persistence. Challenges still remain, but the will is mighty at the foot of Jesus Christ.

28
Rachel's Funeral

The fall of 2016 was when I officially buried Rachel. While I was not anorexic nor routinely tempted by her, I had not gotten rid of her. When I looked in the mirror and saw fatness she was there to smile at my side and when I ran to the point of needing to throw up, she would cheer me on. As I entered into the second year of a serious relationship with Matthew, who was still chasing me and my love without abandon, I knew I had to dispose of Rachel. How could I become a future wife and mother with her hanging out in the corner of my home? She would not allow the weight gain of pregnancy and when mounting stressors got the best of me I knew she would weave her way into every vulnerable place in my mind. Mental disease, as with physical disease, is something you can overcome, but it always remains a part of you. Anorexia will always be a part of my past, but Rachel was not going to be a part of my future.

To once and for all erase the presence and shadow of Rachel, I knew I had to do something drastic. In every journal wherein I located her name, I whited it out or shredded the page on which it was written. And each time her name would creep into my mind, I would exchange the word for "Redeemer." I if heard Rachel murmur at me, I would say, "Redeemer, redemption. Lord, redeem me." I would think of Christ and his love for me. If Satan was real, Rachel was the embodiment of his grand allure. On bike rides I saw her at parks that I passed and at the grocery store when I placed an item in my cart without perusing the nutritional label, Rachel stoically glared at me. I did not know what to do other than in the most obtrusive way, kill her. I had to kill Rachel. *Could I bury her alive? Could I hypnotize my mind to block of the illusions of her presence? What if I bury her? Would I be burying her alive? Well she was never alive to begin with, but...* Yes, yes I could kill her. I decided on the first of October that Rachel was going to die. I would commemorate her death with a funeral and we would never speak again. We would say our goodbyes in a cordial fashion and I would walk away. That would be the end.

October 1st came and I took a backpack full of memories of Rachel. Trinkets that reminded me of her such as bracelets, hair pins, a tennis skirt, tennis balls, old gum wrappers, uneaten packages of strawberry frosted Pop-Tarts, boxes of sugar-free Jell-O, tattered pages from my journals, and billing receipts from the Offices of Dr. Barkens. Barkens was her creator, after all. For a short while I wanted to kill Barkens, too. I wanted to kill the nucleus and then kill its offspring. That would have been murder though, and the construct of Rachel had also given me a targeted enemy in healing. Hate only blackened an atrophied heart.

I set out on my bike with my backpack of Rachel, $5 for a snack if needed, a large water bottle and a black and lime green windbreaker. I rode down towards the riverfront path where I liked to go for long runs. It was weird having Rachel on my back. But as I thought about it, Rachel was always on my back – literally and figuratively - and I needed to shed the excess weight of her toxic friendship. I used the $5 I brought to buy a small, clean notebook and a full pack of Orbit Bubblemint gum at the drugstore off of Wilson Street before I headed to the fateful spot where I had passed out from heat stroke a few years before. A damp, autumn air filled my lungs as I dismounted my bike, set the backpack of Rachel down next to the river and came upon the spot where I vividly remembered throwing up, having diarrhea, and passing out in a rush of chilled sweat. I grabbed a few dead sticks from the trail to use as makeshift shovels and dug a deep hole into the muddy ground near the riverbed dense with worms, ants, shrubs, sinewy tree roots, and roly poly bugs that coiled when my sticks touched them. Flashbacks flooded my mind. I had run on that most acrid day for Rachel. My family at the Sox game. My bright clothing. The blistering heat. The tread bare miles. I felt nauseous. I stabbed at the ground mercilessly. The Earth was working against me and my sticks were not getting the job done. I saw myself hunched over that very patch of earth, hurling bile and losing liquids uncontrollably from my backend. I tore the bike helmet from my head and used its pointed front tip to pierce the ground in fury. Dirt flew to the sides and behind me. Ants, worms, and roly polys burrowed deeper at the disturbance.

Fuck you, Rachel. Fuck you, I muttered underneath my breath. I started crying and I did not know why. But I cast my helmet aside and hands to earth I dug until I had created a hole nearly an arm's length deep. *See this, Rachel? See this?*

This is your new home. This is where you will stay. This dirt hole is for you! I emptied the contents of the backpack into the hole and patted each item in with a fistful of dirt and rotted leaves. I rubbed the snot from my nose on my jacket sleeve and sniffled as I ceremonially buried the visionary temptress that had ruled my life. I put the package of gum on the top of the heap and took out the journal I had purchased. I pulled out a pen from my jacket pocket and on the front cover of the journal I wrote the following message to Rachel: "Thank you. I will miss you, but I have to say goodbye." I wrote in uppercase, bold letters throughout the pages of the small notebook: I WIN. I WIN. I WIN. RACHEL, I WIN. I filled every single page with my vengeance. I returned the pen to my pocket and set the journal in the center of the pile of Rachel's remembrance. I stopped crying. I filled the hole with the dirt I had removed and I proudly patted the Earth with my muddy hands. I traced the shape of an "R" with the sticks on top of her grave and outlined the sides of the mound with a halo of dead leaves. R was dead; she had been safely stowed near the river. I prayed for her as I did all of my enemies. Now, Rachel is only present at that gravesite when I ride or run past her on the river front trail, but she is nowhere else in my life. Rachel is no longer and Rachel never will be again.

29
Tatsimou in my Garden of Heaven

Autumn remained my favorite season. The colors, the foliage, the cooler weather and the reality that Rachel was now underground made that particular fall an even more satisfying one. Each when I was a child, my family traditionally went apple picking – sometimes, more than once. We enjoyed the family bonding experience it provided, not to mention the collected bushels full of fresh, delicious apples we brought home and savored well into the winter months in the form of tantalizing pies, sauces, sweet breads, and jams.

The mesmerizing rows of apple trees boasting the fruit in multiple varieties were often overwhelming at first, but once crowds arrived and the much hoped for gastronomical fantasy was perpetuated by the wafting scent of bakery items, an urgency to collect as many apples as possible would undoubtedly set in for me. And it is precisely at that moment when every suitable apple – red, green or yellow would glow from high branches of the trees and tempt with much-desired satisfaction. A nutrient dense, exceptionally appealing, fall indulgence. In Greek and Roman mythology, apples are upheld as symbols of love and beauty. I adored the tradition of going with my family as a kid. When we were little, Stacey's favorite thing to do at the orchard was to play what affectionately became known as the "Safari-Stacey" game while we were selecting apples. "Safari-Stacey" loved to camouflage herself in-between the heavy, wooden branches of the trees that were cloaked with thick, dark green leaves. Her impish face grinned with pleasure as she giggled from one tree to the next. We usually found her with ease, and reflecting back upon those moments, I find that I still crave the purity of her innocence.

Occasionally, she would pick a few apples that were within her reach, wipe them off on her shirt and give them to Mom or Dad who would then add them to our growing collection of colorful apples bouncing around the orchard in our vintage, fire-engine red, Radio Flyer wagon. My favorite part of the "Safari-Stacey" charade was when she would keep one apple for herself. Then slowly, her brown eyes opened up really wide as she struggled to fit her small mouth around a luscious apple almost as large as her face.

What I remember most is that Stacey's apple-picking approach was different than all of the other apple-pickers at the orchard. She was careful with each and every apple she selected. And even if, heaven forbid, one of the smooth, foggy, wax-covered apples she picked slipped out of her hands, she would gently remove it from the ground, wipe it off on her shirt – shining it the way mom had taught her; and meekly say, "It's okay. Here, Daddy. This one fell on the ground, but I promise, it's okay to take home with us." To that, Dad would respond with a smile as he cautiously placed the apple Stacey supplied him with into the wagon, knowing she was conscious of his every move.

Stacey only picked the few apples she really wanted and judging by the carpet of decomposing apples on the ground, I often concluded that she was the only person in the orchard that ever treated an apple with dignity. Unlike Stacey, Mom was always on the lookout for the deep red, flawless apples; Dennis constantly the challenge of acquiring all of the apples that were out of reach and Dad was usually the camera man and the one hauling the heavy bags of apples we filled just as soon as we overflowed the wagon. As for me, I relished the experience, picking as many apples as humanely possible, fill the wagon and my pockets.

Memories of the powder-blue skies at the orchard speckled by a few billowy clouds that provided an ideal backdrop to the beaming sun ripening the apples that weighed down the upper branches of the trees was like an autumn postcard in my mind. The best apples were always the sunburned ones. With each subsequent year as Dennis grew taller and stronger, my range and selection of available apples from my perch atop his shoulders steadily increased. Despite my snarky complaints at times, I actually loved being on his shoulders. He was strong and muscular and on his shoulders, I became tall and secure. I could reach what all the people on the ground only wished they could have.

On Dennis' shoulders as a young girl, I was able to view the entire orchard. The soft wind shaking the dark green leaves, families with strollers scattered about the orchard, small children nibbling on apples, elderly men and women holding hands and sipping on warm cider, feisty birds singing in the open sky around me and for a few, precious moments I would linger above that layer of air defined by rotting apples. I allowed my lungs to expand as the renewed air entered freely. In the magnified autumn atmosphere, closed my eyes and let go of my stabilizing grip on Dennis' head to reach for the sunburned apples. As a young girl, the orchard was the garden of my heaven.

As apple farms became more and more commercialized the older I became, I no longer wanted to go to the mini-amusement parks with a few rows of trees for apple-picking as an aside to the hay rides, pumpkin patches, gift stores, and apple-launchers. As if the apples were not abused enough? Now, they could be launched towards their destiny of fate – a place far beyond the orchard where they can no longer even hope to be thrown into the cider heap. At best, their flesh would rot and gnats and flies would multiply to cover every visible portion of the exposed, damaged fruit. And then during high school I used to starve myself in preparation for the day we would go apply picking just so I could eat an apple when in the presence of my family at the orchard.

But after several seasons of missing out on apple picking, I was anxious to go again that fall of Rachel's burial. I missed the garden of my heaven that I remembered as a young girl so Mom and Dad desperately searched all over the Midwest to find a traditional, simple, non-commercial-ized apple farm to visit. After vetting every orchard they could find within a 100 mile radius, they invited Matthew and I on a trip to an old-fashioned apple orchard located in Harvard, Illinois. Mom, Dad, Matthew and I enjoyed a two hour, convivial drive to the orchard on a lazy Sunday afternoon taking in the peak fall coloration on the trees and the wafting wooden smell of smoky campfire, the rotting ash cinder of burning leaves. The smokiness clung to my petite nostril hairs and I craved more of it. When we finally arrived at the destined Orchard, I was pleasantly surprised to discover the expansive beauty of rows upon rows of trees, green grass and a small, plain barn and silo reserved for the sampling of hot cider donuts and spiced cinnamon apple cider. There were no apple launchers, commercialized real-estate or over-priced gift stores. My heart was warm and I was in a happy place with my family, my Matthew, and the beauty of God's splendor and provision surrounding me.

We began carelessly traipsing about the orchard, admiring the abundant displays of apples covering endless acres of fields before our eyes. It was a cool fall day, but the sun shone through the clouds to gently warm our skin. As we walked up and down the rows, we carefully filled our bags and indulged in perfectly ripe fruit until we developed much anticipated stomach aches.

Ever content to be apple picking, I do not recall how much time passed. Maybe an hour or two. But in what felt an all too abrupt intermission to our orchard adventure, the sun fell back into the sky as clouds rolled in and hovered over the orchard in a threatening fashion. We dispersed from our apple hunting unit in attempts to gather as many apples as possible before the rain came.

"Better hurry up, kids!" Dad said. "We're at least a half mile away from the car!" We hastily finished filling our bushels as the clouds opened up, first a drizzle, then a most certain downpour. There was no chance we were going to even get remotely close to making it back to the car. I chased down a few stranded apples on low branches and ran towards Matthew, who was a few rows over doing the same thing. His white shirt was drenched and his normally well-styled hair was wet and flat. He had taken his windbreaker off so he could use it to cover my shoulders and keep me warm.

"Let's find your parents," he instructed wrapping his jacket around me and cradling his bag of apples in his left arm. "Your Ma has an umbrella! Come on, let's go!" He said as I worked to nudge a few more apples into my bag. We giggled as my bag was overflowing with apples and we sloshed through the muddied ground towards my parents, who were not far away. Nowhere near any form of shelter, and with only one umbrella, and the strong inkling that the storm would quickly pass, we gathered together under Mom's polka dotted white and navy blue umbrella.

"God has to clean the apples somehow," Mom observed.

"I love the smell and sound of rain," Matthew added. "It soothes me. Even way out here," he continued.

"Oh, me too!" Mom said taking a bite of a half-eaten apple. "You have to try this one!" she urged. For the most part, we were all wet from head to toe, but we stayed under Mom's umbrella anyway.

"Did you taste the Ozark Gold apple?" Dad asked us. "I think that one was my favorite."

"Yes! It was crisp, tart, and most exquisite," I replied.

"I like the Jonathans and Fuji apples," Matthew said. "This orchard is ripe with fruit!" he laughed at his pun. Matthew was ever insistent on being a jokester, bringing levity to all situations, good or bad. I loved that quality about him.

"Very funny," I indulged him. "Clever," I said winking, pressing my wet body into his.

As we huddled under Mom's umbrella, barely withstanding the winds, with nothing to do but wait out the rains in the middle of the soaked apple orchard, I was overcome by the warmth of tatsimou. And Matthew was now a part of it. I had come a long way from humming to the 'tune of tatsimou' that Christmas morning after I returned home following my disappointingly grim first semester at college. Under that umbrella in a heavenly orchard, my parents and the man I would eventually marry were surrounding me in the most indescribable feeling of warmth and love.

I looked down at my muddied purple and teal sneakers and the reflection of my long, narrow face in the gravel filled puddle I was standing in and I thought of Yia-Yia. Of the Friday letters I sent, the foil envelopes, how Papou loved the homemade apple pie Mom made, and that picture of her on the wall of their basement. The idolized portrait of the woman I had become. *Hold on, tatsimou.* I said to myself as I nestled in the middle of the cozy circle of Mom, Dad, and Matthew around me beneath a small polka-dotted umbrella listening to the autumn rains fall upon us as we watched the distant sun peer out from the passing clouds creating soft, misty rainbows in the sky.

"Tatsimou," I said exchanging glances with Mom and Dad with a huge grin on my face. "This is tatsimou!" I felt goosebumps playfully inundate my arms and legs. They smiled back. Matthew knew not what I spoke about, but smiled the way he always did when he heard random "Greek" words being spoken between my parents and me.

"Tatsimou, hold on. Tatsimou, hold on," Dad said as he handed the umbrella to Matthew to hold and extended his arms wider to fully envelop the huddle of our rain soaked love. I felt Dad's warmth and saw the mascara loosening from Mom's ever perfectly painted face. Matthew's left hand was locked with mine.

"Tatsimou, hold on," Mom whimpered and gazed into the double rainbow in the distance.

"Tatsimou, hold on," I followed, looking down at my soggy shoes. "Tatsimou, hold on."

30
From Teacher to Student

The following spring, as my health continued to improve and my desire for achievement in life returned, I prayed about what God wanted for my life. I wanted to know what His plans were for me. He had held my wavering feet steady through caverns of hardship, self-hatred, and illness. And He had lifted me to fruitful summits of redemption. Exceling in my second full-time teaching job, this one at a public school, I itched with each passing day wanting more and wanting something different. The students were uniquely interesting human beings, I received daily accolades for my strong work ethic, and I had a reliable stream of income. Yet each day when I woke up to go to work with lessons planned, ready to teach for the day, I felt a hollow emptiness inside of me. My students were not the problem, nor was the administration or my work colleagues. Sure, I had normal day-to-day work complaints, but nothing that was insurmountable. It was a good job, although I kept having to convince myself that teaching was a respectable career. I constantly justified my growing disdain reminding myself that teaching was a noble profession that allowed me to use my gifts as an empath and leader to touch lives and reach students in a meaningful way. All true statements about what the profession entailed, but nonetheless, the void inside of me continued to grow. Is this it? I would ask myself as I prepared for another day. Is this really it? Is this all there is? Go to work, cash your check, go home, wake up, do it again. And again and again and the same thing for thirty years until you can collect retirement from the state. I never wanted to be a teacher, but was this what I had to do the rest of my life? I was reliant upon the income and the lifestyle really was not all that bad. I mean I had health insurance, a job, and summers off! What's not to love?

However, in daily prayer and penance I continued to seek God's guidance. I was unhappy and discontent and not because I lacked faith in God, but because I did not really feel as though I was using the talents He had given me. I was not making the most of who I was. In a sense, I was not serving His kingdom in the best way I believed myself to be capable of. As my prayers and relationship with God grew more intimate and my study of scripture provided me with a greater understanding of Christ's teachings and His sacrifice, I realized that God puts desires on our hearts with intentionality. God does not create in error. He gives us choices, but He does not make mistakes. I felt as though God was gently tapping my shoulder as if to nudge me to follow my heart. I learned it was up to me to respond to that call He had placed on my heart and to heed that passion he had bestowed upon me. Through growing in the gifts He had given me, I would further grow in Him, His love, and my ability to act as a messenger of His prophecy and Covenant.

Aside from the interest I had developed in fitness, and the education I had pursued to become a professional trainer, what had been on my heart since I was in second grade was writing. In elementary school, I wrote daily poems about my puppies and told stories about alligators eating pancakes on the roof of our house after church, or told elaborate bathroom time stories to Stacey with rubber duck protagonists and the evil, cleansing washcloth antagonists. My nose was always in a book and making up stories was a chief activity for me. As a child, my notebooks were littered with stories, poems, and pictures accompanying short stanzas and prose. In school, I wrote the longest essays and stories of anyone in my class and creative writing was my favorite subject. Yet as I grew older, and even through studying English-in college, the idea of becoming a writer seemed a phony thing to do. Dad told me those "writer folk" are called starving artists. Somehow the warped shelter of a cardboard box was not all too appealing. I mean I learned I could live without food for a while, but probably would not be content being poor and without a home. Writers were pretentious fools. Did I really want to become one of them? I prayed and prayed and prayed. Then I wrote down all of my prayers and prayed some more.

After my relatively lackadaisical efforts to secure work in journalism right after college with my parents urging me to chart a new course that led to teaching, I recognized that tether of creation on my heart had not faded. I had wanted to be a storyteller for as long as I remembered. I dreamed of writing movie scripts, novels, sitcoms, using words to paint original stories. I wanted to go on book tours and share stories of family, travel, home, imagined new worlds, comedy, drama, tragedy, poetry and plays. I wanted more than anything in life to be a writer. But in the midst of recovery from illness, the need for work and the security of what was practical – teaching, I had forgotten that desire on my heart. However, through those prayers and daily litany of questioning, "Is this it? Is there more to life?" I decided it did not have to be "it," or all that was possible unless I allowed it to be. I did not have to stifle that urge to write any longer.

Still teaching full-time, I started writing again and for four months after working both full-time and part-time jobs, I would get home late in the evening and make time to write for at least a half hour per day. I would write whatever would come out. Pencil to paper, I forced myself to make something happen. Whether it was a rant about an event at school or the reincarnation of the rubber ducks of my youth, soon enough I had built up a substantial portfolio of writing, some of which was actually worth reading. I began submitting to literary journals and applying for freelance writing gigs. But work as an English teacher with constant grading and lesson preparation kept getting in the way of my time and creativity, which eventually, drained my aspirations to write. I knew I had to make a decision. Either I was going to go after writing and put my heart and soul into that endeavor or I was going to drop writing, shove it off my mind, and focus on being the best teacher I could possibly be. I did not like being "partially" good at anything. I wanted to be the best. But you can't be the best at everything. My half-assed efforts in teaching and writing simply were not going to cut it for me. I was working at too many things concurrently, and as such, was succeeding at none of them.

The thought of going to graduate school to study writing and linguistics lingered in the back of my mind, probing my attention. The more I entertained the thought though, the more I realized I did not want to go through all of the hoops and application process required to apply to graduate school again. Plus, I knew it was a far off wishful venture. I had applied to several elite writing programs at the end of my undergraduate schooling and had been rejected from every single one, even with the nearly perfect GPA I held. To me, all those rejections indicated that was that sure, maybe I was a good student, but clearly I was not a good enough writer and I could not cut it in those programs. I was ashamed of myself and I did not want to face that kind of rejection again. After all, if I was not good enough then, what made me think I would be good enough five years and a rusty pencil later?

The summer after my second year of teaching in public schools, I tried to keep writing when I could and I was even curiously researching graduate schools. I was so numbed by teaching and I only felt the beating pulse of my heart towards writing grow exponentially. A friend from Texas named Aaron, whom I had known in a college ministry group, came to visit me one hot July weekend that summer. He was a steadfast friend, a Pastor's son with a wonderful family, and a deep thinker with a tender heart. That summer he told me he wanted to visit because he would be leaving the country for a few years to do missions work. I was highly impressed and wished to support him in any way that I was able. That visit, however, ended up not really being about him and his mission. It ended up being about me and it was his visit, which in retrospect, served as a catalyst to change the whole trajectory of my life. I think certain things in life are sanctioned by God. Certain friendships, certain decisions, and the most unexpected events are all part of His great plan. That is all I can figure when I consider the connection Aaron and I had as friends and the trip he made wherein he poured his heart into mine to propel me forward in my dreams.

Sitting in a worn coffee shop together, his shaggy brown hair complementing his piercing dark hazel eyes, 'tough man' ragged jeans and fitted light blue tee with a silhouette of Bruce Springsteen on the front, we reminisced about Bob Dylan and confabulated about memories of our past experiences in college youth ministry. Aaron was into weightlifting and his arguably perfect physique told me he had nothing to learn from me, but he asked anyway.

"At what rep in my sets do you think I should reach my VO2 max?" he asked.

"It depends on how much weight you're using, if you're doing drop sets, supersets, or going for AMRAP (as many reps as possible sets)," I replied. "Whatever you're doing, dude, I think it's working for you," I commented looking at his bulging shoulders, think neck, rectangular face, and prominent jawline. "Looks to me you're killing it in the gym."

He laughed, flattered as any man would be. "So, you dig the guns?" he asked.

"Yeah, Aaron. I know you're all about proportionality and you're getting there, man. I am pretty darn snowed looking at you," I said smiling, knowing even with his short,

5'6" stature he could crush me under the weight of his musculature.

"Never letting me off easy, eh Cladis? C'mon! I've been doing these circuits for months. But yeah my legs need work. You're right on the proportions. I'll get there!" he said only slightly discouraged as we continued to exchange ideas about exercises, workout patterning, and the fitness industry in general for another hour or so. We then talked church, family, and friends and finally we made it around to our other favorite topic, writing. Aaron loved to write poetry and we used to exchange writing back and forth via email when we could. We gave each other feedback and when the rest of the world ignored us, at least we had one audience member to ingest the things we wrote. Aaron knew I was writing more again and not surprisingly, so was he. He was also a self-taught guitarist. Essentially the man was like a mini singer-songwriter version of Bob Dylan. Just more of an intense, Arnold Schwarzenegger, Jesus-loving one. It was quite the combination.

"How's the writing going?" Aaron asked as he looked at me across the table his shaggy hair curling in waves behind his ears.

"Not bad," I said staring at his sturdy shoulders and well-defined pecs. He was only a friend, but men with muscles I had a welling attraction towards. "I have been writing more since school has been out. Mostly poetry. I may dabble into some prose later this summer. How about you?"

"Well you know that part of it. I've sent you pretty everything I have written. Mostly poems, some prose. I wrote a song I want to share before I head back down to

Texas though. Don't let me forget. Wrote up some music to accompany the lyrics. I think you may like it," he said.

"Sounds like you've been more productive than me. Shoot. Keep it up!" I encouraged. "And you sure as heck are not leaving without giving me a show on that guitar! Like Bobby D!" I eased into the language of his musical lexicon knowing comparing him to the likeness of his idol, Bob Dylan, would most certainly inflate his hungry ego.

His dimples grew as he smiled and from his backpack he pulled out what appeared to be a huge stack of papers which he placed in front of me on the table. I stared, chapfallen at the enormous stack in front of me.

"Okay. I've been keeping this one a secret. It's a full manuscript. I want to turn it into a novel someday. Your story – life, school, family, your past – it is what inspired me to write this," he said.

I looked at him, in awe of what was in front of me. I had never ever written anything of that length and I was the one who supposedly wanted to be a writer. "You wrote all of this?" I queried. "Seriously? This is amazing. I was the inspiration? I'm not all that interesting, man. What line of my life did your take for this story?" I asked with expectancy growing in my voice.

"Well that is for you to find out. I want you to read this. When you have the time, of course. I know you're busy. And if you can give me any feedback from your English teacher, intellectual, better-writer-than-me head of yours, I would forever be indebted to you," Aaron said with both humility and noticeable confidence at its completion.

"This is honestly remarkable. I cannot wait to read it. Thank you, Aaron! Have you shared it with anyone else?" I asked.

"In fairness, it's a story that is meant for you. It will make most sense for you. I want you to read it first. Maybe one day I will let the rest of the world be the judge. But right now, just you, Cladis. Okay? Please don't share with anyone else," Aaron persisted.

"Of course. You have my word, Aaron. Now what about that song?"

"You know, Andrea, I believe that pursuing a passion or chasing a dream is the surest way to bring the most glory to God. Don't ever forget that," he counseled.

I nodded in affirmation and we stepped outside, leaving our coffee behind, but the not the vindicating nature of our conversation. Aaron pulled out his guitar, tuning it carefully before he played his song. He called it, "Friends." The lyrics are hazy in my memory bank, but the message was certain. Life had its up, its downs, its highs, and its lows, but if you had a friend, a real friend – one friend who is right there with you in the trenches, the grief, and the celebrations, then you had it all. I did not let him leave before he sang and played the song three times for me in between dabbles of continued conversation. In our constellating, it was all but apparent our friendship was resolute. And through his friendship, I had all I needed to forcefully break out the corner walls of my life.

He returned to Texas and I went back to my life in Chicago, but I read his 96,000 word manuscript. He had written it during the few years we had been apart, only keeping contact through sharing conversations on the phone or via long email messages. Besides Stacey, Aaron had learned a lot about me, my passions, and who I was as a person. He knew of my past and the hopes I had for my future. He had taught me a lot about prayer and even more about fellowship being an integral part of the body of Christ.

I could have finished his manuscript it in one sitting. It was that good. The manuscript he had written held a detailed story of three renegade characters and their adventure through travel, tribulation, mystery, and challenge to fight the dictates of authority. It was heartfelt and moving, but the overarching message was a metaphor for my life and in the final scene the teacher standing behind the desk, who purposely had a name mirroring my own, has a decision to make. She is confronted with an active shooter in her classroom. Part of the scene and the lesson learned from it unfolds as follows:

She lurched forward into a scream for a brief second and her eyes slammed shut – squeezing tears that streamed down her face and wet her hair and caught the curve of her pink pale lips.

The tears leapt off the sharp point of her nose, clipped her chin as it tilted back up to howl at the moon's tiled surface. She doubled over falling to the floor, clutching her gut and the screams went silent as the joy turned to pain and stretched across her tired frame in rippling pleasure.

It was a moment of madness so far removed from this morning's Monday Shuffle.

If something like this, a moment of honesty, a moment of raw expression, a single moment with content worth learning from in an entire school year, had taken place during a normal school day – she'd be quietly removed. If it occurred when the bells chimed at fifty and five minute intervals, when the softball fields were dotted with orange t-shirts for 8 straight periods, when the three lunch hours came with its many sounds and many more smells, when the lockers slammed and the feet pattered quickly past the kissing couples – wrapped in each other's arms unable to bear the coming minutes of separation, if it happened during a day when the acceptable amount of chaos fell into its place she would have been released – considered mentally unstable for the classroom.

The office would be forced to release a statement that Ms. Allie Clayborne was "stepping away" for "personal reasons" and that her "impact would be greatly missed". It's a lie, but they sell it. No one believes it, but they buy it. It's the school lunch principle on a corporate level; we don't consider this a lunch, but we'll gladly pay and swallow for our cafeteria time. I'll scratch your back you scratch mine. I'll slip your wife you slip mine. Confirm my delusions and I'll confirm yours.

On the floor, doubled over in a moment of crippling honesty, because some truths and some denial are just too strong to live with – bifurcation of the mind can only sustain itself so long and then 'can ya say see ya?'; it was like watching two mountains crumble into their own valley – that little blue stream trickling at their base, eroding their foundations out from under them.

On the floor, doubled over, but she'd get a freebie, because four rounds of the six Glock salute will turn her reaction into something that will be considered 'coping', by the office. They'll give her the summer off and expect her to be back, better than ever – ready to teach the little munchkins that charged her room with Guns & Chalk come fall.

On the floor, doubled over, she began to run out of steam. Her tears had stopped in neat little puddles, her lungs with rising and falling as the shakes of her laughter and chaos gave a final rattle for the moment.

On the floor, doubled over, she looked up at those standing over her and said nothing. Her almond brown eyes close fisted about the black pupils, she let her head fall back and the hair that stuck to her face looked like black lightening slashing down the plains beneath her eyes.

On the floor, doubled over, Ms. Allie Clayborne let out a whistle and a sniffle and a groan. "I think… I think if I had been any older, this might have broke me."

We peered at her, curious and fearful.

"There's just so much that happens between graduation and 25, 26, 27… Then suddenly you're thirty and you're locked in."

A whistle.

"And the rest of your life approaches in such a threatening manner; It's a cord wrapped too tight, a blanket too small, a haunt of your youth in which you no longer fit."

A sniffle.

"It's a compromise today for a lifetime of regret tomorrow."

A groan.

Aaron B.D.

In the climactic final scene with a gun to her head, the teacher has to decide if she is going to stay or if she is going to go. Is she going to be behind that teacher behind the desk in thirty years or is she going to be out in the world? Is she going to put her hammer up in protest, or fall back, beaten by the systemic, brain-washing oppression of the school system and the security of job she loathes? The choice is hers. And the salvation of her students rests heavily in her hands.

When I finished re-reading his manuscript a few weeks later, I cried and grinned, and wavered and wondered and then heaved a breath filled with insurmountable joy. I called Aaron to tell him of my reaction.

"I'm Ms. Allie Claybourne, aren't I?" I asked. "It's a compromise today for a lifetime of regret tomorrow," I iterated, repeating the line from the story.

"96,000 words, Cladis. It took nearly 100,000 words to get my point across. I've been hinting at this the last four years! Go get it, Cladis. Don't give up. Hammers in the air! Get after it," he said. His response was all our conversation needed. For a moment it felt like Aaron had a gun to my head in the form of that manuscript he had labored over on my behalf. The point he made was loud and clear. God had spoken with fury through his pen. I knew what I needed to do.

I completed my writing portfolio, asked for letters of recommendation, secured transcripts, wrote over 100 pages of new material for essay submissions and applied to graduate school to attain a Masters of Fine Arts in Writing. But that was not all I did that summer after reading Aaron's story. I finished my own nonfiction manuscript, a project I had once started and set aside back in college, and I renewed my licensure as a fitness professional. Oh, and I prayed. A lot. I talked to God about how I could serve Him with my heart, my experiences, and my life. That goal became my strongest impulse moving forward.

I began that third school year as a high school teacher with trepidation for the work that was ahead, but also with anticipation in my heart. I had polished my graduate school application and at last sent it in for submission. I would know if I was accepted or not by late December. And if I got into graduate school, I was going to cut the cord. Once and for all. I was going to break free from teaching and chart that different course. I was going to put my hammer in the air. If not, I was still going to find a way to chase my dream and keep my hammer in the air.

As I returned to work following the Christmas break holiday, I became somewhat despondent because my assumption was that I had not gotten into graduate school. I would have gotten a response by then and no response usually meant no acceptance. I had poured everything into it, but maybe that everything was not enough, maybe I was still not good enough. I played out every scenario over again and again in my head if there was something I could have done differently and if graduate school did not play out, I could still go after other avenues in writing or make a living, but teaching was stable, secure, and for the most part, easy. I concerned myself with risk and reward.

Is this it? My mind wandered toward dejection again as I watched the first week of January pass with no sign of acceptance or rejection. As 8th hour Friday afternoon rolled around, in what had been a hectic work day, I saw an email come through on my personal account. I was not supposed to check that account during the work day, but my anxiety was too great. I saw a message in my inbox from the Graduate School of Admissions at Fairfield University. I hesitated before opening it. *What's the worst it could say? No? They only sent acceptance letters, right? Maybe part of my application was missing? Maybe...Oh, my gosh! Andrea, open the damn thing! Open it!* I double click on the notification email.

"Dear Andrea E. Cladis," I rubbed my eyes. My fingers were pulsating sweat into the keyboard and mouse. "We are pleased to inform you that you have been..." *Wait? Was I reading that right? I have been what? They are pleased... I have been, I have been...accepted?!* Part of the letter was dedicated to my writing sample and it was evident that the faculty believed it to be marvelous, intuitive, and insightful. "You will be a great fit with our program." MFA programs are competitive and only admit a select number of students each year. And I was going to be one of them. Thus it was, with the greatest sigh of relief I had been accepted into a writing program of my dreams. I nearly screamed into the computer screen and ran out of my classroom right then and there. I all but forgot to take attendance that afternoon.

I would matriculate into the program that upcoming summer and see where things blossomed from there. I did not know how the ending would look, but sometimes the beginning is the most exciting part. I was at last getting my chance to write a new beginning. Five more months remained of teaching before I was going to go after that degree. I was going to close the book on teaching and start writing my very own.

A few weeks later a contract offer for my first full length manuscript submission arrived on my doorstep. Aaron was the first person I told. "Hammers in the air, Ms. Claybourne. Hammers it the air," he said.

31

Write On

My last semester teaching high school English was bitter-sweet for me. I was ready to leave high school in the sense that I hated high school when I first went through it and I had not much cared for it on the other side as a teacher either. But teaching was all that I had known professionally except the part time work I had done in fitness. I invested a lot of myself in teaching and as a result, it mattered to me. I would miss the relationships and the students, reading novels, and sharing my literary knowledge. Yet somehow I knew I had to take a chance on myself. If all else failed, I could return to being a teacher. When doubt crept in and the students were exceptionally kind to me or I knew the reality that failure as artist could also be an outcome, I thought about Aaron, who wrote an entire book as a metaphor for my life persuading me to choose to chase a dream, to not get stuck in the security of a paycheck or the monotony of living in a life that makes me unhappy. I had to keep my hammer in the air.

I officially resigned from teaching and one month later took off to Enders Island, a small island off the coast of Mystic, Connecticut where I would work to enhance my writing through intensive seminars, mentorships, research, and training. As I stepped onto that island for the first time I did not ask the question if this was it or doubt if I would succeed or fail. I knew I was in the midst of pursuing my dream of writing. I had left behind the security of a life that was known and I had stepped out into unchartered waters, and a journey yet unknown. I was writing on an island during the day and spending my evenings in a seaport town observing new sights, sounds, locations, and people. With notebook in hand I knew I was probably going to be poor for a long while, but I was going to be living with gusto the entire time.

After my first summer experience at Enders Island and my entrance into my first semester of the MFA program I realized that I was creating through writing and creating through teaching fitness. The paycheck and income had all but vanished aside from part time work, but I was happy and I was beginning to see the groundwork that God had placed down for my life. Through what I doing through writing, especially the nonfiction Christian book that was to be published, and through work in fitness, was that I was helping myself through the process of using my knowledge to help serve and educate others. Whether I was teaching people about health, wellness, following Christ, or growing through illness, sharing resources and instilling others with purpose and valuable knowledge was pivotal for my continued path towards healing.

Through fitness classes I was an active advocate for health and wellness and through my writing I was creating stories and poems that were slowly seeping into the hands and minds of others, changing perspectives, outlooks, and even changing lives. With my microphone on at the front of a fitness class I was leading, empowering, nurturing, and guiding, reminding people to take the time out of their day to take care of themselves. "Only you can do this for you. Only you can get yourself to the gym. It is only you who can care best for you!" I relayed. Through my illness I had learned the value of health and I wanted nothing more in the world than to share that with others. I went on to become a wellness coach, offering advice for living and executing daily tasks of living life. I honed my focus and specialty on functional fitness – the movements in life that get you from point A to point B. Functional fitness relies on essential movements that illicit comfort in the day to day living of life. That was what I most wanted to teach my clients because of its great merit in all stages of life. I still taught spin, tabata, dance, and high intensity classes, but what mattered most to me was that my clients could stand tall enough to reach the skies and bend down with ease to tickle their toes and then still smile walking with their shoulders back on their way out of class. In my own journey towards health it was the day to day energy for living that had been the hardest to recover. Through proper nutrition and copious amounts of training and exercise I had regained functional fitness. I had to chart a long course to regain that strength and it was strength I never again wanted to lose.

Progressing into my second semester of graduate school, I was doing well enough in fitness and side jobs in writing to afford a small studio space of my own in which I could write. I elected to rent a small space downtown Geneva to set up my very first writer's office. It was to serve as a place where I could go escape, think creatively, and bring new stories to life. Dennis suggested we paint the walls, which were of a dark gray color, and do some remodeling of the space before I moved in. At the time he was spending a few months with our family as he was recovering from a severe depression. The small office space did not need to be painted, though it could stand to be brightened up as Dennis suggested. He knew I loved color and that space was small, dank feeling, and cold. Brighter colors and some mirrors on the wall would open up the space and make it more appealing to work in. And as it turned out, Dennis needed to perform the act of painting just as much as I needed the fully subsume the creative outlet of writing. His paint strokes in my refurbished office represented the heart of his healing as well as my own.

He painted, designing a most beautiful writing space for me. The action was cathartic in every possible way. It brought us closer together as siblings and as friends in its profound symbolism of my own first steps towards achieving a long-awaited dream and as therapy in his life. God's presence was unquestionably felt within those walls. In time, I settled into that office as a space to create poetry, prose, and of course, complete studies for graduate school. It became a creative home away from home with no need for Bubblemint gum nor the presence of an unquenched fire for control to keep me company.

At last, I could see God's hand in everything. From my eating disorder to the love of family to the grief of loss, to friendship and faith, to teaching and fitness. His hand is unfailing in the tapestry of our lives.

32
A Final Conquest: The Finish Line

The more I wrote, the more I wanted to know more of life and all that it was. What I wanted to know more than anything in life was what it was to feel freedom. True freedom. To feel unchained by rules and order, structure and competition, achievement and failure, wealth and poverty, perfection and imperfection, health and illness. I had lived my life in a zone of attainment. Attaining control, attaining education, attaining work, attaining health. But the thing I felt I had attained nothing of was freedom. Sure, there were glimmers and moments of fulfillment, but nothing lasted. I could have claimed a perfect wholeness chasing a dream of writing and finding happiness in my faith, but I still fall short of His glory in occasional doubt, sin, and the unrealistic expectation that God, as a panacea of all, will cure all my problems or clean my slate from any source of discontentment.

I concluded then and would argue now that I don't think true freedom exists. As Bob Dylan famously said, "No one is ever really free, even the birds are chained to the sky." But the liberation I found through running, writing, and teaching others to dance, to move, to connect body and spirit was and still is the closest I have ever come to experiencing the freedom which I desire. It's the physicality of that feeling of freedom which lends itself to what I learned is the most valuable freedom, which is mental freedom. In freeing myself from the ever cumbersome warp of my own mind, I, too, was freeing myself from all of those embedded structures around me that suffocate and stifle.

Persistent as ever, I decided what I needed was a new goal – a sustainable mindset that would create a renewed sense of being. I wanted to find security in that allaying sense of physical contentedness and prove to myself that I was strong enough to go after it and sustain that source of mental freedom. My intrigue for recreational sports and racing had grown exponentially as I become more involved in fitness and I knew that was the route I wanted to take. Completing a short race would not prove anything, and winning a tennis match in an all-women's rich housewife league would leave me feeling empty and not knowing why I had tried so hard. I needed to do something solitary. Something that would be all my own. Something monumental. Something with the potential to shape and change my life. 26.2 miles called my name.

I decided I was going to run a marathon. I was going to see if I could secure that mental clarity and freedom by running a marathon. A what? A marathon? Really, Andrea? Even I doubted myself at first. But the more I thought about the proposition, the more obsessed I got with succeeding at it. OCD and its presence was evermore strong. I would do whatever it took to cross that finish line. I read about training plans, joined a local running group, and got fitted for two pairs of road shoes and trail running shoes. I purchased a Garmin watch to track distance, mileage, time, and pace. I also equipped myself with sport-specific sunglasses, a water bottle belt, thick socks, and a few pairs running shorts designed to prevent chaffing. It was not long before I signed up for my first half-marathon and triathlon. The marathon was to take place in the fall, the triathlon, the following spring. I had six months to train.

I reminisced about the considerable training regimen I had followed the summer before I triumphantly became an Elmhurst College Bluejay and made my debut as a college athlete on the Women's Tennis team. I had proven it to myself then that with enough will I could prevail and I was sure as hell going to prevail once again. The marathon was going to be a race for permanence in healing, dominance of strength, and amplification of self-worth. It would serve as a definitive test of my faith.

On race day, exactly one year to the day of Rachel's funeral, I woke up with the jimjams, a stomachache and a pulsating headache. But I was not cold or unable to move in my bed. I extended my legs under the covers and pressed my arms into a streamline position overhead. The bells on my doorframe jangled and Dad, with excitement only he was capable of having at 4:00 AM whispered into my room, "Time to get up, sweetheart. Today's the day! Are you ready for this race?" I groaned at the time on the clock, and the butterflies swarming my stomach, but it was not a groan of fear or of impending failure that I would be unable to get out of bed.

"I'm ready, Dad. I'm really going to do this," I said as I sat up in bed and looked across my room at the neatly organized stack of race clothing, running shoes, socks, headband, inhaler, water bottle belt, Garmin watch, and my first ever running bib for a marathon. Cladis, #2446. Dad turned on the light in the corner of my room and looked over at me in a fatherly way that beamed of trust, but uncertain worry. Faith, with an undertone of doubt.

"Can I help with anything this morning? What time do we need to leave?" Dad asked, his nerves for me masking his prior excitement.

"I'll try to be ready in about twenty minutes. Are you going to stay with me after check-in?" I asked nervously, desperately wanting his presence that morning.

"I'll be there. Whatever you need, honey. I'm proud of you," he said and kissed me on the forehead before retreating to his room to meet the early dawn and put on some layered clothing to come watch the cool morning race. The race site was about twenty minutes from our home and the course incorporated both open roads and winding paths near the river. I would run past Rachel at mile marker 8. And I would keep running past her all the way through the finish.

As I staggered out of bed, ready to face the race, but not able to quell my nerves and rapid breathing, I entered my bathroom to find the most endearing sight. Adhered to my sink, my mirror, even the toilet and around the shower were hundreds of notes, messages, pictures, accolades and words of inspiration from parents, siblings, friends, relatives, even some of my old high school teachers had written notes. Each note was mounted to cardstock paper in bright colors – yellows, oranges, blues, pinks, and purples. And the biggest note was from Stacey. At the end of her Christ-centered message to me, I was informed that it was she who told all of these people that I was running a marathon. It was she who asked them to write me a note of encouragement and to support me in this life-changing pursuit of physical health. Stacey did all of that. As I began reading the notes from teachers whom I had not spoken with since high school, aunts, uncles, cousins, and friends, my face was overtaken by a cheek-to-cheek smile and my breaths slowed. Never had I felt so loved, supported, and heartened than I did in that moment. I had barely sifted through enough notes to clear my sink to brush my teeth when Dad yelled up to me that it was about time to leave. The rest of the messages would have to wait for later, and I presumed they would be all the more welcoming after I had finished the race anyway.

I finished getting dressed, completing my coordinating outfit with a gray hat that had a pink breast cancer logo on the back. I was wearing that for Mom. I laced up my shoes and took one puff of my inhaler. I would take another a few minutes prior to the race. I quickly went to the bathroom and eliminated everything that was sloshing around in my anxious bowels, knelt for a prayer at my bedside, and went downstairs to leave for the race.

Dad had a few large signs for me in his hands and I left a note on the counter to thank my sister for the colorful messages. The race was so early in the morning and so long in duration that I did not know if she or Mom were going to come watch, but if not, Stacey had given me more adoration than was necessary and I was ebullient and confident from the messages I had read. I could not believe how many people cared about me, loved me, and were rooting for my success!

I was not able to eat anything before the race, but my pre-race meal the night before was full of caloric, nutrient-rich carbs and proteins. I was well hydrated and I was ready to go. Dad and I chit-chatted about fifty yards from the official starting line for the race to distract me from thinking too much. He wrapped his jacket around me to keep me warm as we waited. He coached me to take it easy, to breathe, and to stop if I needed to. He knew I would do none of those things, but he had to tell me anyway. As the National Anthem played and definitive pre-race instructions were given, my nerves were swelling. Dad had to step away from me as the sheer mass of human activity gathered near the starting line. Thousands of other runners were preparing to chart the course of what would be a two to for some, six or seven hour running adventure. I prayed and prayed and prayed. *Lord, see me through this. Lord, see me through this and stay by my side. Lord, give me the strength to get through this race. To cross that finish line in your holy name, Amen.*

Before long, the race was on. Dad ran in the spectator zone alongside me during the first half mile of the race filming me, taking pictures, and cheering me on. I was not embarrassed in the least. He was the best. When I glanced back at him as I made my first turn into the herd of runners, I saw Dad waving, shouting, and crying. His tears made me want to cry and run back towards him. How would I ever repay his unconditional love for me? No matter what was happening, Dad was always there for the storms and the sunshine and for all the crazy things his children sought to do with their lives. Whether that was driving to Indiana and back every weekend or standing on the sidelines of a tennis match or now, a marathon. I internalized his strength as I found my running pace. I hit my groove and with his love bursting from the springs in my feet, I was holding steady. It was happening. *Marathon, I'm coming for you!* I shouted and pumped both of my arms above my head as I lost myself in the throng of people, all shapes and sizes, out to conquer the same monster as I.

Mile one, two, three. I was going strong. Mile four, five, six. I was keeping pace at nine minute miles. Mile seven, eight, nine. My legs began to feel wobbly and I stopped at one of the rest areas to get water and use the bathroom. I got back in the groove, my eyes were watering and my nose was running as I powered through miles ten, eleven, and twelve. Tracking miles in three mile segments forced me to keep moving. Stride after stride, I told myself to just keep running. My pace had dropped to ten minute miles, but I was still moving. At the end of mile twelve, I spotted my Mom, Dad, and Matthew spectating at an open area on the course. I waved and smiled as pain shot up my back and neck. I held my chest and shoulders up to look strong for them as I ran by.

"Go, Andrea! Go! Keep it up! We are proud of you! Go! Go! Go!" They cheered in a swell of affirmations I could hear above the crowd. I was not just doing this race for myself; I was running this race for them. I was running the race to prove that I was strong, that I was capable, and that by their loving hands, and the grace of God, I was a survivor. My body was aching, I felt as though I could easily go to the bathroom again, but I kept pressing forward. Stride by stride watching the sun rise over the foggy riverbank as the brisk morning air swept along the back of my neck. I was squeezing the ends of my long sleeve bright salmon colored running tee in my hands with extra Kleenex stuffed up my arms. I was wearing aqua blue running shorts with salmon accents to match my running tee. The headband I was wearing was also of similar colors, but was tucked beneath my stretchy gray baseball cap that held my iPod in a convenient zipper pocket right underneath my tousled ponytail flopping out. I could feel my breath getting heavier and the dry film on the back of my throat begin to choke off my air supply, but I was okay and more importantly I knew I was going to be okay.

The music beating in my ears helped me keep up pacing and the other runners around me ensured me that I was not alone in the struggle. I looked around on the wooded path noticing the leaves as their tips were ever-so-slightly changing colors signifying the entrance of fall. Change was the one thing I knew I could count on in life. Things, people, and places forever change. But the seasons – fall, winter, spring, and summer, held steadfast to their change. Timing of their entrance might differ, but the seasons could be relied upon. I knew what to expect with the seasons and that was security in change that I could weather. And autumn, as far as I knew, would forever be my favorite. In autumn, everything dies. But everything dies with the graceful color and splendor of warm breezes that turn to cool nights echoed by crunchy, fallen leaves. Everything dies, I thought as I ran. Humans have a 100 percent mortality rate. The green foliage would be gone in a few weeks from that very path. Everything dies, but it's a wondrous death of glowing color. And when the glow fades for winter, it is trusted that the green buds and grasses will spring forth again, being made new the next spring.

I stopped my compulsive mind on that run long enough to see the beauty. To take it in. Most of all, to be attentive to it. Life for me was always put your head down and swim. Put your head down and run. Put your head down. Excel. Achieve, Win. Be the best. That race morning I was not going to excel, achieve, or win anything. The other runners were stronger than me, faster than me, and better trained. I knew that reality well, but I did not care. All I was racing for was the finish. Just to finish the race was going to be more than enough for me. Mental clarity and freedom was being found not in the act of running, but in the act of relinquishing control. That was the secret. That was the freedom.

Blisters popped and puss oozed into my wet socks and the pavement was getting harder as I ran the final half mile of the race. *You can do it, Andrea. You can do it.* I told myself. The finish line was hazy and the huddle of humans waiting underneath the multi-colored orange, green, white, and blue balloon arch at the finish was overwhelming. I could faintly hear the announcer and the music. The wind whipped against my face as I turned onto the large bridge in the center of the town where hundreds of spectators had gathered. 200 yards to the finish. I pumped my arms and closed my eyes tearing out in front of the pack I had been pacing with for most of the race. *Finish line, here I come. Almost there. Almost there.* My heart was escaping my chest, my throat was dry and irritated, the stitch in my left side felt like a knife ripping flesh, but the finish line was visible. I held my breath and sprinted the last 100 yards towards the swarm of human activity, noise, and balloons. I saw Stacey with unexpected tears in her eyes, front and center holding up a sign that read, "Proud of you, Andrea! My sister is amazing!" I ran towards the haze, the sign she was holding, and the neon finish line with more courage than I had ever known.

"Let's give it up for Andrea Cladis of Geneva, Illinois!" The announcer's shout out echoed through the loudspeaker as I crossed the finish line. There was a wave of noise and cheering and I heard my Mom whistling from the side corral of the long bridge and Dad saying, "Let's go, kid! Let's go! Get it done!"

As I crossed that finish line, my face swelled with recovery blood and my eyes blurred momentarily. I checked my Garmin watch. Sub four hours. I made it. I made it. I was breathing and sweating and my heart was beating, well above 35 BPM, and I made it!

Stacey rushed towards me, her face stained with tears and at first I was unsure why. "Tricey! Tricey!" She pressed one of my many nicknames out of her mouth. She was shaken with tears as she embraced me. I watched her perceptively, soon realizing they were tears of joy. In her consummation of innocent perfection, as an angel in my life – the one who humanized me enough to save me from the fate of my eating disorder – I was whelmed by her adoration of me and felt ashamed for all the pain I had subjected her to.

Stacey's tears were of pride and elation and courage as she watched her older sister, once sallow with a failing heart, unable to walk, sipping Gatorade underneath a heavy wool blanket on the couch, and hiding packs of Orbit gum in a shared bathroom to that moment as a witness, watching me have the steadfast endurance to finish a race no one, but Stacey originally thought I was capable of finishing.

Stacey's tears mixed with my sweat as I let my fatigued body fall into the renewed strength of hers. She was my best friend, my closest companion, and the only person in my life who never critiqued me, never queried me, never doubted me, only loved me and prayed for me unconditionally with selflessness of heart. She was my angel on earth. The sound of her sobs matched the pacing of my dissipating breath as my heart wrestled to recover from the stress of marathon mileage. Stacey handed me a cup of cold water, her eyes, wet and bloodshot, but her face absolutely beaming.

"I am so proud of you," Stacey mustered. "You are so strong, Andrea! In all things, God is good! He is good! In Him, it is true, we can do anything," she hugged me again, her happy yellow shirt soaking up my sweat.

"I love you, Stacey. Thank you so much for believing in me and being here for me," I heaved, still catching my breath. I wiped my sweaty face onto my long sleeved running jersey and leaned into her body again for support. "God has healed me through your love, Stacey. He has given me this renewed strength to run and finish the race," I mumbled into her chest. When I had at last gotten control of my breath, I sipped some cool water and removed the wet hat from my head, stepping back from the angel at my side.

Her eyes widened as she looked up and down my body in approval and admiration. "You did it, Andrea. You really did it!" She nictitated to prevent more tears from falling. Mom and Dad were fighting their way through the crowds to reach us. The sounds of the crowd and the race eluded my mind as I looked into Stacey's light brown, inviting eyes. It was a moment of complete stillness as I felt the presence of God. I was most certain of His grace and mercy that late autumn morning. The purity of her virtuous happiness was genuinely endearing, and made my sweat-drenched body and beaten legs feel as if they were floating.

33

The Rearview Mirror: A Lens into Love

The day after I completed my first marathon, I hobbled around cleaning my bedroom with sore, lead heavy legs and found an entry in the form of a letter written to myself in a journal from my freshman year of college. The letter began, "When doubts creep in, insert trust, and when fear whelms, insert belief. And when they both creep in, trust + belief = Faith. For it is then, you must have faith." I tore out the page and adhered it to my bathroom mirror. After I crossed the finish line of that marathon, the secrets and shadows I had come to know so well rapidly diminished in the intensity of their presence. I became so whelmed by the grace of faith, prayer, and the enduring support of my family that permanent healing began. After nearly ten years of struggle for acceptance of my own life, I eventually came to conquer my illness and embrace a different reflection in a mirror of affirmation and not a mirror of constant degradation. Enhanced in self-worth through the empowering act of being loved by another was what ultimately led me to find steadfast security in the affirmation of the rearview mirror.

If you take a narrow lens and start looking back at your life considering where you've been, who you are, and where it is you think you're going, you can ponder the influences and shapes and distances of all the people that have surrounded and created you into the being that you are today. The person you are here in this present moment reading this has gradually been sculpted and defined as you peer into the rearview mirror of your life. You will discover that there is always another new opportunity to experience grace and gratitude, but you can just as easily remain lost because at times it seems impossible to even comprehend how you arrived at the very place and moment in time where you stand.

As for me, the image in my rearview mirror looks a little like this:

She never quite knew what it meant to be in the presence of someone besides a parent or sibling who deeply, wholly, and truly loved her. She had never gone out on dates or had a steady boyfriend. But three years after college and just two years shy of a full recovery from a once life-threatening eating disorder, she discovered that it's not necessarily about what you're doing with your life. It's not even really about who you are. What it is about is the humility of accepting a connection that can't be fully explained. It is something that you want to break down and analyze and try to figure out, rationalize and justify, except for the fact that you cannot. Yet you'll keep trying even though you'll never get there.

For this woman, she looks in the mirror and for the first time she see the reflection of a beautiful woman. She's strong. She's smart. She's intelligent. And no one can tell her otherwise. She has a heart and she cares and she gives of herself. She longs to be loved and longs to be heard. Even though she sees a person of independence often wrought by others as a trait of selfishness, she's surrounded by friends who call her, message her, reach out to her every single day just because they know what she has to offer or say will make a difference in their lives. And as much as she hides away at times or pushes people to distance, they keep prying and though it may take her time, she'll always respond. She'll make her thoughts known and she'll breed that confidence in others. She's a woman of her word. She's a woman others want to know.

Her eyes are brown with maligned dark specks. It's imperfection she now sees as flawless and exquisite. Her hair is long, tangled, tousled, un-styled, but it's perfect for this time and for this moment. She's learned to accept the person that she is and she knows that no one can define her in a tangential, meaningless manner. The worth she has found is in Christ and Christ alone. She now has a man by her side, but she doesn't need the approval of one. However, he has given her the gift of the ability to see that she can be loved no matter what. At any time, on any day, in any state of being, she will be loved. Why? He told her that she deserves that love. She fought this notion day after day after day. And still he stayed. And he told her, I will be there for you. I will always be there for you. I will be on my way. I will see you soon. I will hold you. Wait for you. Protect you. I want to fall asleep next to you and to wake the next day in your arms. I want to be yours. I want you to be mine. Her heart was stolen to Christ's perfect love long ago and she guards it with a closeness that makes it challenging for any man to ever fully make their way in.

As she looks in the mirror, she pulls back her hair, neglecting to brush it because she still has vivid memories of the clumps of hair that once fell from her head as illness took its toll. So instead, she lets the curls fall gently through her hands, those natural waves, with a touch of unfettered frizz; she smiles. Her teeth, once encapsulated by braces, and mouth gear, and torturous appliances that embarrassed her youth are now distant metal memories of the rusted taste of blood seeping from gums dripping a burgundy iron taste in her mouth. Her teeth are white; her smile is wide. Her face has color that it has never before known. She looks on her reflection that was at one time hollow, neglected, a cavern of a dying soul. But what beams back at her in the mirror is a face that is bright. It is full. It's a face that's been kissed, it's been loved, it's seen things it can't remove, but reflects the images of a world that's worth being a part of – a world that she's found her place in.

Pulling her hair back into a loose pony tail with a colorful headband gracing the crown of her head, she finds sparkly purple earrings to match her clothing. Makeup isn't needed on a day like today. All she needs is just the natural glow that she's found in who she is and who she knows she can and will be. She's a woman. She's not a girl. Closing her smile, her pink lips no longer dry, cracked or jaded are lips on a mouth that never fails to speak its purpose. Never fails to provide its intent. It never fails to recognize its force and power.

See? She's a woman who has the power of strength in words. She takes cautious careful care of her body, but even more attention to her mind. She protects her morals, and she uplifts her heart and her soul and her being is well.

Words are her vehicle for action and her roadmap for life. She says, "I'm a teacher, an entertainer. I am someone who has something to say. And others need to hear it."

He calls her when she cries.

He sits with her in her anger.

He waits and waits and waits on her no matter what is going on.

He taught her that to be loved you have to love yourself. And she's teaching him that very same thing.

He says to her, "You are not alone. You will never again have to be alone. I am here. I am yours. I am here." These words they haunt her and humble and confuse her and she speaks them to herself in the days and the nights when she feels hollow or alone or when that park bench tempts the dark places in her mind. She tries to understand his devotion to her, but she can't fully grasp the concept of such a wholesome love. She has been given the unconditional gift of seeing herself as whole through this revelation and this fear-laden, tremble producing notion of love.

Yet the mirror – the once despised mirror – isn't to be feared. And she is not to be feared. At least not by herself ever again. Her eyes glance down from her face to her bronzed body, warmed from miles of biking and running on hot summer days, and she sees tone and muscle where skin and bone used to be; she sees strength and she feels pride. The words fat, ugly, unworthy are nowhere to be found and nor to ever be heard again. Her body is her own. It is her vehicle for life and she will keep it healthy because it's the only one she has. She doesn't admire it for looks; she doesn't maintain an image for the sake of an image. She loves and cares for herself because she deserves that. It's as simple and complex as that.

LESSONS FROM THE MIRROR

Sometimes I think that the Universe has a strange way of surprising us. At one moment, in one hour, in one year, we can expect so little, yet gain so much. In every experience we learn to value all that is that we cannot see. *All that is we cannot see.*

I expect to know. I expect to learn. I expect to grow. And growth is not necessarily an enjoyable process, but it is one that is most necessary for maintaining vitality in our lives.

Perhaps the greatest challenges in life are those which we can't fully explain or understand. I am frustrated and I am raw and I am scared, but I am still me. That mirror says, "Look at you! You gorgeous, loving, hope-filled woman. Look. At. You!"

And I look back and I don't see secrets and I don't see shadows. I don't see those cunning, "tainted" ways of living. I nod and I smile that my hair is out of place, and my sporty shirt says never grow up and my face is slowly welcoming those corner eye creases and somehow it is perfect because this is the way I am supposed to be. This is the way life is supposed to happen. This is the way I've learned to live. And I am happy. I am happy with who I am.

We are not defined by wealth or riches. We are not defined by what we take from others. We are defined by what we give. By who we are and how we live. As for me, I have been given the gift of relentless love from God and my family, and it is that same love I work to bestow upon the most vulnerable people around me. So pause for just a moment and think: How do we see our reflection? How do

297

we keep the light on in our lives? How do we show love to others? What affirmation can the mirror send our way? And in so doing, remember that who we are will always be good enough if we simply let it be. And then we can smile with confidence and boldly pronounce to the mirror of the world, "Let *me* be *me!*"

—

I still can't eat hummus on wheat bread or sliced lunchmeat or even peppers out of a bag without being reminded of the nasty stale smell of the lunchroom bathroom at Park Ridge High school. Orbit gum makes me vomit immediately and any form of peanut butter repulsed me for nearly eight years. I have not stepped on a scale since my senior year in high school. I am terrified to do so. I can't write down what I eat. Ever. But I keep that steno pad tucked under my bed to know I am still in control. Just. In. Case.

On my wedding day as my handsome groom and I cut our decadent chocolate cake with smooth vanilla buttercream frosting, I remember thinking about how badly I wanted to lick all of the frosting off of our cake to honor the sweet satisfaction and nullified emotions from the day. But instead, Matthew held my hand, I calmly ate an entire piece – frosting and all – and danced afterwards, for pleasure, for tatsimou, and not for the destruction of sugared calories.

Epilogue

REMORSE, VICTIM OF

I saw my mother's tears.
I heard my father's pleas.
I felt the plague of guilt.
I knew the lies I told.

cunning words like the blood seeping from my gums
that no one could see
only I could taste.

I knew the taste of Orbit Bubblemint gum
that would keep me from ingesting calories
at lunch.
I felt uncomfortably complacent to the scale holding steady
at 60 pounds.
I heard therapists denying my
humanity.
I saw my glowering face,
the crest of my cavernous collarbone.

I knew my father trusted my every word,
I felt every calorie expand in my stomach, my thighs
I heard arguments about my thin, bony shoulders
I saw the reflection of a sallow girl.

small, protrusive bones in my feet, easily bruised
crescendoing requests to eat
a Honeycrisp apple larger than my fist.
dying would mean freedom.

the constancy of cold
the scalding tea I couldn't swallow,
a mouth lined with cotton.
"What's the matter with you?"

I won control over my mother,
her demand for perfection.

clumps of curly brunette hair carpeted my bedroom floor
me trembling beneath the weight of self-hatred.

mom fading into despair as a poinsettia
exposed to cold, winter air
would I ever be enough?
Whispers wishing to dissolve self.
Whispers wishing to perish into warmth.
Whispers wishing to

SCREAM. OUT. LOUD.

I listened. I believed in
the wishful whispers that told me to
carry on and complete the quest.

The faded whispers,
more muted now at distance,

I still hunger for their restless wish.

About the Author

Andrea Cladis, holds an MFA from Fairfield University and is a Summa Cum Laude graduate of Elmhurst College with degrees in English Writing, Interdisciplinary Communications, French, and Secondary Education. A former journalist and High School English teacher, she currently works as a freelance editor, writing consultant, and fitness professional. She has worked for Delnor Hospital's Marketing and Public Relations Department, for neighborhood magazines, and as a feature writer for Shaw Media. She has been published by SAGE Academic, *The Greek Star*, various literary journals, and online publications including *Thought Catalog, Elite Daily,* and Patch.com. She is also the author of *Finding the Finish Line: Navigating the Race of Life through Faith & Fitness* (CrossLink Publishing, 2017). She has written extensively for online news websites, print magazines, local newspapers, and social media blogs. Known for her local opinion columns, Andrea's writing has been described as "emotive, yet brazen, seasoned with thinly veiled cynicism, and a pinch of sarcasm." Andrea is an Advisory Board Member for Cambridge Scholars Publishing and maintains a personal site about faith, fitness, and writing which can be explored at **www.andreacladis.com.**

36135613R00182

Made in the USA
Middletown, DE
16 February 2019